NATIONALISM AND REGIONALISM IN INDIA

NATIONALISM AND REGIONALISM IN INDIA

The Case of Orissa

SUBRAT K. NANDA

PUBLICATIONS

KALPAZ PUBLICATIONS

DELHI-110052

Nationalism and Regionalism in India: The Case of Orissa

Rs. 690

ISBN: 81-7835-549-3

Published in 2007 in India by
Kalpaz Publications
C-30, Satyawati Nagar,
Delhi-110052
E-mail: kalpaz@hotmail.com

Laser Type Setting by: Rudra Computer Graphics, Delhi
Printed at : Salasar Imaging System, Delhi

Contents

List of Tables

List of Maps

Acknowledgements

On the occasion of the completion of this work I take the opportunity to record my sincere thanks to persons who have been of constant help to me at various stages of this work.

First of all, I express my deep sense of gratitude to my beloved teacher Professor T. K. Oommen for his valuable comments and suggestions on earlier drafts of the work. The idea of working on nationalism and regionalism in provincial context in multicultural/multinational India was conceived while I was studying at Jawaharlal Nehru University, New Delhi. In fact it was Prof. Oommen who motivated me to undertake this study in the context of the East Indian state of Orissa. Without his constant encouragement, valuable suggestions and critical comments it would have been difficult to complete this work. I am also thankful to Prof. Jagannath Pathy of South Gujarat University, Surat for his critical comments on some issues relating to the study of nationalism and regionalism in multicultural context.

I would also like to sincerely thank the Librarians and Staff members of various Libraries and Organisations such as Orissa State Archives, Bhubaneswar; Orissa State Library, Bhubaneswar; Orissa Assembly Library, Bhubaneswar; Board of Revenue Record Room, Cuttack; National Archives, New Delhi; Nehru Memorial Museum and Library, New Delhi; Jawaharlal Nehru University Library, New Delhi; Central Secretariat Library, New Delhi, etc., for giving me access to consult various historical, archival and secondary sources relevant for the purpose of the study.

My friends at Jawaharlal Nehru University, my colleagues at North-Eastern Hill University, and last but not the least my native friends in Orissa have constantly helped and encouraged me in various ways. Hence, my special thanks to all of them.

I owe a debt of gratitude to my family members especially my mother, sisters and my wife Bina for their ungrudging support, inspiration and encouragement. My sweet little daughter Shivangi is a source of inspiration too and hence her name deserves a special mention.I am also profusely indebted to my father, who left for the heavenly abode in May 1996, for his guidance, care and affection that saw me through this work. This work is dedicated to the sweet memories of my father. Finally, I would like to thank Kalpaz Publications, Delhi for taking interest in publishing my work in a very short time. However, the conventional disclaimer applies.

26th October, 2006
NEHU, Tura Campus

Subrat K. Nanda

1

Introduction

1. The Problem

The degree of national unity and the level of political integration that a multicultural country experiences and the amount of threat and resistance, latent or manifest, it receives from its various constituent cultural communities in the process of national consolidation and nation-building are issues of continuous significance in the study of nationalism and regionalism, especially in a country like India. The sources from which such threats and resistances to national unity and integration in multicultural countries result are many and various. One such major source is the conflict arising out of the 'nationality question' of the constituent cultural communities of a multicultural country vis-à-vis their macro-national identity, and another source is the conflict over regional developmental disparities existing in various parts of a multicultural country. While the former gives rise to various regional nationalist movements by distinct cultural communities, the latter leads to growth of regionalism in backward and deprived regions in multicultural countries. These two forms of conflict exert enormous pressure on the stability, unity and integrity in several multicultural countries.

The 'nationality question' in multicultural countries arises from the fact that the people in such countries wish to cling on to both their collective political (state) identity and their respective cultural identities and notions of 'homeland'. In other words, in such countries people by and large wish to express their national identity at both the civil-political and the cultural-primordial level[1]. If this framework is tampered in any form, there would be predictable conflict giving rise to threats and resistances because one or another cultural community may feel deprived objectively or subjectively. The fact that nation and state in these multicultural countries are not co-terminous reinforces this issue further.

The tampering of such a framework precisely occurs when a specific cultural community, by historical accident or by political machinations, remains dominated by another cultural community in one political unit or dispersed into several such units. The common political unit may be either a particular state or a provincial unit therein. Taking advantage of its pre-eminent position the dominant cultural community tries to pose a threat to the distinct identity of the dominated cultural community. The latter responds to this situation by asserting its identity in separatist nationalist terms. The political assertion of such a nationalistic assertion may vary from different levels of political autonomy to provincial autonomy to outright independence. It is this urge to protect one's cultural identity in nationalist sense which gave rise to various nationalist mobilisations in several multicultural countries from time to time.

It may be recalled that most of multicultural countries of the world reeled under colonial rule for a considerable period of their history. Significantly, the tampering of cultural identities in many such multicultural countries occurred for the first time during the period of colonial rule. The colonial administration in most of these countries created artificial provincial units which did not match the cultural-linguistic affiliation and the traditional 'homelands' of the people. This arrangement ultimately resulted in the cumulative socio-economic dominance of the majority community over the minority communities. The domination was felt most acutely in the cultural sphere as the danger of loosing one's identity was very much involved. Small wonder, then, that the minority cultural communities reacted to this arrangement by claiming their territorial-cultural specificity in clear nationalist terms. This nationalist consciousness differed by and large from the national struggle launched at the macro-political level in several ex-colonial multicultural countries to end colonial rule and establish their own sovereign states. It is not surprising, therefore, that in such multicultural countries nationalism assumed a multi-dimensional character and was perceived differently at different context. At the macro-level it was perceived as a united anti-imperialist struggle to liberate the country from foreign rule and establish sovereign state; whereas at the regional cultural level it was seen as movement for self-fulfillment through self-rule for a people living in a culturally distinct homeland. Needless to say nationalism at the macro-political level in these ex-colonial multicultural countries emerged from a shared colonial experience and geo-political unity, and not from a notion of 'pre-existent' nation. In contrast, at the regional cultural level nationalism in these multicultural countries evolved from a distinct cultural-linguistic-territorial identity, that is, a 'pre-existent' nation. The former type of nationalism; conforms to the political brand of nationalism: while the latter conforms to the cultural form of nationalism.

The situation has not changed much after most of these ex-colonial multicultural countries became independent in the periods of de-colonisation. On the other hand, in the post-colonial period the establishment of self-governments and democratic institutions and values in most of these ex-colonial multicultural countries provided added thrust to the nationalist consciousness of several cultural communities including the hitherto subdued and neglected ones. Realisation of this fact seems to have goaded the state leadership of most of these countries to go for provincial reorganisation on the basis of primordial ties. As the primordial ties differ from one country to another, the basis of reorganization also differed accordingly. For example, region was the basis of reorganisation in Indonesia, tribe-cum-kinship in Nigeria, sect and religion in Lebanon, race in Malaysia, language and tribe in Pakistan, etc.[2]

The policy of reorganisation was implemented keeping three ends in view: (a) effecting, wherever possible, co-terminality between administrative unit and cultural unit so that people's aspirations can be largely met and the unity and integrity of the state be maintained; (b) accommodating the whole population on equal footing under one centralising civil-political authority so that one form of civil loyalty displacing all other primordial-cultural loyalties would emerge; (c) and bringing in large-scale state-sponsored modernisation programme so that desirable interaction between social collectivities would be promoted and all types of disaffection resulting from the ties of race, colour, language, religion, tribe, region, etc. would be eventually displaced.

Unfortunately, none of these goals has come true. Not only has the desired co-terminality criterion between administrative unit and culture not been fully met, but also the expected 'displacement syndrome' and the much hoped-for singular loyalty to the state have not emerged.

As far as reorganisation is concerned, the scheme mainly benefited the bigger and/or mainstream nationalities. The smaller and peripheral cultural communities mostly continued to remain in a state of domination-deprivation relation within a multicultural provincial administrative unit. Similarly, the subjection of the culturally diverse people to a common independent state did not destroy their cultural boundaries altogether. Adherence to the broader state identity was not welcomed by these people at the cost of destroying their own cultural identities. The increasing pace of modernization and economic development also could not completely undermine the importance of quest for separate identity. It is true that the process of modernisation has left a drastic impact on pre-modern ascriptive values and institutions existing in ex-colonial world, but the expected "displacement syndrome did not operate as was postulated".[3] Instead of being completely neutralised the cultural identities got invariably re-legitimised on a wider scale under the influence of modernization and economic development. For one thing, in modern times people the world over became increasingly conscious of the practical socio-economic and political advantages (i.e. instrumental pay offs) involved in making language, race, tribe, religion, etc. as viable bases of distinct cultural identities.

In short, one can argue that (a) the continuance of the dissonance between provincial administrative unit and cultural community; (b) the urge to become recognisable entity; and (c) the instrumental advantages in cultural, political and socio-economic terms are the key factors which contributed to the rise of many nationalist movements in ex-colonial multicultural countries even after their independence. As already noted, these movements largely operate within the cultural framework of community identity and that they mostly seek to survive within the framework of a common polity.

It follows that in colonial as well as in postcolonial times people in ex-colonial multicultural countries basically seek to express their national identity at two levels: political/civil and cultural. The former is reserved for the country as a whole and the latter is shown in respect of their specific cultural identities expressed in linguistic, religious and tribal terms. In colonial times people mainly fought at two levels, i.e., against the colonial power and against the people of 'other cultural community'. But in postcolonial and contemporary times the cultural nationalism of the people for their regional-cultural identity is being simultaneously pursued with the broader political nationalism identified with their state.

It is being popularly believed that only the multicultural countries of the ex-colonial world experience regional nationalist movements; the older and well-integrated countries of the West, by and large, remain free from this malaise. Available empirical evidences, however, show that the Western states receive stiff resistance from their people belonging to cultural backgrounds different from the mainstream culture. For example, national movements, latent or manifest, exist among the Scots, Welsh and Irish in the U.K.; French-Quebecois in Canada; German Swiss in Switzerland; Basques and Catalans in Spain; Burgundies and Britons in France, etc.[4] What is, however, disappointing to note is that these nationalisms are dubbed by most scholars, perhaps unwittingly, as regional, sub-regional, sub-national, secessionist or anti-national movements.[5]

It is clear that nearly all multicultural countries the world over face nationality problems. In these countries people in general, barring a few exceptions, want to survive through self-rule within a common sovereign state. This consciousness in turn fosters the notions of 'differential loyalty' and 'differential identity' in most multicultural countries. A.D. Smith, for example, very aptly observes that in multicultural context there exists two polar perspectives on nationalism: statist and ethnicist.[6] According to him, the statists perceive and define nationalism from the point of view of mainstream culture and language and the unity and integrity of the common state. The ethnicists being desirous of maintaining cultural distinctiveness insist that for larger interests not only the distinction between state and nation should persist, but also the state should recognise and carefully nurture and accommodate specific cultural nationalisms existing inside such common states. The statists advocate assimilation of minority cultural communities into the mainstream/majority mould, but the ethnicists consistently resist assimilation with a view to building a nation-state/national state with multiple cultural-national identities.[7]

Again, for the ethnicists merger of distinct and familiar cultural identity in favour of an overarching political-national identity or a somewhat alien cultural mainstream means many things. First, it runs the risk of loss of identity in collective terms and hence autonomy. Second, it amounts to unhindered hegemony of the mainstream cultural-national community. Third, it entails loss of instrumental benefits and of equal opportunity. Finally, it leads to absorption by a culturally proximate community or a threat of domination by a culturally distant community.

Like many multicultural countries, India remained under colonial subjugation for a pretty long time. The colonial administration in India too carved out provinces notwithstanding the socio-cultural composition and the geographical distribution of speech communities. It is well-known that India is the largest multicultural country in the world. The people of India not only speak numerous languages but also they profess different religious faiths and affiliate with various caste, sub-caste, tribal, ethnic and racial groupings. These elements created the mind-boggling cultural diversity in India. Of these elements of cultural diversity in India, language, tribe and to some extent religion are very crucial because they not only define distinct cultural identities but also demarcate specific cultural boundaries/territories traditionally referred to as 'homelands'. Terms like 'desh', 'nadu', 'rashtra', etc. are popularly used in many Indian languages to refer to these traditional cultural homelands[8]. Given this traditional linkage between culture and territory, the artificial provincial arrangement in colonial India led to not only fragmentation of culture and territory of several communities but also juxtaposition of different cultural communities in a single provincial unit or dispersal of one cultural community into several such units. In this scenario, the larger communities having better access to power, privilege and material benefits emerged as dominant communities and their culture and language assumed mainstream status under colonial patronage. On the other hand, the smaller and territorially fragmented cultural communities faced serious threats of extinction of identity. The fear of extinction of identity hence prompted many deprived cultural communities to demand for recognition of their separate identity in a provincial political space within the multicultural set-up.

This very consciousness of protecting and preserving one's cultural identity within a culture-congruent provincial unit gave rise to numerous national movements in various regions in colonial India. The content and goal of these regional national mobilisations, however, differed from the all-India anti-colonial national movement for India's independence. These regional national movements basically aimed at preserving distinct cultural identity and homeland through the provision of internal self-determination inside India. The all-India anti-colonial struggle, on the contrary, aimed at establishment of the Indian sovereign nation-state. Needless to say, the all-India national consciousness emerged from the concept of nation based on the political attributes of sovereignty, secular-democratic values, common citizenship and common legal administrative system; while the regional national consciousness was based on common culture, common language, shared history, common territory, etc. Both these forms of national movement developed in India simultaneously in colonial as well as postcolonial times. As a matter of fact, the national movement seeking internal self-determination in provincial terms continues more vigorously in India after her independence.

As noted earlier, besides nationality problem multicultural countries also encounter the problem of regionalism. Given the free flow of capital and the role of political power, concentration of power and developmental benefits around a few regions in a multicultural country gave rise to regional inequalities. Evidently, people of the less developed and neglected regions would fight for their rights and share in fruits of development and political power. As far as India is concerned, like elsewhere regionalism largely centers on unbalanced regional growth and unequal distribution of political power and administration. Significantly, the unequal nature of regional growth persists in India ever since the colonial period. This has created differential level of socio-economic mobility and differential access to power and in administrative position. This situation of regional developmental disparities aggravated more and more in independent India. As a result, regional discontent and tension are seen in greater intensity in different parts of India since independence. The regional consciousness for developmental benefits, however, differed significantly from the regional national consciousness seen in colonial and postcolonial India. Also, it is noticed that some of these regional struggles for developmental benefits have turned nationalistic in orientation and called for separate province in the Indian union on the basis of a distinct nationality.

Several cases of regional nationalism and regionalism have been noticed in various parts of India from time to time. One of the interesting cases of regional nationalism and regionalism in India is the case of Orissa. The case of Orissa is distinct in several respects. First, the Oriyas as a culturally distinct people suffered from nationality problem in colonial India and regional conflict in post-independent India. Second, the rise of Oriya nationalism in colonial times was the first regional nationalism which demanded internal self-determination in provincial terms in British India. Third, Oriya nationalism succeeded in establishing the first linguistic province of Orissa in British India. Finally, the regional tension seen in the state of Orissa in contemporary period develops the signs of another regional nationalism in postcolonial India. In this study it has been attempted to explore the conditions under which regional nationalism and regionalism have flared up in the state of Orissa in India.

2. The Context

As noted above, this study focuses on the emergence of regional nationalism and regionalism in the context of Orissa in India. The state of Orissa lies in the eastern zone of India. The state has Jharkhand (earlier Bihar) on its north, Chhatisgarh (earlier Madhya Pradesh)[9] on the west and Andhra Pradesh on its south. West Bengal lies to its north-east and Bay of Bengal on the east. The state of Orissa covers an area of 155,707 square kilometers (60,171 sq. miles) and for administrative purposes has been divided into 30 districts[10]. As per the Census of 1991 the population of Orissa stands at 31,512,070 consisting of 15,979,904 males and 15,532,166 females; which is 3.73% of the total population of India. The 2001 Census of India puts the population of Orissa at 36,804,660 comprising 18,660,570 males and 18,144,090 females. This figure accounts for 3.57% of the total population of India. In terms of area Orissa accounts for 4.74% of India's total area[11].

The state of Orissa, as it exists today, has grown out of the earlier reconstitution of Oriya territories at different periods of time. As a separate province in colonial India it came into being in 1936. Then, it comprised six British administered districts. After independence of India, twenty-four Oriya princely states, popularly known as Princely Orissa, were merged with this province of Orissa and thereby the state acquired its present size. The formation of Orissa province in 1936 and its subsequent expansion after independence happened due to two prominent factors: (a) The rise of Oriya national movement in British Orissa; and (b) the emergence of popular democratic nationalist struggles in Princely Orissa. Both the events left lasting impact on the socio-cultural and political realities prevailing in postcolonial and contemporary Orissa. These events also considerably influenced the development of regionalism in the state of Orissa in contemporary period.

For a greater part of their history, the Oriya people enjoyed a considerable degree of political autonomy and cultural unity under different Oriya dynasties. Around the eleventh century the Oriya people emerged as a powerful cultural community with a well-defined language and a definite territory of their own. But the process of disintegration started with the fall of the last Oriya Hindu king. The Oriya territories thereafter passed into the hands of the Mughals, the Marathas and the British successively. It was under the British that the Oriya 'homeland' saw its first systematic territorial disintegration and the Oriya people their cultural fragmentation. The vivisection of Oriya people and their territory can be attributed to the very nature of British conquest.

The British occupied different parts of Oriya territories at different periods and placed them under different provincial administrations. The southern part of Orissa was kept in Madras Presidency, the coastal tract and adjoining areas in Bengal Presidency and the western part under Central Provinces (CP). Besides, a vast part of Oriya homeland was left under the control of the native Oriya princes. This political dismemberment of Oriya territories under the British in the long run posed serious external threats to Oriya identity as the Oriya people were dominated culturally and materially by 'cultural aliens' in every provincial unit they were placed under. Most of the officials who were posted to the portion of Oriya territory kept in Bengal were Bengali migrants. Bengali served as the language of the courts and the medium of instruction in schools. Almost all important positions in administration, law, teaching and clerical services were occupied by the Bengalis. If an Oriya wanted employment with some prestige in administration, he had to virtually turn himself into a Bengali. Similar situation prevailed in the Oriya territories tagged to Madras Presidency and Central Provinces. In the Oriya areas of Madras and Central Provinces the Oriya people were dominated by the Telugu and the Hindi-speaking people, respectively. Under such circumstances, the development of Oriya nationalism in British India was but natural.

The symptoms of Oriya unity began to appear soon after the outbreak of the devastating Orissa famine of 1866. This incipient feeling of Oriya unity soon crystallised into a strong national movement demanding unification of Oriya areas under a separate provincial administration. Initially, the national consciousness among the Oriyas was in the form of reaction to their inferior socio-economic and political positions in every province where they lived as insignificant cultural minorities. But when the Oriya people faced total extinction of their language and culture and hence their identity, they clamoured for formation of a separate Orissa province in British India. The cry for a separate Orissa province in British India first came from the Oriya division of Bengal Presidency. But soon it spread to the other Oriya areas placed under the Madras and Central Provinces. The first step towards formation of separate Orissa province was taken when the Oriya region of Sambalpur was transferred from Central Provinces to the Orissa division of Bengal Presidency in 1905. This was followed by the constitution of Bihar-Orissa province in 1912. Finally, the Oriya national aspiration was realised when six British administered Oriya districts placed under different provincial units were integrated on linguistic basis to form separate Orissa province to protect and preserve Oriya identity.

But the goal of united Orissa still remained incomplete as vast parts of Oriya homeland ruled by the native princes were not included in the new Orissa province. Hence in its second phase Oriya nationalism spread to princely Oriya territories. In this part of Orissa nationalistic upsurge took the shape of an anti-feudal democratic popular movement to free the Oriya people from the tyranny of the native rulers and integrate these territories with province of Orissa. These Oriya territories were integrated with Orissa province during 1948-49.

After integration of nearly all Oriya territories with Orissa province, the goal of Oriya nationalism was almost achieved and with that the question of Oriyas as a distinct nationality was legitimately established in India. Henceforth, nationalism in Orissa assumed the form of an Oriya sentiment which strongly emphasised the distinctiveness of Oriya identity and called for loyalty to Orissa state. It is, however, important to note that the state of Orissa that finally emerged due to the integration of British Orissa and Princely Orissa comprises two distinct regional units, namely, the coastal area and the western region. The coastal area originally comprised four coastal districts of Balasore, Cuttack, Ganjam and Puri. But after the reorganisation of districts in Orissa in 1993 the number of district in the coastal region has gone up to eleven. The district of Balasore was divided to form the new districts of Balasore and Bhadrak. Similarly, the erstwhile district of Cuttack was divided to form the districts of Cuttack, Jagatsinghpur, Jajpur and Kendrapara; while Ganjam was bifurcated to form the districts of Ganjam and Gajapati, the district of Puri gave rise to the new districts of Puri, Khurda and Nayagarh. The western region also originally included five districts of Bolangir, Kalahandi, Phulbani, Sambalpur and Sundargarh. Following the reorganisation of districts the number of district in the western region has also increased to eleven. Excepting the erstwhile district of Sundargarh the rest of districts in the western region were divided to form the new districts. The district of Sambalpur was divided to form four new districts of Sambalpur, Bargarh, Deogarh and Jharsuguda. Similarly, erstwhile Bolangir district was divided to form the new districts of Bolangir and Sonepur; Kalahandi district was divided into two districts of Kalahandi and Nuapada and finally erstwhile district of Phulbani was divided to form the new districts of Boudh and Kandhamal. It may, however, be noted that in this study the erstwhile undivided districts comprising the coastal and western regions have been used for the purpose of our analysis. The remaining districts of Orissa, namely, Dhenkanal (now includes the new districts of Dhenkanal and Anugul), Keonjhar, Koraput (now forms the new districts of Koraput, Nabarangpur, Malkangir and Rayagada) and Mayurbhanj do not form a part of either the western region or the coastal region and hence not included in the framework of the study. These two conspicuous regions of Orissa—coastal and western—form two compact units in terms of geographic, demographic, linguistic and socio-cultural characteristics and they experienced differential rate of socio-economic development and political mobility at different periods of time. Compared to western region, the coastal belt of Orissa remained economically more advanced, politically dominant and culturally pre-eminent. In the perception of western Oriya people the unification of Oriya territories led to the domination of coastal belt over western region of Orissa. They further claim that Orissa state is solely identified with coastal Oriyas who because of their economic, political and cultural pre-eminence perceive themselves as the mainstream and hence the vanguard of Oriya nationality. It may be noted that due to early British penetration coastal Orissa experienced improvement in transport, communication, irrigation facilities, spread of education and media activities. On the contrary, western Orissa, which remained mostly under native rule of the Oriya princes, received low level of socio-economic development and opportunities. This regional disparity widened further after independence as the coastal region continued to receive better official attention from all successive governments in Orissa state. Further, as compared to the coastal area the western region has a substantial tribal and scheduled caste population. This has serious economic, political and social implications as far as regional disparities between the two regions are concerned. The fact that the tribals are abysmally poor makes this area comparatively less developed than its coastal counterpart.

Besides the socio-economic disparities, the two regions reveal considerable political inequalities since colonial times. Expect for the Sambalpur district, the rest of the areas in the western region experienced the traditional domination of the princes; while the entire coastal region experienced the legal-rational bureaucratic domination of the British rule. The historicity of the context thus gave the coastal people a position of political advantage. Since independence the coastal region continues to dominate in the assembly and the ministry and also affects decision-making, policy-making and opinion-making.

This regional socio-economic and political imbalance led to the rise of regional discontent and separatism in western Orissa despite the overarching linguistic homogeneity in the state of Orissa. The regional consciousness is further reinforced by some cultural and historical factors. For example each of the two regions is associated with a local speech/dialectal form, i.e., 'Sambalpuri' speech with western region and 'Kataki' or coastal speech with coastal region. This natural clubbing of local speech with a particular region tends to sharpen the regional differences more and creates attitudinal sub-culture and insider-outsider dichotomy in each region. In terms of history there exist some regional differences too. Historically, the coastal and the western regions belong to the territories of the erstwhile kingdoms of Utkal-Kalinga and Koshal respectively. These differing regional historical traditions not only help in regional identity formation but also provide favourable grounds for articulating regional consciousness in western Orissa. In recent years regionalism in western Orissa has taken a nationalist turn as a section of people in western Orissa began thinking in terms of a separate state within the Indian Union on the ground of their newly constructed Koshali nationality based on Koshali language and culture.

This development not only gives rise to a parallel nationalism in Orissa but also it impairs the unity and integrity of Oriyas as a distinct nationality and Orissa as well-integrated province within Indian Union. Thus, while in colonial era the threat to Oriya identity came from external sources, the threat in contemporary times comes largely from regional forces from within. At one point of time, the internal regional threats originated from regional disparities and political-attitudinal conflict between the people of coastal and western region; but recently the threat is coming from the development of Koshali nationalism within the Oriya society. It is in this sense the analysis of nationalism and regionalism in the context of Orissa in India makes an interesting study.

3. Objectives, Questions and Hypotheses

The present study is conducted with the primary objective of bringing into focus the emergence of nationalism and regionalism in the case of Orissa within the multicultural context of India. Attention has been mainly focused on the development of Oriya nationalism in colonial period and the emerging forces of regional conflict existing between the coastal and western regions of Orissa in contemporary period. Emphasis has also been placed on the possible impact of regional conflict on the Oriya national identity. It is also attempted to reveal the nature and trend of pan-Indian nationalism vis-à-vis regional nationalism seen in various parts of India. It is in this context the study tries to spotlight on the distinction between all-India nationalism and regional-nationalism by associating the political content of nationalism with the former and the cultural content with the latter.

The study thus aims:

(a) To examine the dynamics of the notions of 'differential loyalty' and 'differential national identity' which exist in multicultural polities?

(b) To conceptualise and contextualise nationalism and regionalism in multicultural countries.

(c) To distinguish regional nationalism from regionalism and the broader nationalism seen in multicultural situation.

(d) To study the conditions under which nationalism and regionalism emerged in Orissan context in India.

(e) To bring into focus the extent of socio-cultural differences and the levels of socio-economic and political disparities existing between the coastal and the western regions of Orissa.

(f) To underline the impact of regional forces on the Oriya national identity and the development of political unity and integrity in the Orissa state.

The following questions are addressed during the course of the study:

- Should the movement launched by the Oriyas to retain their linguistic-cultural identity be called a national movement considering the fact that nationalism in India is associated with the all-India anti-colonial struggle for independence and later with an 'Indian consciousness'?
- Can the Oriyas be called a nation vis-à-vis the Indian nation? If so, in which sense?
- Does a regional national movement seeking separate provincial unit in multicultural polity such as India deserve the qualification of nationalism? If so, in which sense?
- In which sense can a national movement be distinguished from a regional movement in multicultural context?
- Is the emergence of regionalism in western Orissa related to feeling of relative deprivation? If so, in which areas the deprivation is felt more acutely and in which it is less?
- Is regionalism in western Orissa posing threats to Oriya nationality?
- Is regionalism in western Orissa heading for another regional nationalism?

The major hypotheses of the study are the following:

- Co-existence of several nations/nationalities under one political roof may lead to nationalistic mobilisation by the deprived nation/nationality.
- Quest for identity along national lines results when a peripheral community distinguished by subjective-objective criteria faces threat to its identity from a dominant community. The threat may come from all directions, but is more acutely felt in the cultural sphere.
- Concentration of political power and socio-economic development in one region may lead to protest and separatism in neglected region within a socio-linguistically homogeneous provincial unit.
- Disaffection resulting from wide differences in cultural identity poses greater challenge to political unity than tensions arising out of regional economic and political disparities.

4. Sources of Data

Data required for this study have been culled from several sources. Primary and secondary as well as qualitative and quantitative data have been used in different measures. Two types of primary data – historical and sociological – have been used. The primary historical data include the published historical records, proceedings, administrative reports, letters, archival materials, manuscripts, biographies, case histories etc. Historical data are collected from Orissa State Archives, Bhubaneswar; Board of Revenue Record Room, Cuttack; National Archives, New Delhi; Nehru Memorial Museum and Library, New Delhi; Sahitya Academy Library, New Delhi; Central Secretariat Library, New Delhi and State Museum Library, Bhubaneswar. Biographies and case histories are mainly collected from the personal library of ex-princely rulers.

Observation and interviews (with the help of an interview guide) are the chief methods used for collection of sociological data. It consists of two sections of open-ended question items and is primarily used to elicit information, attitude, opinions from knowledgeable persons, local leaders, women activists, student leaders pertaining to various issues relating to regional conflicts and regional imbalances between coastal and western regions of Orissa.

Most of the data on customs, social structure, local culture and forms of speech are obtained through observation of and interviews with the local people. Most of the information on associations and clubs was obtained by attending many association meetings and from several pamphlets, leaflets pertaining to their activities. Party literatures, memoranda, representations are collected from party offices and from persons involved in political activities and from student leaders.

Apart from this, library sources particularly books, journals, articles, census reports, Orissa statistical abstract, agricultural statistics relevant for the purpose have been extensively used. More emphasis has been put on published material and documentary evidences while discussion with political leaders and local persons has been used in a limited scale to present the study in its right perspective.

5. Plan of the Study

The study is organised into three parts and eight chapters including the conclusion. The current chapter under the title 'Introduction' deals with the statement of the problem, area of the study, objectives, questions and hypotheses and a general outline of chapter contents. Chapters two and three in part one offer some conceptual clarifications and theoretical understanding concerning the relevant key concepts and theories on nation, nationalism, region and regionalism. The major emphasis in these chapters has been on the multi-dimensional character of nationalism and its distinction from regionalism. Broadly speaking, two aspects of nation and nationalism– political and cultural– have been identified for the present purpose, while regionalism is basically dealt with as a form of in-group-out-group conflict arising out of regional imbalances existing within the territorial boundaries of a nation/ nationality. It has been stated that in the case of rise of nationalism threat to distinct cultural identity is the key variable, whereas protection of material interest of a neglected region is the salient variable in the rise of regionalism.

The chapters in part two examine the factors responsible for the growth of nationalism in the Oriya territories in colonial period and regionalism in contemporary Orissa. Chapter four tries to bring into focus the distinctiveness of Oriya nationhood prior to the British conquest and its subsequent vivisection under the colonial rule, a fact responsible for the rise of Oriya nationalism. Attention has been primarily focused here to study development of Oriya nationalism as a form of cultural nationalism seeking to retain distinct cultural identity of the Oriyas in a demarcated politico-administrative unit in India. Chapter five analyses the spread of nationalism to the Oriya-speaking areas under the princely states, a fact which led to the enlargement of the erstwhile Orissa province thereby making it co-extensive with its cultural-linguistic and physical boundary. The rationale behind this chapter is to study the differential growth of nationalism in these two parts of Oriya homeland, which had its bearing on the growth of regional diversity and regional tension in the later periods.

Chapter six discusses the extent of socio-cultural differences, socio-economic disparities and political inequalities existing between the coastal and western regions of Orissa. The main thrust of the chapter is to verify the issues of relative deprivation which exists in western Orissa. While the socio-economic and political indicators have been treated as the crucial variables in giving rise to regionalism in western Orissa, the socio-cultural, historical and geographic variables are treated as the reinforcement variables. In chapter seven, the process of articulation of regional aspiration has been discussed. The chapter mainly highlights the major regional demands and the process of development of separatist attitude on the part of a group of western Oriya people. Regional mobilisation is discussed broadly under two heads: the demand for greater regional autonomy for development and the demand for separate state on the basis of a distinct Koshali nationality. It has been attempted here to show how regionalism in western Orissa is tending towards another regional nationalism.

In the concluding chapter in part three some general observations and concluding remarks have been made on the basis of the analysis done in the preceding chapters. The major emphasis in the conclusion is to situate Oriya nationalism vis-à-vis Indian nationalism and to show the degree of specificity and commonality that the Oriya national movement shares with other such national movements in India. The chapter also focuses on the impact of regional consciousness on Oriya national identity.

Notes and References

1. See for details, Clifford Geertz, "The Integrative Revolution: Primordial Sentiments and Civil Politics in New states" in C. Geertz (ed.), *Old Societies and New States*, Amerind, New Delhi, 1971, pp. 6-7.
2. *Ibid.*
3. See, T.K. Oommen, "Insiders and Outsiders in India: Primordial Collectivism and Cultural Pluralism in Nation-building", *international Sociology*, Vol.1, No.1, 1986, p. 54. See T.K. Oommen, "Conceptualising Nation and Nationality in South Asia", in S.L. Sharma and T.K. Oommen (eds.), *Nation and National Identity in South Asia*, Orient Longman, Delhi, 2000, pp.1-18.
4. See for details T.V.S. Satyamurthy, *Nationalism in the Contemporary World*, Frances Pinter, London, 1983; A. Birch, *Nationalism and National Integration*, Unwin Hyman, London, 1989; Tom Nairn, *The Break-up of Britain: Crisis and Neo-Nationalism*, New Left Books, London, 1977; H. Seton-Watson, *Nations and States*, Methuen, London, 1977. James Minohan, *Nations without States: A Historical Dictionary of Contemporary National Movements*, West Port, Greenwood Press, 1996
5. See, for an exception, T.K. Oommen, *Citizenship, Nationality and Ethnicity Reconciling Competing Identities*, Polity Press, Cambridge, 1997.
6. A.D. Smith, 'Nationalism', *Current Sociology*, Vol. XXI, No. 3, 1973, pp. 5-185.
7. *Ibid.*
8. See, T. K. Oommen, "Nation, State and Ethnicity: Towards a Conceptual Clarification and an Empirical Explication", *Social Action*, Vol. 38, Oct-Dec, 1988, pp. 333-43. According to Oommen, 'desh' implies not merely a territory but also a people, language, style of life, pattern of culture; in fact a nation in the European

sense of the term. See also Madhav N. Deshpande, "Nation and Region: A Socio-linguistic Perspective on Maharashtra", in Milton Israel (ed), *National Unity: The South Asian Experience*, New Delhi, Promilla Publishers, 1983, pp.71-91. He observed that the word 'nadu ' in the name Tamilnadu was expressly intended by the Tamil leaders to express the idea that their homeland is a nation. He also mentioned that the word 'rashtra' in Marathi language means nation and from this word the name Maharastra, meaning 'Great nation', was derived. For a recent articulation on this point also see Jagannath Pathy, "Tribe, Region and Nation in the Context of the Indian State, in S. L. Sharma and T. K. Oommen (eds) *Nation and National Identity in South Asia,*Orient Longman, Delhi, 2000, pp. 97-111.

9. It may be noted that the Jharkhand and Chhatisgarh regions of the erstwhile states of Bihar and Madhya Pradesh have been constituted into separate states of the Indian Union as per the Bihar and Madhya Pradesh Reorganisation Act of 2000.

10. Originally there were 13 districts in Orissa. But with effect from 1st April 1993 the number of district in Orissa has increased to thirty. However, the data on regional socio-economic disparities presented in chapter six of this study mostly reflect the situation prevailing in the 13 undivided districts of Orissa and not the newly created districts. The new districts created in 1993 were carved out of the sub-divisions of the earlier 13 districts. Some new districts have been created out of a single sub-division of a former district, while the other new districts have been formed by joining two or more sub-divisions of a former district. The original 13 undivided districts are Balasore, Bolangir, Cuttack, Dhenkanal, Ganjam, Kalahandi, Keonjhar, Koraput, Mayurbhanj, Phulbani, Puri, Sambalpur and Sundargarh. The newly created districts are Anugul (formerly part of Dhenkanal district), Bhadrak (formerly part of Balasore district), Jagatsinghpur, Jajpur, Kendrapara (formerly parts of Cuttack district), Khurda, Nayagarh, (formerly parts of Puri district) Gajapati (formerly part of Ganjam district), Rayagada, Malkangiri, Navrangpur (formerly parts of Koraput district), Bargarh, Deogarh, Jharsuguda (formerly parts of Sambalpur district), Sonepur (formerly part of Bolangir district),

Nuapada (formerly part of Kalahandi district) and Boudh (formerly part of Phulbani district, now renamed as Kandhamal district). In chapter six, for the purpose of showing regional disparities between coastal region (which formerly comprised the districts of Balasore, Cuttack, Ganjam and Puri) and western region (which originally comprised the districts of Bolangir, Kalahandi, Phulbani, Sambalpur and Sundargarh) of Orissa, the socio-economic data of 2001 census for the new districts of these two regions have been combined for convenience.

11. *Census of India*, 2001.

2

Nation and Nationalism: A Conceptual Analysis

Analysis of nationalism in multicultural context such as India needs a proper understanding of the terms nation and nationalism. Broadly speaking, in multicultural context two perspectives are followed to define the terms nation and nationalism: (a) the civil framework of state; and (b) the cultural framework of the mainstream nation.

According to the first perspective, the people of a multicultural state, regardless of their cultural differences, are referred to as the nation; whereas the provincial units in the state are viewed as 'regions' notwithstanding the fact that in most cases such units contain culturally distinct nations within their fold. In the same manner, nationality in such state is interpreted in terms of citizenship and the territorially specific cultural identities are dubbed as regional or ethnic identities. Loyalty to the state and a sense of unity among the people are perceived as hallmarks of nationalism; while striving to maintain cultural identity at the regional/provincial level is considered as manifestation of regionalism.

According to the second perspective, the mainstream nation in multicultural state (e.g., Hindi-Hindu combine in India; English-Protestant combine in UK; WASP in USA; Fulani-Hasua in Nigeria, etc.) is referred to as the legitimate nation and all other smaller and peripheral nationalities (e.g., Scots, Welsh, Irish in UK; Francophone in Canada; Ibo in Nigeria; Tamils, Oriyas, Punjabis,

Kashmiris, etc., in India) are termed as regional or ethnic groups. By the same logic, the culture of the mainstream group is viewed as the 'national culture' and its language as 'national language'; while the minority cultures and languages are treated as mere regional offshoots. Assimilation into mainstream culture and language are perceived as genuine commitment to nationalism, whereas resistance to assimilation is categorised as expression of regionalism.

The above two perspectives not only confuse nation with state and mainstream culture but also undermine the multi-dimensional character of nation and nationalism. To avoid this conceptual ambiguity, it is necessary to evaluate nation and nationalism in correct perspective.

1. Understanding Nation

The concept of nation is crucial to the growth of nationalism as a sentiment/ideology or as a movement. However, the concept of nation appears to be very elusive precisely because: (a) several criteria such as geographic, demographic, socio-cultural, legal-political, economic are being used to define nation; and (b) in modern discourses for all practical purposes nation is conflated[1] with the concept of state. The conflation of nation with state not only dilutes the understanding of the term nation but also blurs the distinction between nation and state.

Etymologically, nation is derived from the Latin word 'nasci' or 'natio' (i.e. birth or race) or the French word 'nascion' (i.e. to be born) and originally meant a group of people born in the same place and territory; the political condition (i.e. sovereignty) was not a necessary element.[2] By seventeenth century the term nation came to be referred to describe the inhabitants of a country.[3] This means that in its original conception the ethnic-racial or cultural content of nation was in vogue. But with the rise of nationalism in 18th-19th century Europe, the political meaning of nation became preponderant. This is so because development of nationalism in Europe has led to the establishment of a new political entity called the nation-state, i.e., a culture-congruent sovereign state.[4] With this development the political content of nation assumed saliency and the criterion of sovereignty became identified with the term nation.

A closer scrutiny, however, reveals that historically the process of nation-state formation in Europe followed two distinct routes: state-to-nation and nation-to-state. A.D. Smith referred to these two processes as 'civil-territorial' model and the ethnic-genealogical model of nation-state formation.[5] According to him, the former model emphasized the universalistic political properties of nation such as common citizenship, popular sovereignty, equal legal rights and common administrative provisions; whereas the latter model, stressed upon the cultural attributes of nation such as distinct cultural traits and linguistic unity. The civil model was heavily influenced by the classical-liberal tradition espoused by the writings of the social contract theorists Hobbes, Locke and Rousseau.[6] The ethnic model originated in the nationalist tradition of renaissance Europe and it owed much to the writings of Fitche, Herder, Hegel's metaphysics and the social theory of Otto Baur, Lenin and Stalin. Following the civic model, England, France, Holland and the US established themselves as distinct nation-states under centralized constitutional states. But the ethnic model was realised in Germany, Italy and East European countries. Here national consciousness arose from a 'pre-existent nation'. In the countries where the civic model was realised, massive state-sponsored nation-building programme through cultural homogenisation was undertaken to mould the people around a dominant nation (e.g. English in Britain, French in France, Spanish in Spain, etc.) and make the state co-extensive with a national base. Despite this, most of these states retain their multi-national composition even today.[7] The civil-territorial and the ethnic-genealogical models finally led to the formation of nation-states in Europe and with that nation became at once a cultural and a political entity. When the referent was citizenship nation meant an organised political community of citizens, and when the referent was cultural identity it meant a culturally and linguistically homogeneous people. This suggests that the idea of equating nation with state originated with the formation of nation-states in modern Europe.

But the experience of many non-European countries revealed a slightly different trend. Here the nation-states emerged through the incorporation of several nations, nationalities, ethnic groups, tribal groups, etc. Hence in this case nation did not become at once a cultural and political entity, nor did the state become coextensive with a national base.

In the case of Third World[8] countries the civic and cultural models were realised differently at different levels. In these countries, nation at the broader state level meant a political unit comprising culturally heterogeneous or homogeneous citizens; whereas at the regional level, nation meant a territorially-based distinct cultural community. Unlike European experience, here the distinct cultural communities did not tend to produce their own states but rather preferred to co-exist under a common state. These differential notions of nation continue to exist in these countries even today. The experience of the Third World countries thus brought to the fore three notable elements: (a) a political nation can emerge by incorporating several cultural communities; (b) a cultural nation can exist without a state of its own; and (c) nation and state is not always co-terminous.

In sum, if nation in Europe emerged as a sovereign political entity, in most non-European countries it acquired a sovereign political form at the macro level and a cultural form at the regional level. Similarly, nationalism in these counties aimed at a common sovereign state at the macro level and culture-congruent provincial units at the regional cultural level. The differing experiences of both European and non-European countries thus testify that nation can be conceptualised in both political and cultural terms.

The interpretation of nation in political and cultural sense is also discernible from some major writings on nationalism. J.S.Mill, for example, wrote:

A portion of mankind may be said to constitute a nationality if they are united among themselves by common sympathies, which do not exist between them and any others, which make them cooperate with each other more willingly than with other people, desire to be under the same government and desire that it should be government by themselves or a portion of themselves exclusively.[9]

Hobsbawm noted that, "any sufficiently large body of people whose members regard themselves as members of a 'nation', will be treated as such". He further argued that nation is "a social entity insofar as it relates to a certain kind of modern territorial state".[10] Benedict Anderson, one of the most famous contemporary scholars on nationalism, defines the nation as "an imagined political community, and imagined as both inherently limited and sovereign".[11] According to Anderson "nation is imagined because the members of even the smallest nation will never know most of their fellow-members, meet them, or even hear them, yet in the minds of each lives the image of their communion. In fact, all communities larger than primordial villages of face-to-face contact are imagined".[12] Anderson further observes that:

Nation is imagined as limited because even the largest of them encompassing perhaps a billion human beings, has finite, if elastic boundaries, beyond which lie other nations. No nation imagines itself coterminous with mankind. It is imagined as sovereign because the concept was born in an age in which Enlightenment and Revolution were destroying the legitimacy of the divinely-ordained hierarchic dynastic realm. Finally, it is imagined as a community because regardless of the actual inequality and exploitation that may prevail in each, the nation is always conceived as a deep, horizontal comradeship.[13]

The above definitions especially that of Mill restrict the concept of nation to the subjective-political variables such as consciousness, general will, common government, sovereignty and citizenship. Such subjective-political definitions of nation tend to be one dimensional in nature and they suffer from several limitations. First, these subjective-political definitions confuse nation with state. Not all nations are state endowed; in reality a nation may form a part of a state, may be coterminous with it or may extend beyond it.[14] Second, these definitions put maximum stress on sovereignty and citizenship. In fact, sovereignty and citizenship are the salient attributes of a state and not a nation. A nation essentially refers to a culturally homogeneous people of a given territory. Finally, these definitions emphasise that common interest or general will is a key attribute of nation. But the fact of the matter is that common interest is not fixed, it changes from time to time and from one context to another.

Scholars following the cultural interpretation, however, try to lodge the concept of nation on somewhat more concrete or objective cultural criteria such as common language, common religion, common culture, shared history, descent, myths, memories and common territory. Stalin, for example, defines nation as a "historically evolved stable community of people, formed on the basis of a common language, territory, economic life and psychological make-up manifested in a common culture."[15] According to him, none of the above characteristics is by itself sufficient to define a nation. However, he argued, if any of these characteristics is absent, the group ceases to be a nation. Stalin's definition does not include historical tradition, religion or common government

William Patterson, another exponent of cultural notion, defines nation as "...a people, folk, held together by some or all of such more or less immutable characteristics as common descent, territory, history, language, religion, way of life, or other attributes that members of a group have from birth onward."[16] The problematic aspects of this definition are the notion of immutability and the attribute of religion.

Ernest Gellner, a notable European scholar on nationalism, also emphatically stressed the cultural content of nation. He observes that, "two men are of the same nation if and only if they share the same culture, where culture in turn means a system of ideas, signs and associations and ways of behaving and communicating."[17] He further suggests that "...a mere category of people occupying a given territory or speaking a common language, or practicing a distinct culture becomes a nation if and when the members of the category firmly recognize certain mutual rights and duties to each other by virtue of their shared membership of it."[18] For Gellner, then, cultural and psychological elements are the key attributes of nation. But Gellner's argument is based on the limited experience of the industrialised parts of the West where states are sustained by languages and cultures shared by all and transmitted to all through systems of mass education. This shows that Gellner restricts his analysis of nation to high-literate cultures only. Basically, he treats nation and state as identical units. He sees nation as a culture-congruent polity in which the boundary of the state is co-terminus with the cultural boundary of a specific people. To him the normative idea of nation in its modern sense presupposes the existence of a state, intended or real. It seems, then, in Gellner's analysis a nation arises only within a state framework, that is, a people united by common culture and literary language can constitute a nation only when they form a state. This argument again places sovereignty as the key variable of nation.

This conceptualisation is fraught with the following difficulties. First, Gellner equates state with nation and argues that common literary language and cultural homogeneity are the pre-requisites for the existence of a state. This situation largely entails in most of the western states. But in many non-western countries of the world the state is not based on a common literary language or common culture. Hence, linguistic uniformity and cultural homogeneity can not be considered as the sole prerequisites of state-formation in many parts of the world. By the same logic, sovereign state structure can not be considered as an essential condition for the existence of a nation. Second, Gellner reserves the term nation for 'high-literate' cultures; and for him, only the industrial societies produce this type of mass cultures. The 'agro-literate' societies according to him do not represent mass cultures and hence cannot be qualified as nations. If one follows this argument then a substantial number of people in most of the countries in Africa, Asia, and Latin America would be excluded from the ambit of the term nation. In these countries numerous people speak several distinct languages but do not possess literary cultures. Hence, Gellner's definition cannot be applied to many countries in the non-European parts of the world.

Perhaps, the most forthright statement on the cultural view of nation came from the writings of A.D. Smith. Set in cultural pluralistic tradition, Smith distinguishes two types of nation: civic (or political) and ethnic (or cultural). The civic type according to him originates from a civil-territorial base and the ethnic type from an ethnic-genealogical or 'demotic' cultural base. The sovereign states represent the civic type and the smaller nations contained within such states constitute the ethnic type. He observes, "..for small nations, their cultures and history have become both means and end of their existence... for it defines their very *raisen d'etra* as separate units".[19]

He further argues once a civic nation consolidates, it tries to look for ethnic past to root the nation in a cultural space. Similarly, once an ethnic nation crystallizes into a state, it tries to transcend the ethnic past and evolve into a civil society.[20] Hence in both cases, the essential attribute of nation is located in cultural homogeneity. Smith further adds that cultural distinctiveness is not enough, the desire to obtain self-rule is inherent in many ethnic or cultural nations. This desire originates from their ability to form and sustain a state which in turn is derived from a concept of 'home territory' and a distinct cultural identity.[21] Most ethnic nations, however, prefer to realize their desire for self-rule by retaining their cultural-territorial identity within the federal framework of a civic nation. For Smith, then, the goal of self-determination is not always one of independent statehood; this can very well be achieved in terms of political autonomy within a sovereign polity. In order to be called a nation a people should not only possess a common cultural identity but also a desire and capacity for self-rule, in independent or autonomous terms. This conception of nation is different from civic nation which is based exclusively on independent statehood. Smith's dual conception of nation applies to several countries in different parts of the world.

2. Nation and State

A nation crystallizes into a state once it acquires a sovereign political structure over its territory. This is, however, not to say that the terms state and nation mean the same thing. The distinction between state and nation is strikingly noticed in multi-national and multicultural states. Even in the mono-national and mono-cultural states, the nation can be conceptually differentiated from the state.

As a matter of fact, state exclusively implies a sovereign legal-political structure and it is overwhelmingly linked with the institutions of legitimate power and authority. According to Weber, state refers to that agency within the society which possesses the monopoly of legitimate violence.[22] Pye defines it as "a legal concept describing a social group that occupies a defined territory and is organised under a common political institution and an effective government."[23] Bhikhu Parekh defines the modern state "as an association of individuals".[24] It is clear that the concept of state is basically political in content and it refers to a people organised under a government which exercises sovereignty over a defined political boundary. What is common to the people of a state is citizenship which necessarily implies a territorial base. Hence, sovereignty, citizenship, political territory are the major attributes of state; of these sovereignty is the critical variable, while the rest two are emphasised in order to make the exercise of sovereignty effective. It is sovereignty which distinguishes a state from a nation and from other forms of social organisations exercising social power. A nation in strict sense is a cultural entity surviving within a geographical base; it may or may not have its own state. A state, on the contrary, is exclusively a political entity and it implies a variety of political structures: empires, kingdoms, principalities, city-states, republics, federations and confederations. Further, a state is differentiated from a nation in that the former refers to a 'political homeland', i.e., an instituted legal-political boundary vested with sovereignty and the latter refers to a 'cultural homeland', i.e., an ancestral or adopted territory.

Nation is not only distinct from state, but also from nation-state and national state. A nation-state is a state in which only one nation exists. That is, it is a state where the 'political homeland' of the people is perfectly aligned with their 'cultural homeland'. This concept of one-nation, one-state hardly exists in reality. Most of the contemporary states are either multinational or multicultural. A national state is a state in which one nation is overwhelmingly dominant with some rights granted to the smaller nations and cultural minorities.[25] The dominant nation calls itself the mainstream nation and identifies itself with the state.

The distinction between nation and state can further be clarified once we look at the possible manner in which state and nation are combined in different parts of the world. Some of these combinations are as follows:[26]

(1) One-nation, one-state. This variety is a misnomer. Nowhere in the world has conformity to this norm existed. Yet Japan and Sweden can be cited as examples notwithstanding the presence of Korean minority in the former and the Palestinian refugees in the latter.

(2) One nation divided into two or more states for ideological and geo-political reasons (e.g. pre-unified Germany, former Vietnam, and the two Koreas).

(3) Part of a nation constitutes a sovereign state and the other part either forms an autonomous administrative unit in another sovereign state or remains attached to it (e.g. Bangladesh and West Bengal and Tripura in India; Ireland and Northern Ireland in UK).

(4) One nation is divided between two sovereign states and constitutes administrative units in each of them (e.g. Indian Punjab and Pakistan Punjab).

(5) One nation is divided into several administrative units in a sovereign state (e.g. Hindi-speaking states in India).

(6) One nation fragmented into many sovereign states (e.g., Kurdistan in Iraq, Iran, Syria, Turkey and Afghanistan).

(7) One nation fragmented into many provincial administrative units of a sovereign state (e.g. former Jharkhand region dispersed into the provinces of undivided Bihar, Orissa, Bengal and undivided Madhya Pradesh in India).

(8) One state and many nations. This has the following varieties:

    (a) One state comprising of two dominant nations (e.g. Malays and Chinese in Malaysia; Anglophones and Francophone in Canada, Tamils and Sinhalese in Sri Lanka, etc.).

    (b) One state and several nations with one being significantly dominant (e.g. English in UK; French in France; Spanish in Spain, etc.).

    (c) A number of distinct nations forming a state (e.g. India and former Soviet Union).

(d) Parts of different nations came to constitute a state for geo-political reasons (e.g. Switzerland).

(e) One state comprising many smaller nations with no one being dominant (e.g. most African states).

(f) A set of migrants drawn from a variety of nations constitute a state (e.g. the USA).

It is clear from the above that nation and state can be combined in a variety of ways; a nation-state refers to only one such combination. Hence, the principle of co-terminality between state and nation is not an essential condition for the survival of nation. A nation can very well survive without a state of its own.

To recapitulate, nation was originally understood in cultural terms. But with the emergence of the so-called nation-states in Europe and America, the cultural content of nation was sidelined and its political content became dominant and as a result of this development nation through out the world came to mean an organised political grouping of citizens of a sovereign state. However, the consolidation of many multicultural states in different parts of the world has made the cultural and political notions of nation very clear. This apart, the ongoing demands for separate provincial units by several deprived cultural communities in a multicultural state as well as the process of nation-building in it re-emphasised the cultural dimension of nation. As a result, nation came to be interpreted in a dual manner – cultural and political.

The political connotation of nation has two sub-types. The first type includes sovereign states comprising culturally different people and the second type includes cultural communities having their own sovereign states. In both instances, however, sovereign state structure is singled out as the critical factor in nation-formation. But the fact remains that nation at root is a cultural entity; and the political approach by putting the accent on sovereignty has excluded many cultural communities from the ambit of nation.

The cultural interpretation, on the other hand, does not emphasise sovereignty as an essential or a sufficient condition for the existence of nation. It locates nationhood in the attributes of distinct culture, shared past, common language and territory. Again, it stresses that a nation may organise itself into a state, or forms a part of state, or split up into two or more states, or remains without any political structure of its own. In short, the cultural approach of nation seems to be pluralistic in orientation.

It follows that both approaches differ so far as the critical variable of nation is concerned. The political approach locates the critical variable of nation in independent statehood and citizenship; whereas the cultural approach locates the critical variable of nation in the notion of distinct identity and unities of culture, language and territory.

On the basis of the foregoing discussion nation can be classified into two major types: civil or political and cultural or ethnic. The political nations are sovereign entities and they refer to both mono-cultural and multicultural states. The cultural nations are territorially distinct cultural communities without their own states. In most cases these cultural nations survive as provincial units in large states. These cultural nations are referred to by many as nations without states.

Following the cultural interpretation, nation in the present study is defined as a social collectivity sharing common culture and common past, recognised by its members and by others as different; having a uniform communication medium (usually a mother-tongue); occupying a naturally owned or effectively controlled geographically contiguous territory; showing a strong sense of unity from within and feeling of separateness from without; and desiring for legitimate political authority in independent or autonomous terms.

This definition includes both objective and subjective conditions of nation. The cultural and spatial variables conform to the objective condition; the sense of unity, feeling of separateness and the desire for political legitimacy conform to the subjective condition. It may be noted that nation exists both as a subjective and an objective reality. While the objective markers define the boundaries of a nation, the subjective elements help internalise these boundaries into the collective psyche of its members.

Each nation is defined and determined by unifying its members from within and by differentiating them from other groups. It is true that the perception of difference in most cases accrue from a feeling of relative deprivation. So, the concepts of 'we' vs. 'they' or 'us' vs. 'them' are central to the growth of a nation.

However, the notion of 'we' vs. 'they' is also found among groups resembling nation. How then can we distinguish that element which is necessary, though not sufficient, in defining nation? That distinguishing feature is a desire for political self-determination (i.e. self-rule). But the desire for political self-determination can be found in a variety of cultural groups. Should such groups then be called nations? The answer is no, because to be effective, political self-determination requires the essential condition of 'home territory'. To quote Oommen, "even if all other attributes are present together a nation does not come into being unless it establishes legitimate claim over a territory which in turn provides it with the potential to state-formation."[27] This means that cultural distinctiveness and desire for political unity have no meaning without a territorial base. For example, prior to the formation of Israel the Jews were hardly called a nation because they lacked a definite territory. This means that cultural distinctiveness and desire for political self-rule have no meaning without a territorial base.

The major attributes of nation thus are:

(a) **Distinct culture:** It refers to demotic vernacular cultures. For maintenance of cultural distinctiveness, certain pre-requisites such as minimum size, physical concentration and constant interaction have to be met.

(b) **Common communication medium:** It provides the modus operandi for group interaction and for transmission of cultural symbols. It may include (i) a mother tongue, or (ii) a lingua-franca used by all diverse groups in a given territory.

(c) **Territory:** It refers to the physical as well as the cultural-linguistic boundaries of a community. A definite territory imbibes a sense of 'homeland' in the minds of the people.

(d) **Common past**: Human roots come from their social origins and shared history. The latter comprises symbols, legends, myths, memories, golden ages, common suffering, and national heroes. Where no such things exist, attempts are made to create them so as to root the people in a common past. Historical root is as important as cultural and territorial roots.

(e) **Psychological unity:** It stems from 'consciousness of likeness' and 'consciousness of difference'. The former is based on common characteristics prevailing among group members and the latter grows from perception of difference from others.

(f) **Potentiality for self-rule:** Besides being a cultural unit, a nation is viewed by its members as a political unit. So, it is essential that to be a nation, a group must possess the potentiality for political self-determination in independent or autonomous terms.

(g) **Economic viability:** Economic viability provides a nation with the power to sustain itself independently without outside interference.

3. Nation and Nationality

Nation is also closely associated with the concept of nationality. In political sense nationality is mainly interpreted as membership in a nation which is mostly understood in citizenship terms. But an examination of facts suggests that nationality has been viewed in various ways.

In its original German conception, nationality refers to nations which failed to establish their own states.[28] But as a matter of fact, aspiration for statehood is not an essential condition for a nation to exist. In another sense, nationality refers to membership in and identification with a particular nation-state. In this sense, the term connotes two meanings: political, which is expressed in citizenship terms and cultural, which indicates identification with a community which shares a distinct culture, common language and specific home territory. In mono-cultural states these two dimensions of nationality are blended together. But, in multi-national and multicultural states the political and cultural dimensions of nationality are clearly visible. In the UK, for example, there is a tendency to distinguish nationality as citizenship from nationality as cultural identity. One can be British as well as English or Scottish or Welsh at the same time. While the British identity reflects political expression of nationality, the English or Scottish or Welsh identity reflects cultural expression of identity. These two notions of nationality—political and cultural—operate in somewhat different forms in India as well.

Nationality also means the quality or consciousness of being a nation. In this sense, it refers to a people whose members are united by certain cultural, linguistic and territorial bonds. In yet another sense, nationality refers to national minorities who have no territory of their own, but broadly identify with the state of their location. In this sense nationality connotes an ethnic group.[29]

The Marxists see nationality in terms of shared cultural ties and linguistic unities; whereas a nation is considered by them as a politico-economic unit.[30] According to this argument, nationality existed prior to capitalism, but nation as politico-economic unit emerged in the age of capitalism.

From the political perspective nation and nationality are regarded as separate entities; the former connotes a political unit endowed with sovereignty and the latter indicates distinct cultural community not endowed with sovereignty. In this sense, the culturally diverse people of a multicultural state are labeled as nationalities; and the political state containing these culturally diverse people is referred to as the nation.

But from the socio-cultural point of view, nation and nationality appear to be more or less same. The only distinguishing factor is that in the case of nation, the subjective consciousness of the people is clearly manifest and that the unit with which they identify possesses the potentiality for self-rule. Not all nationalities are capable of forming viable self-ruling units. Hence, a nationality becomes a nation only when it possesses potentiality for political self-rule in independent or autonomous sense.

In the light of the discussion in the preceding pages, the following general points can be made:

1. Nation can be conceptualised both in political and cultural sense. In political sense nation can be conceptualised following a set of political variables such as sovereignty, citizenship, common administrative-legal system, common solidarity, etc., and in cultural sense nation can be conceptualised using a set of cultural criteria such as common language, common culture, shared history, ancestral homeland, etc. In the multicultural context nation assumes a political form at the macro level and a cultural form at the regional-cultural level.

2. Nation and state need not be always co-terminous. They can be combined in various ways. A state may comprise a single national unit or it may contain several nations as well as cultural, racial and linguistic minorities. A nation becomes a state by securing sovereign political structure. But not all nations tend to produce their own states; some nations prefer to co-exist as provincial units under a common political roof.
3. The principle of congruity of political sovereignty and cultural homogeneity should not be taken as an essential condition in the understanding of nation. A nation is essentially a territorially-rooted cultural community having a strong sense of separateness and a capacity for self-rule.
4. Potentiality for self-rule is crucial to the understanding of nation. But self-rule should not be analysed in sovereign terms only, it can be realised in autonomous terms as well. Sovereignty is an essential feature of state and not nation.
5. Both political and cultural varieties of nations exist in the world. The sovereign states comprise the political nations and the territorially distinct cultural communities in a sovereign state constitute cultural nations

4. Nationalism: The Theoretical Perspectives

As noted earlier, the concept of nation (political or cultural, real or imaginary) lies at the root of all nationalisms. In some cases national consciousness may precede nation-formation, while in some it may originate from a pre-existing nation. The idea of nation, however, does not necessarily give rise to nationalism. Certain other conditions have to be met for nationalistic ideology or movement to grow.

Some scholars treat nationalism primarily as a 'form of politics', which aims at capturing state power.[31] Some writers are concerned with nationalism as a 'state of mind', as the expression of national consciousness.[32] Most writers focus on the multi-dimensional aspects of nationalism, depending upon the context one or another dimension of it assumes saliency. For example, Coleman has identified five different brands of nationalism in Nigeria: African, Nigerian, Regional, Tribal and Cultural.[33] Probably, the most commonly held view about nationalism is that it arises from some sort of national identity (pre-existent nation), or that it is a search for such an identity.

As far as theories of nationalism are concerned, there exist three major varieties: Liberal theories, Marxist theories, and the Cultural-pluralist theories.[34] The Marxist theories see nationalism exclusively in terms of class and class conflicts.[35] On the whole, the Marxists denounce the bourgeois character of nationalism. True, the nationalist ideals are mostly transmitted from the elites to the masses. But to construe all-nationalism-as-bourgeois-and-therefore-bad is to ignore the mass character of nationalism. Again, the fact that certain classes play a decisive role in a nationalist movement does not mean that nationalism is a class phenomenon. In fact, class like gender, sex, age, etc. creates intra- and not inter-community cleavages. It is linguistic cleavages and cultural differences which create inter-community conflicts. Further, as an ideology, nationalism places self-determination at the centre of its concern. Naturally therefore nationalism cannot be interpreted in class terms.

The liberal and cultural-pluralist theories examine nationalism in different perspectives. The liberal theory, in the main, claims that the root to nationalism is the idea of nation consisting of citizens of an independent state. That is, as a movement, or as an ideology, nationalism is always related to a sovereign-state-seeking goal. Hayes, for example, argues that nationalism as a political doctrine envisages the principle of 'national congruence' which says that a national unit should be congruent with a sovereign state, and that all cultural groups worth self-governing should be constituted into sovereign states.[36]

Hans Kohn, the leading liberal theorist, quite explicitly states that "in all nationalisms activities are directed towards the sustaining of the nation-state; where the nation-state is non-existent, the group satisfies itself with some form of autonomy or pre-state organisation, which, however, always tends at a given moment to develop into a sovereign state".[37] Kohn's nationalism thus is founded upon the concept of nation-state as the supreme source of political legitimacy. Kohn further states that the quest for political self-determination is invariably linked with quest for cultural self-determination and vice-versa.

Ernest Gellner, a notable figure among liberal theorists, observes, "nationalism, as a sentiment or as a movement, is primarily a political principle which holds that the political and national unit should be congruent."[38] Gellner considers nationalism as a distinctive species of patriotism. The units with which this distinctive form of patriotism identifies its loyalty are: (a) culturally homogeneous; (b) socially anonymous; (c) educationally developed; (d) normatively of 'high' culture; and above all (e) politically independent. He further claims that nationalism emerges only in the milieu where the existence of the state – intended or real – is taken for granted.[39] Taken to its logical conclusion, this argument postulates that nationalism arose precisely because of the violation of nationalist principle, and the said principle was violated by the emergence of modern states. Three points are clearly discernible from Gellner's analysis of nationalism: First, nationalism is a theory of political legitimacy which requires that political boundary should not cut across the cultural boundary. Second, it is the mismatch between nation and state which gives rise to numerous national movements. Third, he acknowledges the cultural basis of nation but advocates that only the high-literate-industrial cultures are capable of constructing nationalism mainly because these cultures through their means of common language and shared cultures are capable of sustaining independent states.

Like Gellner, Hobsbawm also uses the term nationalism to mean primarily a principle which holds that the political and national unit should be congruent[40]. John Breuilly, another great exponent of the liberal theory, defines nationalism as a term "used to refer to political movements seeking or exercising state power and justifying such actions with nationalist arguments".[41] According to him a nationalist argument is a political doctrine built upon three basic assertions: (a) there exists a nation with explicit and peculiar character; (b) the interest and values of this nation take priority over all other interest and values; and (c) the nation must be as independent as possible, this usually requires at least the attainment of political sovereignty.[42] In short, the telling point in the argument of liberal theory is that nationalism is simply inconceivable without the idea of independent state.

The above conceptualisations on nationalism suffer from a number of difficulties. First, the idea that independent state formation is inherent in all types of nation has been disproved several rounds over, especially in the multicultural context. Second, Kohn's argument that cultural self-determination in all nationalisms is linked with political self-determination in independent terms has also not come true in different parts of the world. Finally, Gellner's view that only industrial cultures can produce nationalism is based on limited observation of European societies and is not applicable to many other parts of the world including India. Nationalism in most parts of the world has developed from agrarian cultures and vernacular languages.

It may be observed that three nationalist traditions have influenced the liberal theory: the liberal nationalist tradition of West Europe and the US, the cultural nationalist tradition of Central and East Europe, and the anti-colonial nationalist tradition of the Third World. Accordingly, the liberal theory is divided into three sub-types: (a) liberal-political, (b) liberal-nationalist, and (c) anti-colonial. The idea of independent state is common to all these variants of liberal theory of nationalism, but they differ from each other in regard to their conceptualisation of nation and their context of analysis.

The liberal-political type originated in the US and West Europe and it owed much to three epoch-making universalistic political struggles: the English Revolution of 1668; the American War of Independence of 1776 and the French Revolution of 1789. These major events gave birth to a nationalist ideology which includes the following elements:

(a) A nation is a political unit comprising equal citizens.

(b) Political authority derived from the people is the only legitimate authority.

(c) Loyalty to the nation is the supreme form of loyalty and the interests and values of nation take precedence over all interests.

(d) The nation must be as independent as possible. This usually requires at least the attainment of political sovereignty.

To put differently, this nationalistic ideology embodied three novel ideas: a new concept of loyalty; a new basis of political legitimacy and a new type of state-formation. The new concept of loyalty called for replacement of the older form of loyalty to the monarch or ruling class by loyalty to the nation. The new basis of legitimacy rejected political authority based on divine sanction and natural right and implied that the collective personality of the people was more important. The new form of state-formation called for constitution of states along national lines, usually conforming to one-nation, one-state norm.[43]

This nationalist vision swayed almost all parts of Europe, America and the Third World. But the definition of nation, the course of nationalism and the set-up under which nationalism operated differ in almost all of them. For example, in USA, nation referred to the people regardless of their cultural composition. In Western Europe, nation meant a political unit but closely interpreted in terms of the dominant nation (e.g. English in Britain, French in France, Spanish in Spain, etc.). But in Germany, Italy, East Europe and the Balkans, nation referred to a distinct people speaking the same language and sharing the same culture. Finally, in the Third World, nation implied a political unit composed of people belonging to diverse cultures, languages, religions, races, etc.

Nationalism took a state-to-nation route in the USA; a state-to-nation (via the dominant nation) route in Western Europe; a nation-to-state route in Central and East Europe; and finally a colony-to-nation route in the Third World. These different routes of nationalism can be attributed to the origins of nationalism under different conditions. Nationalism emerged in the USA from political unity and widely accepted democratic values; in the Western Europe it emerged from political unity and a national consciousness broadly centering around the dominant nation; in Central and East Europe it evolved from pre-political unity based on common cultural-linguistic identity; and in the former colonies it grew from political unities created by the colonial states, geographical bonds persisting since time immemorial and the commonly shared anti-colonial experiences. Hence, the nomenclatured variants: liberal-political, liberal-nationalist and anti-colonial forms of nationalism.

For analytical purposes, the state-to-nation and the colony-to-nation types of nationalism can be classified as 'political nationalism', and the nation-to-state types of nationalism as 'cultural nationalism'. Cultural nationalism may follow a nation-to-state path, or it may seek an administrative or provincial unit within a common sovereign state. Needless to say, the former type is based on the broad political attributes of nation and the latter is based on the cultural specificities.

If in the US political nationalism led to the formation of the American state, in Europe states were formed pursuing either political or cultural nationalism. But in the Third World these two forms of nationalism were pursued differently at different levels by the people of the same country. Political nationalism here was seen at the broader level and it originated from a political view of nation engulfing the entire country; while, cultural nationalism was seen at the regional-cultural level and it evolved from a cultural view of nation. The former aimed at establishment of independent state and the latter maintenance of cultural distinctiveness. But unlike Europe, in the Third World cultural nationalism did not exclusively tend toward independent state-formation.

The cultural-pluralist theory of nationalism differs drastically from the liberal position. It states that nationalism can very well exist without any motive for political self-determination in independent terms. People can be politically mobilized for achievement of internal self-determination within the provisions of self-rule inside the political structure of a common sovereign state. This theory sees nation primarily as a homogeneous cultural unit with or without state structure. Additionally, it stresses the multi-dimensional or the pluralist vision of contemporary nationalist ideology. It claims that both political and cultural nation and nationalism can and should harmoniously co-exist in a single sovereign state.

To explicate their position, the cultural-pluralists refer to the numerous national movements which existed or continue to exist in many multicultural states. The chief advocate of this theory is A.D. Smith. Initially, Smith supported the liberal position and argued that real nationalism is always linked with a goal of sovereign state, and anything resembling nationalism which appeared in ancient or medieval times are but forms of 'ethnocentrism' or 'ethnicism'.[44]

But as a point of departure, Smith later noted that nationalism grows out of some oldest feeling or primeval desires of human beings, and that it need not necessarily be linked with concept of sovereign statehood. He wrote, "...nations like Scotland and Catalonia opt to remain within wider states, and even welcome two circles of national loyalty."[45]

He further stated, nation-state model is nowhere realized. On the contrary, most states are multi-national and varieties of nationalism with varying objectives are found in them. According to Smith the primary objective of contemporary global nationalism is a nationalist vision of a plurality of unique and free nations under a single sovereign state[46]. Like Smith, several other scholars also focused on the varying aspects of nationalism. Snyder, for instance, noted that most national movements operating within the boundary of larger states aim at political autonomy and not outright independence.[47] Birch's study on the national problems in UK, Australia and Canada has reiterated the above position.[48] Edmonds observed that given the barrier to national unity, the Kurds of Iraq and neighboring countries have opted to remain as autonomous units within large states.[49] In short, the cultural-pluralist theory mainly argues that distinct cultural identity may not exclusively be used for achieving sovereign statehood; it can be directed at autonomy as well. In the same vein, cultural nationalism can serve as a necessary ingredient of political nationalism.

It may be recalled here that political nationalism in the ex-colonies aimed at transforming the colonies into sovereign states and the subjects into citizens. In contrast, cultural nationalism in ex-colonial countries broadly followed two courses. In some cases it emphasised sovereign-state seeking goal and in some it demanded culturally homogeneous provincial units. A third variety of cultural nationalism also emerged in these countries. This variety of nationalism dwells heavily upon the dominant majority culture and tries to identify itself with the whole state.

It follows that four types of nationalism are seen in the multicultural ex-colonial countries of the Third World: (a) broader political nationalism enveloping the whole population; (b) cultural nationalism seeking sovereign states; (c) cultural nationalism seeking provincial units within common sovereign state; and (d) cultural nationalism of the dominant nation identifying with the whole state. Hence, in the multicultural context of the Third World nationalism can neither be interpreted exclusively in political terms nor equated with a sovereign state seeking goal only.

In sum, the experiences of different countries of the world suggest that political nationalism invariably tends towards a state-seeking goal; whereas the goal of cultural nationalism varies from achievement of autonomy to outright independence. Brubaker remarks that nationalism in post-communist Europe and Eurasia differs sharply from the state-seeking and nation-building nationalism of Western Europe[50]. To explain why nationalism has taken different forms in different countries, Michael Hechter in his recent work offers an analytical typology of nationalism. Hechter argues that "if nationalism is collective action designed to render the boundaries of the nation congruent with those of its governance unit, then a simple analytic typology of nationalism flows directly out of this definition".[51] He identifies four types of nationalism: state-building, peripheral, irredentist and unification. State-building nationalism is embodied in the attempt to assimilate or incorporate culturally distinctive territories in a given state. It is the result of the conscious efforts of central rulers to make a multicultural population culturally homogeneous. Peripheral nationalism occurs when a culturally distinctive territory resists incorporation into an expanding stat, or attempts to secede and set up its own state. Irredentist nationalism occurs with the attempt to extend the existing boundaries of a state by incorporating territories of an adjacent state occupied principally by co-nationals. Finally, unification nationalism involves the merger of a politically divided but culturally homogeneous territory into one state. In this case the effort to render cultural and governance boundaries congruent requires the establishment of a new state encompassing the members of the nation.[52] Beiner notes that in multi-national or multi-ethnic states both civic and ethnic nationalisms are seen.[53]

5. Modernist and Primordialist Debate

The liberal and cultural-pluralist theories of nationalism also differ on the question of whether nationalism is modern or primordial (or ancient). The liberal theory adheres to the modernist position, but the cultural-pluralist theory subscribes to the primordial viewpoint.

The modernist position holds that far from being a natural social reality and a historical constant, nationalism is clearly a contingent phenomenon created in modern times. Three modern factors accounted for its growth: (a) industrial capitalism, which replaced the older feudal society; (b) bureaucratic centralism, which established representative government and constitutionalism; and (c) utilitarian secularism, which promoted use of vernacular language and spread of secular education.[54] The interplay of these modern factors gave rise to a political doctrine which postulated that sovereign states should be created on cultural basis. According to the modernists, nationalism precisely grew out of this political ideology of organising modern states along cultural lines. Kohn, for example, stated that consciousness about one's linguistic and territorial identities existed among certain peoples in earlier times (e.g. ancient Greeks and Jews), but these elements were never used for political mobilisation and therefore cannot be termed as true nationalism.[55] This shows that the cultural dimension of nationalism existed before, but its political dimension assumed saliency in modern times as the desire for organising cultures into unified sovereign politico-economic units was felt.

Perhaps the most succinct exposition of the modernist viewpoint came from the writings of Anderson and Gellner. According to Anderson, the most notable figure among modernists, the decline of religious authority and the rise of secular capitalism under the novel technology of print media in the modern era made it possible to imagine communities at once sovereign and homogeneous. Such 'imagined communities' or nations came to serve vital psychological, political and economic needs under modern conditions.[56] In other words, nations developed as necessary component of industrial society. Anderson places greater emphasis on the constructed nature of culture and on the role of print capitalism to the development of nations. On the cultural front, Anderson argues that pre-national culture was religious culture. Nations replaced this religious culture with their own uniquely constructed national cultures.[57] On the whole, Anderson places print capitalism at the core of his theory of nationalism.

Gellner too points out that nationalism as a sense of attachment to one's language and territory is created under conditions prevalent in modern industrial societies; modern societies require homogeneity, mobility and literacy to sustain an industrial economy.[58] Modern states created the nationalism by homogenising their populations through mass and standardised secular education. For Gellner, then, the modern forces of industrialisation and the agency of modern states have created nationalism and not followed it. Gellner categorically mentioned that nations, like states, are a contingency, and not a universal necessity. Neither nations nor states exist at all times and in all circumstances.[59] Deutsch also believes that new modes of communication unleashed by the modern societies promoted the spread of nationalist ideals.[60]

In short, the modernists argue that nationalism as a political creed appeared only in modern times. Consciousness about cultural and territorial identity existed in pre-modern times, but the consciousness to constitute distinct cultures into independent states came in modern period only, and this consciousness is nationalism. For the modernists the past is largely irrelevant. The nation is a modern phenomenon, the product of nationalist ideologies, which themselves are the expressions of the modern industrial society. Hence, nations are phenomena of a particular stage of history, and embedded in purely modern conditions.

The primordial view states that independent state structure is not an essential condition for the existence of nation or the rise of nationalism. It is cultural distinctiveness, territory, language and sense of solidarity that give rise to nationalism, and these traits are as natural as human speech, sex, family and geography. Influenced by Shills' work on civil, sacred and primordial ties,[61] the primordialists in general maintain that nation is a human constant even though its form and content change over time and space. In other words the primordialists argue that nations are timeless phenomena. Tom Nairn, for example, notes that the urge to constitute groups along national lines is inherent in mankind like infantilism or dementia.[62] Armstrong argues that nations as cultural entities even existed before the birth of nationalism in modern times. Most of these nations did not have their own states.[63] He strongly emphasized that nationalism grows out of some enduring bonds of myths, memories and symbols.[64] Kedourie took national divisions, national character and nationalism for granted, even if he deplored its harmful effects.[65] Satyamurthy also emphatically focuses upon the naturalness of nation.[66] Billig suggests that nationalism exists at all times in less visible forms which he defines as 'banal nationalism'. He argues that far from an ideology of the peripheries, nationalism is always present even in the developed west.[67]

To the primordialists, nation as a unique socio-cultural unit and nationalism as a group sentiment exists in all ages, but nation-state as a new sovereign socio-political unit emerged only in modern period. They argue that nation-state emerged as nationalism acquired a political character in modern era and culture became the basic organising principle of state formation in modern times. They further contend that the modernists are concerned with the form of nationalism that produced the nation-states; but a particular form of nationalism producing nation-state can not undermine the cultural dimension of nationalism that unites people and marks off nations.

On the whole, the primordialists emphasise the 'perennialness' and 'naturalness' (immutability) of nation and nationalism. But some primordialists do not support the latter view. Smith, for example, observes that nations and nationalism always existed in human history, but they are not something 'fixed out' there. That is, nations and nationalisms are not static categories, to be achieved once and for all. He argues that nations are both mutable and durable; myths, memories, cultural symbols and even language can be reconstructed and redefined.[68] He further adds that nation and nationalism are not as modern as the modernists claim. Modern nationalism derives its content and inspiration from 'demotic' cultures and nations need cultural cores, i.e., ethnic past to survive. Nations need homelands, not just terrain on which to nurture identities but historic landscapes in which the ancestors of a specific people lived and which they carry in their hearts.[69] Thus nation and nationalism are janus-headed, i.e., they are at once modern and primordial.[70] Renan also points out the importance of both past and present in the formation of nation. According to him, nation is a soul, and two things constitute this soul: one lies in the past, i.e., possession of rich legacy of memories, and the other is present day content, the desire to live together.[71]

On the basis of the foregoing discussion, the following observations can be made:

1. Like nation, nationalism can be interpreted in both political and cultural sense. While political nationalism invariably aims at sovereign statehood, the goal of cultural nationalism varies from political autonomy to outright independence.
2. As a political ideology, or as a political movement, nationalism is purely a modern phenomenon. However, in its political sense nationalism emphasises co-terminality between culture and polity.
3. The concept of nation is the key to all nationalisms. In some cases national movement may precede nation-formation; and in some nation may precede national movement. In other words, national movement can grow from an existing cultural identity, or it may lead to search for such an identity. It is also possible that nationalism may grow from concept of nation based purely on political attributes.
4. Nationalism based on distinct cultural identity may not always be used for political mobilisation demanding sovereign statehood; it could as well be used for demand of separate provincial unit in a sovereign polity. This variety of nationalism is seen mostly in the multicultural countries such as India.

Keeping the foregoing discussion in mind, nationalism in the present study is defined in the following manner. As a sentiment, nationalism involves loyalty to, and identification with a particular nation: political or cultural. As a movement, nationalism can be defined as:

(a) a collective mobilisation on the part of a people inhabiting a given territory and sharing an identity based on either common will and political unity; or shared culture, common language and common descent to gain independence as sovereign states; or,

(b) a collective mobilisation on the part of a territorially rooted cultural community seeking to retain its identity within the purview of self-rule in provincial terms inside a sovereign polity.

To conclude, it can be argued that nationalism, as an ideology or as a movement, seeking to attain independent statehood on the basis of civil-political notion of nation can be termed as political nationalism. This variety of nationalism is exclusively oriented to state-building and it views nation as a community of citizens of an independent state. But, nationalism based on cultural view of nation seeking to maintain cultural distinctiveness within an independent multicultural state can be termed as cultural nationalism. This form of nationalism sees nation as a homogeneous cultural unit and it basically emanates from cultural pluralism and a selective adoption of historical and territorial symbols existing in several multicultural countries in the world. In several multicultural countries cultural nationalism is largely restricted to the demand of autonomy, self-determination within the provisions of provincial rule.

In multicultural countries mostly four major types of cultural nationalism appear: irredentist, autonomist, separatist and secessionist. The irredentist nationalism strives to unify the territories of a divided nation. Depending upon the situation, it may demand its own sovereign state or a separate politico-administrative unit in a sovereign state. Separatist and autonomist types aim at various forms of self-ruling units for safeguarding cultural identity and political autonomy within a sovereign state. But the secessionist type always develops independent state-seeking goal. Interestingly, in multicultural states the broader political nationalism is identified as 'nationalism proper', while nationalism seeking to maintain separate cultural identity in a politico-administrative space is perceived as false or negative nationalism.

As noted earlier, the idea of nation does not *per se* give rise to nationalism. Similarly, co-existence of several nations under one political unit may not create nationality problem. For nationalism to grow, perception of relative deprivation must exist. Where nationalism emerges from a pre-existing national identity, deprivation is seen more in cultural terms; but where nationalism is directed towards a search for such an identity, deprivation is calculated in economic and political terms. In the latter case the people in question try to reconstruct a separate national identity so as to protect their economic and political rights. The process of deprivation may involve three broad patterns:

(a) There may be material deprivation but no cultural deprivation. Such a situation may not necessarily lead to a national movement because the nation in question may adopt various pressure tactics to obtain material benefits. But should the nation in question realise that one or another nation is blocking its development, it would try to assert its separate identity.

(b) There may be cultural but no material deprivation. Such a situation will lead to a national movement as the question of losing one's identity into another is involved here.

(c) Both material and cultural deprivation exist in various forms. This situation leads to an intense form of nationalism, because the nation in question faces a 'double deprivation'.

Apart from deprivation, other factors like socio-economic transformation, spread of education, cultural and political awakening, presence of an articulate leadership, and above all, wide cultural differences between peoples also play crucial role in growth of nationalism.

Notes and References

1. See T.K. Oommen, *Citizenship and National Identity: From Colonialism to Globalism,* 1997, New Delhi, Sage, pp. 47-58.
2. *International Encyclopaedia of Social Sciences*, New York, 1968, pp.3-7. Also see *Oxford English Dictionary*, Vol.X, London, 1989.
3. Walker Conner, "A Nation is a Nation, is a State, is an Ethnic group, is a...", *Ethnic and Racial Studies*, 1 October 1978, pp.381-82. Also see Mostafa Ejai and Cynthia H. Enloe, "Nation States and State Nations", *International Studies Quarterly*, 13 June 1969, pp.141-42.
4. On the origins of nation-states in Europe see Rupert Emerson, *From Empire to Nation*, Boston, 1960; C. Tilly (ed.), *The Formation*

of National States in Western Europe, Santa Barbara, 1980; Elie Kedourie, *Nationalism*, London, 1960; Hans Kohn, *The Idea of Nationalism*, New York, 1961; See also his *The Age of Nationalism*, New York, 1962; Boyd C. Shafer, *Nationalism: Myth and Reality*, New York, 1955; *Report of the Royal Institute of International Affairs on Nationalism*, London, 1939.

5. See for details A.D. Smith, *The Ethnic Origins of Nations*, London, Oxford University Press, 1986, especially Chapters 6 and 9. But Oommen argues that the entire European experience cannot be grasped through these twin processes. There have been state-renouncing nations such as Wales and Scotland in U.K. and Catalonia in Spain, etc. This trend is also much more prominent in South Asia. For details, see T.K. Oommen, *Citizenship, Nationality and Ethnicity: Reconciling Competing Identities*, Cambridge, Polity Press,1997, pp.34-35.
6. On the contribution of the Social Contract Theorists on Nationalism, see *Report of the Royal Institute, op. cit.*, Chaps.1, 2 and 3.
7. See on the multinational character of Western States Tom Nairn, *The Breakup of Britain*, London, 1977. Walker Conner, "Nation-Building or Nation-Destroying?", *World Politics*, 24, 1972, pp.319-55; A.H. Birch, *Nationalism and National Integration*, London, Unwin Hyman, 1989; A.D. Smith, *The Ethnic Revival*, Cambridge, Cambridge University Press,1981.
8. On the Third World Nationalism see E. Kedourie (ed.), *Nationalism in Asia and Africa*, London, 1971; Samir Amin, *The Arab Nation*, Zed Books, London, 1978; J.S. Coleman, *Nigeria: A Background to Nationalism*, University of California Press, Berkeley, 1958.
9. J.S. Mill, *Considerations on Representative Government* (1861), New York, 1958, Chap.16.
10. See Eric J. Hobsbawm, *Nations and Nationalism Since 1870:Programme, Myth and Reality*, Cambridge, Cambridge University Press, 1990.
11. See Benedict Anderson, *Imagined Communities: Reflections on the Origin and Spread of Nationalism*, (rev. ed.), London, Verso, 1991, pp. 5-7.
12. *Ibid.*
13. *Ibid.*

14. L.W. Pye, *Politics, Personality and Nation-Building*, Princeton, 1968, p.334.
15. J. Stalin, "Marxism and National Question", *Collected Works*, Vol. 3, Moscow, 1953-55, pp.300-84.
16. William Peterson, "On the Sub-nations of Western Europe" in Nathan Glazer and D.P. Moynihan (eds.), *Ethnicity: Theory and Experience*, Harvard University Press, Cambridge, 1975.
17. E. Gellner, *Nations and Nationalism*, Oxford, Basil Blackwell, 1983, p.7.
18. *Ibid.*
19. See A.D. Smith, *Ethnic Origins, op. cit.*, p.217.
20. *Ibid.*, Chap. 9.
21. *Ibid.*
22. Max Weber, *From Max Weber: Essays in Sociology*, Routledge and Kegan Paul, London, 1947.
23. Pye, *op. cit.*, p.334.
24. See Bhikhu Parekh, *Rethinking Multiculturalism: Cultural Diversity and Political Theory*, 2000, New York, Palgrave, p. 181
25. Paul Brass, *Language, Religion and Politics in North India*, New Delhi, 1974, p.9.
26. This typology is an adoption and extension of the combinations of nation and state formulated by Oommen. See T.K. Oommen, "Political Alienation and the Internal Threats to the Indian Nation-State: Towards a Non-Alarmist Perspective", *The Indian Journal of Social Science*, Vol.2, No.2, 1989, p.133.
27. See, T.K. Oommen, Social Action, *op. cit.*, p.336.
28. See, Report *of the Royal Institute of International Affairs, op. cit.*, Chapter 1. Also see Peter Worsely, *The Three Worlds: Culture and World Development*, Chicago, 1974, pp.247-48.
29. See T. K. Oommen," State, Nation and Ethnie", in P. Ratcliffe (ed.), Race, *Ethnicity and Nation*, London, Univ. College London Press, 1994, pp.26-46.
30. See P. Chatterjee, "Bengal: Rise and Growth of a Nationality", *Social Scientist*, Vol.37, August 1975, p.68. Also see Jairus Banaji, "Nationalism and Socialism", *Economic and Political Weekly*, 7 September 1974, pp.1538-9. According to this perspective, "nationalities... are separate linguistic; cultural and ethnic

formations which existed prior to capitalism and will continue to exist for an indefinite period under socialism. Nations, on the other hand, are constituted by a historical process specific to the early stages of capitalism and their unit is a politico-economic unit embodied in and mediated through the state". In other words, nationalities are cultural groups and nations are specific forms of states constituted along cultural homogeneity or common solidarity in capitalist society.

31. See John Breuilly , *Nationalism and the State*, Chicago, University of Chicago Press, 1985.
32. For details see L.L. Snyder, *The Meaning of Nationalism*, New Brunswick, 1954. According to him, after the rise of nation-states in the era of rising capitalism, nationalism tends to be irrational and xenophobic.
33. Coleman, *op. cit.*, pp.169-70.
34. On theories of nationalism, see A.D. Smith, *Theories of Nationalism*, London, 1983, pp.27-150 and 153-229; *Nationalism*, Current Sociology, *op. cit.*, pp.45-95.
35. On Marxist Theories of Nationalism see Horace B. Davis, *Towards a Marxist Theory of Nationalism*, New York, 1978; James A. Blaunt, *The National Question*, London, 1987, Chaps. 2, 5 and 7. According to Blaunt the class-struggle theory of nationalism represents the main line of Marxist thinking since Marx. But some Neo-Marxist like Poulantzas and Debray believe that nationalism emanates from the nation as a primordial entity. The British Marxist Tom Nairn in his work *The Breakup of Britain, op. cit.*, holds that nationalism is autonomous from class struggle and is in essence and origin, an idea. But Blaunt, *op. cit.*, Chaps.3 and 7 criticizes the neo-Marxist by arguing that nationalism is a form of class struggle.
36. C.J. Hayes, *The Historical Evolution of Modern Nationalism*, Macmillan, New York, 1948.
37. See for details Hans Kohn, *The Idea of Nationalism, op. cit.*, p.16. Kohn also sees Nationalism as a state of mind seeking to establish a state. He defines nationalism "as a state of mind, permeating the large majority of a people and claiming to permeate all its members; it recognises the nation-state as the ideal form of

political organisation and the nationality as the source of all creative cultural life". *Ibid.*, p.16. For an evaluation of Kohn's ideas on Nationalism, see, Ken Wolf, "Hans Kohn's Liberal Nationalism: The Historian as a Prophet", *Journal of the History of Ideas*, Vol.37, 4, 1976, pp.651-72. Both Kohn and Hayes identify nationalism with more universal political values. However, both the writers pointed out the distinction between Western or 'open', and Eastern or 'closed' forms of nationalism. They argue nationalist doctrine in the former stresses citizenship and subjective choice and in the latter emphasises cultural identity as an objective fact.

38. Gellner, *op. cit.*, p.1:
39. *Ibid.* p.7.
40. Hobsbawm, *op. cit.*
41. See Breuilly, *op. cit.* p. 3.
42. *Ibid.*
43. On the Liberal-political nationalism see the works of Kohn, *op. cit.*, Kedurie, *Nationalism, op. cit.*; H. Seton-Watson, *Nations and States*, London, 1977; Emerson, *op. cit.*; and John Breuilly, *Nationalism and the State*, *op. cit.*
44. For Smith's earlier ideas on the distinction between nationalism and ethnocentrism see his, *Theories of Nationalism, op. cit.*; and "Ethnocentrism, Nationalism and Social Change", *International Journal of Comparative Sociology*, Vol.13, 1, 1972. However for his later viewpoints (i.e. nationalism originates from the primordial entity called nation) see *Ethnic Origins, op. cit.*; *Ethnic Revival, op. cit.*; and *Nationalism and Modernism: A Critical Survey of Recent Theories of Nation and Nationalism*, Routledge, London, 1998.
45. Smith, *Ethnic Origins*, p.154.
46. *Ibid.* p. 211
47. L.L. Snyder, *Global Mini-Nationalism: Autonomy or Independence*, Greenwood Press, Westport, 1982.
48. A.H. Birch, *op. cit.*
49. C.J. Edmonds, "Kurdish Nationalism", *Journal of Contemporary History*, Vol.6, 1962, pp.87-107.
50. Rogers Brubaker, *Nationalism Reframed: Nationhood and the National Question in the New Europe*, Cambridge, Cambridge University Press 1994.

51. Michael Hechter, *Containing Nationalism*, New York , Oxford University Press, 2000, pp. 15-17.
52. *Ibid.*
53. Ronald Beiner, ed. *Theorising Nationalism*, Albany, State University of New York Press, 1999.
54. Smith epitomised these events under the term 'triple revolution': economic, political and cultural. E. Hobsbawm, however, categorised them as 'double revolution': economic and political. See for details A.D. Smith, *Ethnic Origins, op. cit.*, Chap.6; E. Hobsbawm, *The Age of Revolution: 1789-1848*, New York, 1962; "Some Reflections on Nationalism", in T. Nossiter and others (eds.), *Imagination and Precision in Social Sciences*, Faber & Faber, London, 1972.
55. Kohn, *The Idea, op. cit.*, p.37.
56. Benedict Anderson, *Imagined Communities: Reflections on the Origin and Spread of Nationalism*, London, Verso, 1991.
57. *Ibid.*
58. Gellner, *op. cit*, see conclusion.
59. *Ibid.*
60. K. Deutsch, *Nationalism and Social Communication*, Cambridge, 1953. In fact, all the conservative mainstream writers and some neo-Marxists like Poulantzas, Davis and Nairn argue that nationalism is an idea concerning a specific form of modern policy and that it originated in Europe and was exported to other countries under the influence of modernization and communication.
61. Edward Shills, "Primordial, Personal, Sacred and Civil Ties", *British Journal of Sociology*, Vol.3, 1957, pp.130-45.
62. See Tom Nairn, *The Breakup, op. cit.*, p.359.
63. See John Armstrong, *Nations Before Nationalism*, Chapel Hill, 1982.
64. Armstrong, *op. cit.*
65. See, Kedourie, *Nationalism, op. cit.*, p.9. According to him, humanity is naturally divided into nations, that nations are known by certain characteristics and that the only legitimate type of government is national self-government. The central theme of his argument is that political authority exercised by principalities, city-states and empires is illegitimate.

66. Satyamurthy, op. *cit*
67. See Michael Billig, *Banal Nationalism*, London, Sage, 1995.
68. See A.D. Smith, *The Ethnic Origins of Nations, op. cit.*, pp.6-13; also see his, "Gastronomy or Geology? The Role of Nationalism in the Reconstruction of Nations", *Nations and Nationalism*, Vsol. 1, No. 1, 1994, pp. 3-23.
69. Smith, *The Ethnic Origins, op.cit.*
70. *Ibid.* pp. 212-14.
71. See Ernest Renan, "What is a Nation ?" in Eley, Geoff and Suny, Ronald Grigor, ed. *Becoming National: A Reader*, New York, Oxford University Press, 1996. pp. 52-54.

3

Region and Regionalism in Multicultural Context

As far as the term regionalism in multicultural context is concerned there is enormous conceptual ambiguity for a variety of reasons: first, the distinction between regionalism and regional cultural nationalism gets blurred as the provincial units in multicultural states organised mostly on primordial-cultural basis are treated as regions; second, study of regionalism in this context utilises different sets of criteria to analyse the term region; third, nationalism shown by the smaller and peripheral cultural communities in these states are dubbed as expression of regionalism from perspective of the state and the mainstream culture and language. All these create confusion in the understanding of region and regionalism in multicultural situation. It is therefore relevant to have a conceptual clarity to understand these terms in proper sense in multicultural context.

1. Defining Region

Odum and Moore in their compilation on American regions listed several definitions on region. According to them, the common aspects in many definitions involve, "some spatial generalisations, that is, a set of geographical traits which define and distinguish a particular area and give it a distinct character."[1] Norton Ginsberg, the geographer, remarked, "there is no universally accepted definition of the region, except as it refers to some portion of the surface of the earth."[2] B.S.Cohn notes, "most definitions of regions begin with a geographic component and develop out of the relationship between geographic features and man's adaptation to physical environment."[3] The Penguin Dictionary of Geography defines region as "an area of the earth's surface with one or more features or characteristics (natural or the result of human activity) which give it a measure of unity and make it differ from the areas surrounding it. According to the criteria used in the differentiation, a region may be termed cultural, economic, morphological, natural, physiographic, political etc.; and a region may be identified by a single, multiple or total attributes."[4] The International Encyclopaedia of Social Sciences defines region "as a homogeneous area with physical and cultural characteristics distinct from those of neighbouring areas."[5] In this sense, region connotes an amalgam of spatial, physical and socio-cultural features.

Joseph Schwartzberg defines region "as a perceived segment of the time-space continuum differentiated from others on the basis of one or more defining characteristics." These characteristics and the region they define may be of many types: natural (e.g., tropical rain forest region); political (e.g., Orissa, Calcutta city, a district, etc.); economic (e.g., wet rice area, coal mining area, etc.); cultural (e.g., area of the Tamil or Bengali speech).[6]

On the basis of their recognition, Schwartzberg classified regions into: 'naively given', 'instituted' and 'denoted'.[7] He argues that the same entity (e.g., India or USA) can be described under each of these types. A 'naively given' region is one which is recognised as a meaningful territorial entity by the people who live there and/or by other people to whom it is of some concern (e.g., the concept of 'desh' in India) such regions persist in the psyche of the people and held by consensus. Cohn referred to this as "subjective region".[8]

Instituted regions are so called because they are instituted by human agency as distinctive and discrete units limiting the aerial extent of operation of certain functions. These include particularly the territory of the states and their administrative divisions and sub-divisions and similar units instituted by religious bodies or other social organisations. The Republic of India and its provincial units come under this category.[9]

The denoted region is of the kind which is purposefully delimited by scholars and planning authorities concerned with particular problems. Spate's 'physical regions',[10] Grierson's 'linguistic regions',[11] Karve's 'kinship regions'[12] and Schwartzberg's "caste and cultural regions'[13] are of this type.

On the basis of their delimitation denoted regions are commonly classified as 'formal' or 'uniform' and 'functional' or 'nodal'. A formal region is one which is defined on the basis of homogeneity within specified limits, with regard to one or more variables existing over its entire extent. Climate regions based on specified combinations of temperatures and rainfall are of this type. Regions classified on the basis of economy, language, culture and religion fall in this category. A functional or nodal region is recognised on the basis of organisation, internal flows, and quite often the existence of a focal or nodal place, e.g., service area of a newspaper or radio transmission, etc. From a taxonomic point of view regions may be categorised as 'generic' and 'specific'. A generic region refers to a class with similar properties, e.g. hill region, dense forest region, etc. Specific regions are one of a kind, e.g., the deccan lava plateau.[14]

According to Schwartzberg, regions have extensions both in time and space; otherwise there would be no need for historical atlases. Thus like nation a region is not a fixed category; it undergoes changes over time and space.[15] Thus, in Schwartzberg's analysis, a region may have several connotations. But Cohn argues that for most social scientists the conceptualisation of region involves basically non-physical phenomena. He observes, "although logically a definition of region refers to some portion of the surface of the earth, the geographic component is the beginning point for us rather than an end in itself."[16] Because, in a region so defined, there may exist within its boundary a set of homogeneous socio-cultural traits which are not found in contiguous areas and, therefore, set the people inhabiting the region off from other such regions.

Keeping this in mind, Cohn divided regions into: historical, linguistic, cultural and social-structural. A region may be identified by any or all these variables.

A historical region is one in which there are sacred myths and symbols, held by significant groups within the area, regarding the relationship of the people to their past and the geographical entity. Examples of such regions in India are Bundelkhand or Rohilkhand in U.P., the Koshal area in Orissa, etc.[17]

A linguistic region can be sub-divided into three types: (a) literary standard; (b) regional or dialectal standard; and (c) the broad linguistic families. More often than not the linguistic region reinforces the cultural and structural or even the historical regions.[18]

A cultural region is one in which there are widely shared and recognised cultural traits and patterns of behaviour, particularly among the common people. Descriptively, one or two kinds of behaviour, customs or traits are taken as diagnostic of regional culture. For example, Gods, Goddesses, rituals, myths, fairs, festivals, dress, jewelry, house types, etc. are considered as important cultural items.[19]

Structural regions are differentiated in terms of groups of associated structural variables such as caste ranking, family type, forms of marriage, kinship patterns, etc.[20] Marriot's "caste ranking and community structures in five regions of India and Pakistan"[21] is one of the leading example of this type.

It follows from the above discussion that region can be conceived in various ways. However, the geographical component is common to all types of region. This means that region is essentially a spatial category which is homogeneous in certain respects. The common elements which determine a region may be geographic, economic, political, socio-cultural or all of these. A geographic region is characterised by certain climate type, terrain, soil, flora, fauna, etc. An economic region is distinguished by the major form of economic activity or economic resources available in the area. A political region is identified on the basis of administrative criteria and legal-political jurisdiction. A socio-cultural region is characterized by certain socio-cultural peculiarities like cultural practices, speech forms, life-styles, forms of marriage, caste and kin groupings. In addition, there can be planning region, broadcasting region, transport region, military region, service region, communication region, and educational region and so on.

It may be recalled here that the concepts of state and nation also involve a territorial element. How then can a regional territory be distinguished from a national or state territory? A national territory basically implies a culture space over which people have a moral claim. A state territory denotes a defined political boundary over which state has a legal claim to exercise the monopoly of legitimate power.[22] A regional territory, however, may form a part of national or state territory, may be co-terminous with the territory of a nation or a state or may extend beyond it. For example, in the international sphere a region may comprise a group of sovereign states having common political, economic and cultural interests.

It may further be observed that from a strict socio-cultural viewpoint, the distinction between a region and a nation in multicultural context is blurred. For, what is referred to as socio-cultural region from official or the mainstream community's perception may be viewed as nation from people's point of view, no matter, however sub-standard their culture or language appears to be in the perception of mainstream community. Again, if one restricts the term nation to mean only the 'literate culture' and reserves the term region for folk culture, then several cultural communities worth self-governing would be excluded from the category of nation. The best way to avoid the confusion is to treat region as geographical entity and nation as distinct cultural entity or independent political unit. To put differently, the term region can be invoked when the referent is a distinct area, and nation can be invoked if the referent is a distinct people, culturally homogeneous or heterogeneous. To cite one example, the Oriya-speaking area denotes a linguistic region; the state of Orissa is a political region; and the Oriya linguistic community is a nation. This is, however, not to suggest that a distinct cultural or linguistic community may not have internal regional variations in terms of cultural practices, customs, traditions, dialectal or colloquial standards, forms of marriage and social ranking. In this sense a region denotes a sub-culture within a larger culture. In this study the term region is used to mean a distinct area in a country, nation, province or part thereof characterised by special physical, socio-economic and socio-cultural characteristics.

2. Understanding Regionalism

The existence of a region, objective or subjective, does not *per se* give rise to regionalism. It is the nexus between people and their socio-economic and political environment which gives rise to regionalism. As a sentiment regionalism grows out of an attachment to, and identification with, a particular region,[23] developed or backward. But as a movement, regionalism is linked with the phenomenon of relative deprivation primarily in material terms which in turn arises from differential rate of socio-economic development and political mobility between regions. Socio-cultural peculiarities and physical characteristics provide the psychological input in a regional mobilisation. Also they are the basis around which regional identities are formed, but they do not by themselves create regionalism. A regional movement is conditioned more by economic and political phenomena. Regionalism grows only when a region remains economically backward and politically discriminated. In a regional movement the regional identity is invoked to meet some economic and political ends. Several scholars supported this argument. Cohn, for example, remarks that regionalism is, "a conscious or unconscious development of symbols, behaviours and movements which are designed to mark off groups within some geographical boundary from other for political, economic or cultural ends."[24] This means that regionalism is a set of 'attitudes' or 'feelings' or 'action imperatives' which are used by a people inhabiting a contiguous region to promote their socio-economic, political and cultural interests.

Regionalism is also referred to as, "a manifestation of federalism or an intermediate stage between administrative decentralisation and federalism. It involves such diverse problems of modern political and cultural life as those of minorities, local self-government, autonomy, and earth and local patriotism."[25] Further, the mere presence of socio-economic and political inequalities is not enough to create regionalism. Inequalities have to be perceived in relative terms. As a matter of fact, the essential pre-requisites for the growth of regionalism are: (a) perception of deprivation by an important section of people of the concerned region; (b) rise of an articulate regional leadership; (c) presence of a reference group against which the development of the region can be contrasted. It is clear that regionalism is essentially guided by perception of relative material deprivation; the primary concern is development of the region and increased political participation.

It is worthwhile to examine briefly some of the theoretical perspectives to substantiate the above argument. There are four major theoretical perspectives on regionalism: Liberal-economic, Behavioural-democratic, Internal colonialism and Marxist.

The liberal-economic perspective states that as capitalist development is uneven in nature regional disparities are bound to emerge given the uneven development caused by the free flow of capital and investment choices depending upon the economic factors available in a region.[26] This theory accepts the inevitability of unequal regional development. It attributes regionalism to the simple rational economic analysis which accompanies laissez-faire economic activities. It therefore suggests that the interventionist role of the state is essential in correcting the regional imbalances.[27] But what the liberal theory seems to have overlooked is that the growth of regional disparities is a function of the nature of power structure existing in a given state which in turn is influenced by the social structure of that region. In other words, the role of political economy of an area is important in creating as well as ameliorating regional disparities. It is the decision-makers and planners who influence the quantum of development in a particular region. Further, the liberal theory fails to explain why development benefits do not accrue to a people of an industrially developed region.

The behavioural-democratic perspective, while acknowledging the inevitability of regional inequality and the ameliorative role of the state, advocates for a multiple or pluralistic power base to reduce regional imbalances and correct uneven nature of capitalistic development.[28] It argues for competitive political elites belonging to various regions to compete for and bargain with the state power structure for re-distribution and reallocation of scarce resources. So, competitive politics on regional basis is the answer to the solution of regional inequality. Both the liberal and behavioural perspectives hold that manifestation of regionalism is a type of interest group activity.

The theory of 'internal colonialism' stresses that regionalism is a product of a real or perceived sense of exploitation of the peripheral regions by the core regions of a state.[29] This argument claims that the core regions secure an advantageous position during the initial periods of modernisation and thereby come to dominate the peripheral regions. It also states that there exists an elite pluralism in the core regions, that is, the group which dominates in the economic mainstream also wields importance in the cultural and political spheres, leading to cumulative dominance.

The Marxist perspective attributes regionalism to the experience of relative deprivation which is felt most acutely in the peripheral regions. This perspective sees regionalism as a form of politics, that is, a class struggle to capture state power. It is a class struggle between the mainstream bourgeoisie which holds the core region and the oppressed people of the peripheral regions.[30] It views the rise of regionalism as an expression of critical consciousness. That is, regionalism is a form of protest by the oppressed regions against the core region. The Marxist perspective therefore suggests that restructuring of the economic and power structure is the only measure to arrest regional imbalance.

The liberal perspective sees income redistribution as a method to curtail regional imbalance. The Marxist paradigm, however, regards it as an instrument to perpetuate the dependency and backwardness of the deprived region. Further, the Marxist paradigm welcomes state's interventionist role as far as such a policy is meant for correcting regional imbalance by halting concentration of wealth in one particular region.

Regionalism has different ends in various countries. For example, in France regionalism meant a protest against over-centralisation of power and administration in Paris, over-emphasis on Parisian culture. The movement aimed at the free development of local culture and talent, revival of local dialects, publication in local newspapers and above all decentralisation of power and balanced economic growth.[31] In Germany, regionalism aimed at reorganising the old state boundaries.[32] In Britain, it meant administrative devolution and a new framework for local government.[33] In Denmark, it was directed to a folk revival combined with scientific agriculture.[34] In USA, regionalism is expressed in terms of inter-state conflict.[35] In the Third World, crystallisation of regionalism begins with modernisation and westernisation.

As noted earlier, in multicultural context regionalism is often confused with regional cultural nationalism seeking politico-administrative unit. But the fact of the matter is that regionalism differs from regional cultural nationalism in that the latter implies search for identity and desire for political self-rule by a culturally distinct people in an independent state. In other words, assertion of identity in distinct cultural terms signifies regional cultural nationalism, whereas protest against socio-economic exploitation and political inequalities experienced by a neglected or dominated region characterizes regionalism. In the case of regional cultural nationalism, the critical factor is protection of cultural identity; whereas in regionalism the critical variable is protection of regional developmental interests.

Further, in a multicultural country regionalism like regional nationalism may also be linked with goal of politico-administrative unit, but the crucial difference is that in the case of the former such a demand is based on regional identity and the factor of development, and in the latter the demand is based on distinct cultural nationality. It is also possible that regionalism can be transformed into regional cultural nationalism. This happens when a distinct national entity crystallises within a region. A distinct national entity crystallises in a region precisely when the people begin to standardise their language/dialect and differentiate their culture to such an extent that a sense of unity within them can be established and genuine cultural differentiation from others can be made.

3. Nationalism and Regionalism: The Indian Situation

Generally, the study of nationalism and regionalism in India follows two broad approaches: the nation-state approach and the multi-national approach. The former is heavily influenced by the political interpretation of nationalism and regionalism, but the latter adheres to the Marxist and Cultural-pluralist interpretations.

The nation-state approach sees India as a single nation consisting of people (i.e. citizens) belonging to diverse cultural, linguistic, religious, ethnic, caste, tribal and racial backgrounds. The major attributes of Indian nationhood in terms of this approach are located in popular sovereignty, common citizenship, secular-democratic institutions, common administrative and legal systems, on one hand, and the culture, language and religion of the mainstream community, on the other.

This analysis sees regionalism in terms of cultural pluralism. It states that in India cultural pluralism in terms of linguistic, religious, ethnic, caste, racial, and tribal diversities creates and strengthens various forms of regionalism such as linguism, ethno-nationalism, sub-nationalism, cultural nationalism, localism, sectionalism, separatism and secessionism. It also suggests that conflicts arising out of socio-economic and political disparities existing within or between regions are forms of sub-regionalism.[36]Weiner, for example, pointed out that regionalism real or imaginary, is often cultivated by the politics of scarcity.[37] This approach further states that regionalism indicate a combination of forces which pose internal threat to Indian nation-state. Selig Harrison, for example, argued that the reorganisation of Indian provinces on cultural basis laid the foundation of regionalism and contained the seeds of national disunity and disintegration.[38] Thus viewed all forms of regionalism in India are considered as bad from the point of view of Indian nation-state.

But Iqbal Narain argues that, "the quest for regional identity is not necessarily anti-thetical to the urge for a national identity; the two can co-exist in a situation of a mutually rewarding partnership." He further noted that in India, and elsewhere, regionalism has both a positive and a negative dimension. Negatively, "it reflects a psyche of relative deprivation and positively, it embodies a quest for self-fulfillment on the part of the people of an area."[39]

In short, the nation-state approach emphasises precisely two points: one, it views the Indian state as representing the Indian nation and treats all forms of mobilisations for assertion of cultural identity as expressions of regionalism; two, it advocates that regionalism essentially creates divisive tendencies within the Indian state. Needless to say, this approach confuses state with nation and nationalism with regionalism.

The multi-national approach advocated by the Marxist and the cultural-pluralist, on the contrary, sees India as a political entity consisting of a multiplicity of nations organised under a common government. This view holds that although India is a historically unified civilization and a compact geographical unit, yet it has never achieved cultural unity at any stage of her history. As a political unit, India emerged only during the periods of anti-colonial struggle for independence. The Indian Marxists[40] reject the existence of an Indian nation as there is no common language or common culture available in India. They prefer to term the distinct cultural communities in India as nationalities and not nations. This argument on the part of the Indian Marxists seems to have come from the idea that nation is a politico-economic unit which emerged only in the capitalist era, but nationality is a unique cultural group that existed prior to capitalism.

The cultural-pluralists view India as a state with multiple centres of culture. It states that an effective Indian nation in civil-political sense can be built by accommodating specific cultural identities existing in the Indian union. This requires, in theory as well as in practice, creating multiple power base for multiple centres of culture. That is, cultural communities capable of self-rule should be granted such right.[41]

In general, the multi-national perspective holds that the emergence of regional cultural nationalism in India can be attributed to the disjuncture between cultural homeland and political autonomy. It is the desire for maintaining cultural distinctiveness within a provision of self-rule under the broad Indian identity which gives rise to such nationalisms. These nationalisms operate within the framework of cultural nationality.

This approach considers regionalism in the context of developmental disparities and political inequalities existing between regions. In India, there exist several regions which differ in terms of socio-economic development and access to, and regulation of, political power. Hence, it is not cultural pluralism but regional disparities which account for regionalism in India. Although local cultures, speeches, customs, traditions, beliefs and myths influence the formation of regional identities, yet regionalism basically emanates from deprivation in economic and political terms.

Following the multi-national approach regionalism in this study is seen as a movement or a sentiment arising from unequal regional development and distribution of political power. Variables like language, religion, ethnicity and tribe create regional cultural nationalism and not regionalism.

4. Determinants of Regionalism in India

A regional movement has both an instrumental and a symbolic dimension. While the cultural factors, real or imagined, focus upon the symbolic dimension, the socio-economic and political disparities highlight the instrumental dimension. However, it is the instrumental dimension which is the critical variable in the growth of regional movement. Keeping these considerations in mind, the major determinants of regionalism in India are examined as under:

(a) **Geographical Factor:** Regional identity and regional consciousness relate to a specific geographical area. But the territorial dimension is not central to its being. Physical distinctiveness of a region does not create regionalism automatically. The geographical distinctiveness gives a symbolic identity which needs economic and political props for its resurgence from time to time.[42] For example, the old geographical boundaries of the ex-princely states still haunt and are implied in defining regional identity in India.

(b) **Historical Factor:** Common historical experience often buttresses regionalism by way of creating differences in social heritage, attitude, myths and symbolism. The Shiva Sena movement in Maharashtra in West India, for example, used the historical symbols of the great Maratha Empire to stimulate Marathi sentiment against the outsiders, especially the Tamils in Bombay. The Dravidian movement in South

India similarly drew inspirations from Dravidian history and culture.[43]

(c) **Socio-cultural Factor:** Socio-cultural differences between regions fan regional feeling to some extent. Socio-cultural symbols often provide the necessary inputs for identity-formation for a people living in a particular region.[44] It may be observed that a culture may contain various sub-cultural zones within its area. Likewise, a linguistic community may show dialectal diversity or colloquial variation within a geographical area. This means that people speaking the same language or sharing a common culture may show diverse cultural practices and speech forms depending upon their regional affiliation. The differences are seen mainly in the spheres of customs, traditions, social practices, beliefs, rituals, rites, fairs, festivals, ceremonies, food, dress, deities, institutions, values, speech, agricultural equipments, mode of cultivation, housing patterns, etc.

These cultural ingredients of a regional sub-culture basically originate from 'oral', 'folk' or 'little' tradition and are treated as variants of the mainstream culture or the 'great tradition'. Usually, the language and script of the mainstream community are used for official purposes and the mainstream culture is used to homogenise the people. This policy creates a situation of negligence and inattention to the regional sub-cultures and languages which in turn motivate the people of a region to agitate against the mainstream cultural hegemony. Several regional movements in India such as Vidarbha, Telengana, Saurashtra and Uttarakhand used sub-cultural elements to further their interest vis-à-vis the mainstream group.

Regional caste, sub-caste and kinship differences also motivate regional feeling within a broad socio-linguistic area.[45] Caste is a factor of regional tension in a number of states in India. For example, mutual hostility exists between Vokkaligas and Lingayats in Karnataka, Jats and Yadavas in U.P., Kammas and Reddis in Andhra, etc.

(d) **Socio-economic Factor:** Socio-economic imbalance between regions is the crux of regionalism in India. In India the resources are scarce and the demands disproportionate and ever-growing on account of acute competition among individuals, groups and regions within a state. Demands for distributive justice thus get generated and assume the form of a regional movement. Most regional movements demanding separate statehood are based primarily on unfair and uneven distributions of developmental benefits.[46] Even common language and culture cannot prevent inter-regional competition. Nothing perhaps illustrates this point better than the Telengana and Vidarbha movements. The simmering discontent in the depressed regions of Bihar, Madhya Pradesh, Maharashtra, Gujarat, Uttar Pradesh and Rajasthan further reinforces this point.

In the context of development two forces are working in India: (a) economic integration through central planning and (b) free flow of capital, a pre-requisite for development.[47] The former is heavily influenced by the political economy of an area. The region which wields effective political power gets maximum developmental gains. This is an all-India phenomenon. The system of planning in India envisaged the whole country as a single economic unit and its constituent provinces as regional economic units. This system has neglected the development of the regions within a province. An excessive bias towards centralism resulted in a tendency to regard the units merely as supplicants of the system. The core regions within the states also get maximum attention as compared to the peripheral regions. This inbreeds centralisation in planning and development. The politics of planned development thus completely changed the nature of development. Given the differential rate of political modernisation and participation, the politically motivated developmental schemes would inevitably create regional socio-economic disparity.

Regional imbalance is also inherent in the pattern of capital investment and distribution. The uneven nature of capital investment is bequeathed to India by the colonial government.[48] Regionalism within the Indian states is thus the outcome of some real or perceived sense of internal colonialism, the result of unequal sharing of developmental benefits.[49] As Azam noted, "association of planning with political processes was one of the chief factors that creates economic regionalism, the political manifestation of which have largely contributed to inter and intra-regional conflicts."[50] Narain states that "regional pressures emanating from economic compulsions are mere bargaining centres than secessionist moves."[51]

While economists, planners and bureaucrats would suggest strategies to arrest regional imbalances, it will be the task of political decision makers to see that policy decisions move in the direction of balanced development without any bias for or against any particular region. This requires effective state leadership to bring in balanced regional development. For this purpose two conditions have to be met. First, for balanced development, the concept of region has to be redefined combining socio-economic and socio-cultural factors. In India there are regions within states as well as those which extend beyond them. Planning to be successful has to take the socio-economically backward regions into account. Second, the concept of development based on the nodal region theory has to be recast. This theory postulates that development gradually percolates from the nodal or core region to the peripheries. This often does not happen in reality. In many states though developmental efforts have increased in every successive planned period, its benefit has percolated more to the already developed area.

(e) **Political Factor:** The political component of regionalism is important even though politics does not so much create as accentuate it.[52] In a sense, all regionalism is a form of politics, i.e., politics of nativism. In political sphere, regionalism is against centralisation of power and administration. It stands for more federalisation of power and administration. Over-centralisation leads to bureaucratism and concentration of power in one region which in turn results in lopsided development.

The central and state planning in India is politically influenced and political discrimination creates developmental hiatus between regions. The regional elites exploit the economic discontent and political disadvantage of the people to gain some instrumental payoffs. It may be noted that power and administration are important means for the fulfillment of regional aspiration that are usually used by the ruling elites in favour of one region and at the cost of other. The regional political parties, therefore, clamour for a pluralistic power base. Thus regionalism within a province thrives on real or fancied charges of political discrimination.[53] For example, rivalry between the factions within the Congress led to the Telengana agitation in Andhra.

Thus, regionalism is a kind of counter-political movement which aims at greater economic development and effective political rights and participation under the federal structure of a state or provincial government. It may also demand a separate administrative unit on the basis of economic backwardness and political discrimination of a region.

With this conceptual background emphasising the distinction between political and cultural interpretation of nation and nationalism, on one hand, and the distinction between regionalism and regional cultural nationalism, on the other, the emergence of nationalism and regionalism in Orissa in India is analysed in the following pages.

Notes and References

1. Quoted in Richard D. Lambert, "Methods of Determining Regions with Special References to India" in R.I. Crain (ed.), *Regions and Regionalism in South Asian Studies: An Exploratory Study*, Duke University, 1967, Programme in South Asian Studies, p.271.
2. Quoted in B.S. Cohn, "Regions Subjective and Objective: Their Relation to the Study of Modern Indian History and Society", in Crain (ed.), *op. cit.*, pp.104-36.
3. Cohn, *ibid.* p.104.
4. See Audrey N. Clark, *Penguine Dictionary of Geography*, Penguin Books, London, 1990.

5. *International Encyclopaedia of Social Sciences*, Vol.13, 1968, p.268.
6. J. Schwartzberg, "Prolegomena to the Study of South Asian Regions and Regionalism", in Crain (ed.), *op. cit.*, pp.86-101.
7. *Ibid.*, pp.89-91.
8. Cohn, *op. cit.*
9. Schwartzberg, *op. cit.*, p.90.
10. O.H.K. Spate, *India and Pakistan*, London, 1954, pp.352-63.
11. G.A. Grierson, *Linguistic Survey of India*, Calcutta, 1922, especially Vol.1.
12. I. Karve, *Kinship Organization in India*, Poona, 1953.
13. J. Schwartzberg, "The Geography of Caste in the North Indian Plain", in B.S. Cohn et. al. (eds.), *Social Structure and Change in Indian Society*, Chicago, 1968, pp.103-25.
14. Schwartzberg, *op. cit.*, p.91.
15. *Ibid.*, pp.91-92.
16. Cohn, *op. cit.*, p.118.
17. *Ibid.*, p.106.
18. *Ibid.*, p.107.
19. *Ibid.*
20. *Ibid.*, p.108.
21. Quoted in Cohn, *ibid.*, p.108.
22. See T.K. Oommen, *State and Society in India: Studies in Nation-Building*, New Delhi, 1990, pp.10-11.
23. Schwartzberg argues that just as regions may be conceived at any scale, so also regionalism can vary, theoretically, from parochial loyalty to the village or urban neighbourhood, at one extreme, to one-worldism, at the other. At the scale of the nation-state, regionalism takes the form commonly known as nationalism. See Schwartzberg, *op. cit.*, p.95.
24. Cohn, *op. cit.*, p.121.
25. *International Encyclopaedia of Social Sciences*, Vol.13, New York, 1968, p.208.
26. See D. Smiley, *Canada in Question: Federalism in the Eighties*, McGraw Hill, Toronto, 1980.
27. J. Lele, "Regional Disparities and National Identity in Maharashtra", *Journal of Social and Economic Studies*, Vol.3, No.2, April-June 1986, pp.175-89

28. D. Baskin, "American Pluralism: Theory, Practice and Ideology", *Journal of Politics*, 32, 1970, pp.71-95.
29. Michael Hechter, *Internal Colonialism*, Routledge and Kegan Paul, London, 1975, pp.8-10.
30. See Lele, *op. cit.*, pp.177-79 and J. Alam, "Class, Political and National Dimensions of the State" in A. Majeed (ed.), *Regionalism and Developmental Tensions in India*, Cosmo Publications, New Delhi, 1984, pp.37-51.
31. See V.L.S. Prakasa Rao, "Regional Concept: A Short Review Note", *Indian Statistical Institute, Regional Survey Unit*, Calcutta, n.d., p.5, quoted in Cohn, *op. cit.*, p.130. Rao points out that there is a cycle of regionalism. The cycle begins with the revival of poetry and language and ends with plans for the economic invigoration of regional economy, with proposals for more political benefits.
32. Rao, *op. cit.*, p.5.
33. *Ibid.*
34. *Ibid.*
35. See, S.E. Finer, *Comparative Government*, Penguin Books, Middlesex, 1975, pp.189-90.
36. For details, see Iqbal Narain (ed.), *State Politics in India*, Minakshi, Meerut, 1967; Myron Weiner (ed.), *State Politics in India*, Princeton University Press, Princeton, 1968; A.P. Padhi (ed.), *State Politics in India: A Case Study of Orissa*, B.R. Publishers, New Delhi, 1985.
37. M. Weiner, *The Politics of Scarcity*, Asia Publishing House, Bombay, 1963.
38. Selig S. Harrison, *India: The Most Dangerous Decades*, Princeton University Press, Princeton, N.J., 1968.
39. See Iqbal Narain, "Regionalism: A Conceptual Analysis in the Indian Context" in A. Majeed, *op. cit.*, pp.22-23.
40. Irfan Habib, "Emergence of Nationalities", *Social Scientist*, August 1975; E.M.S. Namboodripad, "Class Character of the Nationalist Movement", *Social Scientist*, August 1975; A.R. Desai, *Social Background of Indian Nationalism*, Popular Prakashan, Bombay, 1966; Nihar Ranjan Ray, *Nationalism in India*, Sir Syed Ali Publications, No.4.
41. See for details T.K. Oommen, "Insiders and Outsiders: Primordial Collectivism and Cultural Pluralism in Nation-building",

International Sociology, Vol.1 (1), 1986, pp.53-74; M.N. Srinivas, "Towards Smaller States", *Times of India,* 14 August 1969; Rajni Kothari, "National Unity in Danger: A Case for Smaller States", *Times of India*, 10 February 1968; Balraj Puri, "A Case for Sub-States", *EPW*, 12 December 1970. Khan, for one, advocated that "the process of restructuring of the Indian federation is not yet over" and he makes a plea for further restructuring in terms of smaller and medium-sized states as "the problem is really not of numbers but of the reorganisation of the Indian federation based on objective criteria of socio-economic homogeneity and felt group identity in order to provide a more responsive infrastructure for an industrial breakthrough and modernisation". See R. Khan, "The Regional Dimension", *Seminar*, No.164, April 1973, p.36.

42. Narain, *Regionalism, op. cit.*, p.23.
43. *Ibid.*
44. A.K. Chatterjee, "Sociological Context of Regionalism in India – A Conceptual Framework" in Satish Chandra et. al. (eds.), *Regionalism and National Integration*, Alakh Publishers, Jaipur, 1976.
45. See on the caste factors of regionalism P. Brass, *Factional Politics in an Indian State: The Congress in Uttar Pradesh*, Oxford University Press, Bombay, 1966; E.F. Irschik, *Politics and Social Conflict in South India*, Oxford, Bombay, 1969.
46. I. Narain, "Cultural Pluralism and National Integration in India" in K.R. Bombwall (ed.), *National Power and State Autonomy*, Minakshi, Meerut, 1978, p.186.
47. See Kauser J. Azam, *Political Aspects of National Integration*, Minakshi, Meerut, 1981, p.124.
48. Krishna Bhardwaj, "Regional Differentiation in India – A Note", *EPW*, Annual No.1982, Vol.17, pp. 605-14.
49. A. Pant, *op. cit.*
50. K. Azam, *op. cit.*, p.125.
51. Narain, *op. cit.*, p.187.
52. *Ibid.*, p.188.
53. A. Mudalkar and R. Vora, "Regionalism in Maharashtra", in A. Majeed, *op. cit.*, p.92.

4

Rise and Growth of Oriya Cultural Nationalism in British Orissa

In chapter two it is seen that nation and nationalism can be interpreted in political and cultural ways; nation can be either defined in terms of certain political variables, or, on the basis of a set of socio-cultural criteria such as common language, shared culture, common territory and a shared history.

It is also argued that political approach examines nationalism in the context of sovereign state; while cultural perspective interprets nationalism as a form of mobilisation by a nation/nationality to maintain cultural distinctiveness within a politico-administrative space inside a common sovereign polity. In this cultural sense the concepts of nation and nationalism have been used in this chapter to analyse the emergence of nationalism in British Orissa within the multicultural framework of India.

1. Colonial Rule and Orissa

It is well-known that national consciousness among many culturally distinct nationalities in India grew in the wake of colonial rule. As noted earlier, the colonial ruler in India created administrative provinces which fragmented territorial boundaries of several cultural communities. This situation had created and perpetuated a fear of lose of identity in the minds of the dismembered and neglected nationalities who in turn began to assert their cultural personality by invoking a sense of indigenous cultural defense and by demanding provincial political space for their respective communities. This very consciousness of protecting one's cultural identity within a culture-congruent provincial space emerged as a form of cultural nationalism in different parts of India during colonial period. The Oriya national movement was such a case in point, although the circumstances which led to its emergence were in many ways different from other such regional national movements.

(a) Territorial dismemberment and colonial exploitation

As a socio-culturally distinct people, the Oriyas enjoyed great political and cultural unity under different native Hindu dynasties. Several powerful kingdoms and empires such as Kalinga, Utkal, Odra and Kosal flourished in different periods in the Oriya-speaking region. The territorial extent of these kingdoms stretched from the river Ganga in the north to Godavari in the south and Bay of Bengal in the east to Amarkantak Hills in the west.[1] The glory of Orissa shot into prominence under the illustrious Oriya Emperor Kharvela whose empire in India stretched from the eastern coast to the western coast and from Mathura in the north to the Pandya kingdom in the south.[2] After Kharvela, Orissa once again became famous under the imperial Gangas. In 12th century, Anantvarman Chodagangadev, the founder of Ganga dynasty, united the territories and the people of Kalinga, Utkala, Odra and Kosala into one political unit called "Odradesa" with capital at Varanasi Cuttack (present Cuttack city).[3] Around this time the use of pure Oriya language gradually began. Thus under the Gangas, the Oriyas emerged from a heterogeneous society to a distinct people with a well-defined language and a definite territory of their own.

The cultural distinctiveness of Oriyas continued to grow further under the Gajapatis who succeeded the imperial Gangas in Orissa. Remarkable developments in Oriya language and literature were made during the Gajapati rule.[4] However, towards the end of the Gajapati rule the political boundaries of Orissa had shrunk to its geographical limits and it roughly coincided with the cultural boundary of the Oriya speech community. After the downfall of the Gajapatis in 1568 the land of Oriyas came under the Muslim rule. The downfall of Gajapati Empire resulted in the emergence of several independent principalities in the northern, western and central parts of Orissa. At the same time, the remnants of Orissa Empire got confined to the coastal plains.

In 1578 the Oriya-speaking land consisting of the coastal parts and the smaller principalities came under Mughal rule. For the purpose of revenue, the Mughals divided the Oriya territory into two political divisions: the 'Mughalbandi' and the 'Garhjats'.[5] The 'Mughalbandi' constituted the coastal region and it was ruled directly by the Mughals. The 'Garhjats' comprising the princely states were ruled by the native chiefs under the overarching imperial Mughal suzerainty. The Marathas, who conquered Orissa in 1751, retained the same Mughal system for the purpose of administrative convenience and political expediency. While they ruled Mughalbandi directly, the Garhjats were separated and left in the hands of the Oriya chiefs who ruled on a hereditary basis by paying fixed tributes to the Marathas.[6]

But under the British the Oriya territory was systematically fragmented. The land of Orissa came under British occupation in a piece-meal fashion and different parts of Oriya territory conquered at different times were placed under different administrations. For example, Medinipur and Jaleswar in the north were tacked to Bengal in 1765; Ganjam and Koraput in south Orissa were annexed in 1776 and placed under Northern Circar and Vizagpatnam agency of Madras Presidency respectively. The coastal areas consisting of the districts of Balasore, Cuttack, Puri and the tract of Khondmal were taken from the Marathas in 1803. These areas constituted the Orissa division of Bengal Presidency.[7] Besides these areas, the princely states of Orissa, which formed a vast part of Oriya territory, were conquered in different periods from 1803 to 1818 and were placed under British paramountcy.[8] These states were also placed under various administrations at different times. For example, the states which acknowledged British supremacy at the time of conquest of coastal Orissa were placed under the Orissa division of Bengal Presidency.[9] The state of Sambalpur along with its five tributaries was first placed under the Chhotanagpur division and later in the Central Provinces (CP) till they were finally transferred to the Orissa division.[10] Four Oriya states remained with Singhbhum district under Chhotanagpur division.

Thus by 1862 direct British administration was confined to the following Oriya-speaking tracts: (a) the three coastal districts of Balasore, Cuttack and Puri of Orissa division in Bengal Presidency; (b) the district of Sambalpur in Central Provinces; and (c) the district of Ganjam and Koraput tract in Madras Presidency. The rest of the Oriya territory remained under the native princes who ruled in their land as subordinate allies to British paramount power.

Shortly after their occupation the British thought of extending Bengal regulations to both Orissa division and the princely states. But as the princely areas were kept separate from the British administered Orissa division they thought it proper to extend Bengal regulations to the latter. While doing so the British had two aims in mind: one, to exact optimum revenue from the Orissa division and two, to follow a conciliatory policy towards the local chiefs.[11]

The extension of Bengal regulations to Orissa division was done with total disregard of the local conditions. It brought in its wake several serious changes in judicial, police and land revenue administration. As far as land revenue administration was concerned, the short-term settlements introduced in 1805 and the long-term settlement in 1837 caused serious economic hardship to the local peasantry.[12] The assessment of land was made without proper investigation of the land and of the paying capacity of the people.[13] To make the matter worse, the British introduced a new coin currency in 1809 replacing the old 'cowry currency' and stipulated that the payment was to be made in cash and not in kind.[14] The new coin currency gave rise to great financial burden and caused a good deal of chaos and confusion among the peasantry.

Not only that, the British also set up monopoly over salt trade. The establishment of salt monopoly not only robbed the local population of their alternative occupation but also made the basic food item a scarce commodity. Further, the declining salt trade resulted in growing the pressure on land which in turn led to low productivity and excessive fragmentation in land. Absentee landlordism coupled with administrative apathy further slowed down the pace of agricultural productivity.[15] The increased burden of land revenue resulted in accumulation of arrears and non-payment of it led to auction of native lands. This way for the first time the Oriya land holders were dispossessed of their traditional hereditary lands.

To compound the problem further, the British substituted the traditional Oriya revenue officers by the Bengali officials and record-keepers.[16] These often corrupt and mostly greedy Bengali officials took to fraudulent means of inheriting landed properties in Orissa by taking advantage of the unscrupulous British officials and the defenceless Oriya peasantry. They made every effort to sell out the defaulting estates through auction at Calcutta.[17] All these developments had serious repercussions on the agrarian economy of Orissa which started to tamper steadily under colonial weight. The situation ultimately led to an open revolt, popularly known as the 'Paik rebellion' of 1817.[18]

It is clear then that the Oriyas under the British administration went through a complete process of structural disintegration, cultural fragmentation and economic exploitation. These conditions in the long run posed serious threats to Oriya identity.

(b) Intellectual and material development

The revolt of 1817 exposed to a great extent the flaws in early British administration in Orissa. It also brought to light the perils of bringing in the cultural outsiders who practically turned Orissa into a colony within a colony and deprived the Oriyas of their native lands and lucrative government jobs. This necessitated the government to re-orient its policy towards the Oriya people. Henceforth, lucrative government jobs were offered to Oriyas so as to acquaint themselves with the system of administration. The appointment of Chaturbhuj Patnaik in 1835 as settlement officer at Khurda marked the beginning in this regard.[19]

The missionaries who came after the rebellion also worked for the development of vernacular and English education in Orissa.

In 1823 they opened one English Charity School at Cuttack. They also established the first printing press in Orissa in 1837.[20] The same year, Oriya replaced Persian as official and court language of the government.[21] Induced by the missionaries, the government took some interest in imparting English education to the local people. Consequently, the government established in 1835 one English school at Puri which was closed down shortly.[22] In the following years some Commissioners like Henry Ricketts and G.F. Cockburn took active interest and through their generous efforts both English and vernacular schools were opened at various places in Orissa. In 1841, the government took over the Cuttack missionary school and renamed it as Cuttack English School. Gradually, the demands for English education increased in other parts of Orissa.

The Wood's dispatch of 1854, which revolutionised modern education in India, had its impact on Orissa too. But except for starting some vernacular schools here and there, nothing significant was done under the scheme to revolutionise education in Orissa. Thus by 1857-58 there were three Zilla schools in Cuttack, Puri and Balsore, one Anglo-vernacular school at Bhadrak and 26 other vernacular schools in the whole Orissa division.[23] With education slowly making its way and government jobs getting available to the local people, a radical change among the Oriyas had begun. However, the early development in education and employment was marred by a dreadful famine which struck Orissa in 1866 catching both the government and the people unawares and taking a heavy toll on human lives. Under its influence about a third of the population died and millions were left destitute.[24] Popularly known as "Na'anka Dhruviskya" (as it fell in the 9th renal year of King of Puri), this famine was commonly attributed as a man-made disaster mainly caused by the official inattention, lack of infrastructure facilities, failure of crops, shortage of food grains, low level of literacy and inept handling of relief works.[25] Referring to the administrative negligence, Sir Stafford Northcote, the then Secretary of State for India, said in British Parliament, "This catastrophe is a monument of our failure."[26]

The impact of the famine was far-reaching. First, it aroused considerable mass discontent and resentment through out the length and breadth of British Orissa. Second, it brought a new sense of realisation upon the British government regarding the defects in its administration. Third, it forced the government to take some steps in matters of development of education, transport and communication network. In the post-famine period, Orissa was directly linked with Calcutta, both physically and administratively. Besides, the idea of reorganising the province of Bengal was also mooted. The Secretary of State for India suggested that the province of Bengal be divided so as to relieve it of its unnecessary administrative and financial burden.[27] But while Assam and Chhotanagpur were made into separate commissionership, the status quo for Orissa was maintained.

Nevertheless, the chain of events that followed the post-famine period opened up a new era in the history of Oriya people. Not only the Oriyas of British districts received greater official attention, but also a new sense of nationalistic consciousness began to dawn upon them in this period. The period also witnessed noticeable spread of western education, import of liberal and progressive ideas, development of transport and communication, restructuring of public opinion through press, clubs and societies, etc.

Progress of education, especially higher education, received greater attention in the post-famine years. Grant-in-aids were made available for publication of Oriya text books and subsequently a number of Oriya text books were published during 1867-68.[28] By 1868-69, the total number of schools rose up to 44 which included 24 Government schools and 20 grant-in-aids schools.[29] In 1868 Cuttack Zilla School was raised to the status of High School and a college class was opened in the school. The same year a formal training school for teachers also started.[30] At the same time, steps were taken to set up English schools in Ganjam and Sambalpur. In 1872 the Government took interest in opening schools in rural areas and provisions were made to provide scholarship to meritorious students. The Cuttack High School was elevated into a college in 1876 and it was named after the then Commissioner T.E. Ravenshaw.[31]

Besides, female education was also encouraged by the Government. The significant step in this direction was the opening of Cuttack Hindu Girls' School in 1869 (later renamed as Ravanshaw Girls' High School in 1913). Efforts were also made to establish girl's schools at Berhampur, Sambalpur and Balasore.[32] Thus, education in British Orissa progressed steadily by the end of 19th century.

Along with education Oriya literature also made considerable progress in the post-famine era. Oriya novels, drama and short stories highlighting the evils of colonial rule and extolling the history, language and culture of Oriya people came up in increasing numbers. Radhanath Ray's "Chilika" and "Mahayatra Mahakavya", Madhusudan Rao's "Bharat Bhraman" and Fakirmohan's "Mamu", "Lachhama", etc. were outstanding writings of the day.[33] Fakirmohan's writings in particular introduced lots of social content to Oriya literature. His writings heralded a new literary tradition in Oriya language free from Bengali influence.[34]

Progress of education also promoted prospects of employment. Prior to the famine period the Mukherjees, Banarjees, Ghoses, Boses and such other Bengali surnames preponderated in the list of subordinate officials.[35] The Oriyas lost ground to the Bengalis when it came to the knowledge of English. But the situation slowly improved after 1866 with the spread of school education among Oriyas. Henceforth Oriyas were preferred more in local jobs. Some British officials like F. Gouldsbury, G.F. Cockburn and T.E. Ravanshaw took keen interest in providing suitable jobs to the Oriyas.[36] Such appointments gradually improved the economic position of the Oriyas.

In the areas of press and communication satisfactory development was also made in the last quarter of 19th century. Except for a few missionary periodicals like "Gyanaruna" (1849), "Prabodhchandrika" (1856) and "Arunodaya" (1861), the Oriya newspapers focusing on the local issues were almost non-existent in 19th century. The first Oriya newspaper, 'Utkal Dipika', edited by G.S. Ray made its appearance on 4 August 1866 from Cuttack Printing Company.[37] Soon after the publication of 'Utkal Dipika', a chain of newspapers came out in British Orissa. Of these, 'Sambad

Bahika' in Balasore, 'Sambalpur Hitaisini' in Sambalpur and 'Asha' in Ganjam played a crucial role in shaping public opinion. These newspapers covered topics concerning the economic, social and educational problems of the Oriyas.[38]

Further, the government attention to communication led to improvements in road transport, postal services, irrigation networks and railways. A coast canal connecting river Hooghly with river Matai near Balasore was constructed by the end of 19th century. The Bengal-Nagpur railways linking Calcutta with Cuttack and Puri was inaugurated in 1905.[39] All these developmental works provided additional employment opportunities and added to the rising standard of living of the local population. Moreover, better means of communication helped in great interaction among the people.

With the expansion of mass media and communication network, voluntary associations of various kinds began functioning in British Orissa. Some of the earliest associations were the 'Utkal Bhasa Unnati Bidhayan Sabha' founded at Balasore in 1866, and the 'Cuttack Society' founded in 1868.[40] The members of landed aristocracy and political chiefs mainly dominated these associations. But gradually the situation changed and many other associations with varied cultural, economic, political and literary interests came into being.[41] These associations made sustained efforts to bring about a metamorphic transformation in public opinion and provided the requisite forum for likeminded people to come together for exchanging ideas concerning local issues. The right to cultural self-determination became the reforming spirit of most of these associations. People from various cross-sections such as landlords, educated elites, peasants, students, and women joined these associations in large number. Of all these associations, "Utkal Sabha", presided over by the noted Oriya nationalist Madhusudan Das, was the most significant in view of its role in awakening the masses.[42] In fact, it was the only association which drew membership from various quarters of Oriya society.

Thus, one finds that by the third quarter of 19th century a social climate favourable for the development of national awakening was available in British administered Oriya districts.

The spread of English education, better means of communication, employment opportunities, growth of press and associations and clubs of various types provided the pre-requisites for forging a sense of unity among the culturally fragmented and politically dismembered Oriya people under British rule. The growth of a self-conscious educated middle class in particular helped in spreading the message of Oriya unity.

2. Language Agitation

At the time when the Oriyas of the British administered areas were experiencing a new sense of awakening under the impetus of new socio-economic forces unleashed by the colonial administration, some Calcutta-bred Bengali chauvinists, in collaboration with a few Bengali migrants in Orissa, seriously attacked the distinct status of Oriya language and thereby challenged the very foundation of Oriya nationality. These Bengalis waged a sinister campaign in the 1870s to abolish Oriya language from the schools and courts in the Orissa division of Bengal presidency. The anti-Oriya campaign of these Bengalis came at the time when the Oriyas hardly recovered from the shock of the catastrophic famine of 1866. Obviously, therefore, the attack on Oriya language created much flutter and triggered off Oriya national aspiration on a wider scale.

In the opinion of the Bengali chauvinists, since Oriya was a vulgar/corrupt dialect of Bengali, it was no longer necessary for the Oriyas to read and write through Oriya medium. As a matter of fact, the Bengalis in India experienced faster development due to their early association with the British. This historical fact made the Bengalis socially powerful and culturally dominant. In the colonial period wherever the Bengalis migrated they tried to impose their language and culture on the local population. The Bengalis followed the same track in Orissa under British patronage.

Bengali migration to Orissa started from the 13th century. Those who came during the time of Chaitanya adapted themselves into Oriya culture and society. But the Bengalis who came with the British during the 19th century, unlike the earlier settlers, emerged as usurpers, intruders and exploiters. Initially, these

Bengalis came to British Orissa in search of jobs and business opportunities, but as they found the local situation agreeable they started to impose Bengali language and culture on the local people. They made all possible effort to culturally absorb the Oriyas into their fold. Taking advantage of their influential positions in government jobs, especially in administration and education, they made all facilities available to educate their children in Bengali medium and forced the Oriyas to study through Bengali in their own homeland.

Oriya replaced Persian in 1837 as the medium of instruction and administration in the Orissa division. The Bengalis, however, did not favour the decision of the government. From time to time the Bengali chauvinists made serious attempts to get rid of the Oriya language. For example, in 1841 and subsequently in 1848 the Bengalis persuaded the Government of Bengal to instruct the Commissioner of Orissa to supply Bengali text books to Oriya schools on the ground that Oriya language was more akin to Bengali and therefore could be written in Bengali script irrespective of the fact that Oriya had a distinct script of its own.[43] However, the Commissioner of Orissa F. Gouldsbury did not agree with the proposal. In his reply to the Government he wrote, "...if such a measure will be taken then the natives of Bengal will find themselves supplanted in the public offices of Orissa." He further pointed out that, "...knowledge of Oriya, which is the vernacular language of the land is of first importance to the Government and people of Orissa."[44]

Accordingly, the idea of supplying Bengali text books was dropped and provisions were made to produce sufficient number of Oriya text books and steps were taken to equip the officials with the knowledge of Oriya. The government's favourable gesture to Oriya language aroused suspicion among the Bengalis as they perceived in it a threat to their dominant economic and cultural positions in Orissa. Hence, the Bengali opposition to Oriya language continued unabated. The situation came to a boiling point in 1870 when R.L. Mitra, an eminent historian from Calcutta and the author of "Antiquities of Orissa" remarked in one of his speeches at Cuttack that,

Oriya is more closely related to Bengali than any other vernacular of India and the relationship is most probably is that of the mother and daughter and not of the sisters. And, if this be admitted, it must follow that as in Assam, Sylhet and Cooch Behar, so in Orissa, education should be conducted in Bengali and not in Oriya.[45]

In his anti-Oriya campaign, Mitra received tremendous support from some Bengali immigrants settled in Orissa. For example, R.C. Bhattacharya, a deputy inspector of schools at Balasore, published a booklet entitled, "Odia ek Swatantra Bhasa Nai" (Oriya is not an independent language) and put forwarded several arguments in favour of his claim.[46] Encouraged by this, some Bengali people in Orissa started a signature campaign in favour of Bengali language.[47] This action raised a storm of protests among the Oriyas. To counter the Bengali claim, the Oriyas launched a "save Oriya campaign" throughout the Orissa division. To defend their language they demanded the appointment of Oriyas in the education department and competence of Oriya language for the non-Oriyas living in British Orissa. The then Commissioner of Orissa, T.E. Ravanshaw, supported the Oriya cause wholeheartedly and urged that the Bengalis should learn the local language to get themselves acquainted with the local situation.[48]

At the time when the Oriyas were agitating over the language issue in the Orissa division of Bengal Presidency, the Chief Commissioner of Central Provinces arbitrarily decided to replace Oriya by Hindi as the official language in the Oriya-speaking district of Sambalpur with effect from 15 January 1895.[49] The Central Provinces government maintained that since Sambalpuri-Oriya was different from the standard coastal Oriya and was more akin to Chhatisgarhi Hindi, the changeover would pose no problem to the people of Sambalpur and would also help the smooth functioning of the local administration.

To restore Oriya language in Sambalpur, the local Oriyas organised strong protest movements and led several demonstrations to the authority. The Oriya leadership argued that although the form of Oriya spoken in Sambalpur was much influenced by Chhatisgarhi Hindi and therefore appeared to be different from coastal Oriya speech, yet the Oriyas of Sambalpur subscribe to the standard Oriya language for the purpose of both reading and writing. They further claimed that if mutual intelligibility of language was the criterion for the changeover, then the same logic should have been applied to Hindi and not to Oriya only. It was further alleged that the influence of Chhatisgarhi on Sambalpuri-Oriya was not very much due to mutual borrowing, but due to the arbitrary placement of Sambalpur under Central Provinces for a quite long time.

Further, the decision to replace Oriya in Sambalpur violated the general rule of the British government of encouraging the local vernacular language. In a memorial sent to the then Viceroy Lord Elgin, the Oriya people of Sambalpur asserted that, "the denial to the people of the use of their mother-tongue is the worst form of gagging and is yet unknown in the most despotic form of government."[50] The imperial government, however, approved the C.P. government's decision in toto. As a result of this, the number of non-Oriya schools and Hindi-speaking officials increased in the region. This raised a fear among the Oriyas of Sambalpur that sooner they would be reduced to a linguistic minority in their own locality, besides being a numerical minority in the province as a whole.[51] A local newspaper, 'Sambalpur Hitaisini', reported that, "the replacement of Oriya would deprive a large section of the Oriyas to get education in their own mother tongue."[52] It also drew the attention of the local people to the language agitation in the Orissa division where Oriya language became the victim of Bengalis. The literary writings of Gangadhar Meher, a noted Oriya poet from Sambalpur, inspired the people further to rally round the cause of their mother tongue.[53]

Not only in Orissa division and Sambalpur the Oriyas faced the risk of losing their language, but in Ganjam also they experienced a similar treatment. The Telugus, who held important positions in government jobs, courts and schools in Ganjam, induced the provincial government of Madras to replace Oriya by Telugu in Ganjam.[54]

The Oriya language thus came under serious external threats in all parts of British Orissa. The threats to Oriya language motivated the articulate section of Oriyas to assert their identity in clear nationalist terms. Three sets of objective markers: (a) unique history, (b) distinct language and (c) specific cultural tradition were prominently invoked for this purpose.

(a) Unique history: The historical roots were emphasised to highlight the exemplary tradition of the Oriyas as conquerors, empire-builders and maritime traders. The glories of past Orissan Empires under the legendary Oriya Emperors such as Kharvela, Chodagangadev and Kapilendradev were brought to the limelight in order to stress the unique Oriya historical tradition. The military might and the maritime power of the ancient Kalinga kingdom, the famous Kalinga War of 261 B.C., and above all, the conquest of Magadha by Emperor Kharvela were stressed to reactivate the people about their glorious past.[55] The leading Oriya newspaper 'Utkal Dipika' drew the attention of the Oriya people to their glorious past and urged that the memories of ancient and medieval Orissa should be taught in the schools to inculcate among the youth a deep sense of Oriya national feeling. Attention was also focused on the temple architecture of the Ganga period and the great artistic and literary tradition of the Gajapati period.[56] In short, the historical legacy of the Oriyas provided a vast pool of symbols which were used to create a strong sense of Oriya unity.

(b) Distinct language: It was claimed that, Oriya not only had a separate existence but even regarded as older than Bengali considering its great many archaic features. For example, John Beams, a noted British Philologist, in his reply to R.L. Mitra's remarks on Oriya language observed that,

At a time when Oriya was already a fixed and settled language, Bengali did not exist. The Bengalis spoke a vast variety of corrupt forms of Eastern Hindi. It is not till recent time we find any thing that can with propriety be called a Bengali language. Thus, the arguments voiced by Mitra and his followers are profoundly destitute of philological arguments.[57]

He further noted that the New Indo-Aryan languages descended from various 'apavramsa' which started roughly from 1000 A.D. The Eastern group of New Indo-Aryan languages comprising Oriya, Bengali, Assamese, Maithili etc. descended from

'Magadhi Apavramsa', which owed its origin to 'Magadhan Prakrit'.[58] Because of the common parent, Oriya like Assamese showed greater affinity to Bengali and for this reason Oriya was often treated by Calcutta pundits as dialect or daughter of Bengali language.

The domiciled Bengalis supported Beam's arguments and identified themselves with the interest of the Oriyas. For example, the editor of 'Utkal Dipika', G.S. Ray condemned the ignorance of R.L. Mitra regarding the origin of Oriya language. Another Oriya newspaper, the 'Sambad Bahika', stated that, "...no doubt Bengali and Oriya have some similarities due to their common origin but this does not mean to say Oriya is a dialect of Bengali."[59] British official L.S.S. O'Malley argued that Oriya was not only differentiated from its neighbours by grammar, idioms and phraseology but by a distinct script also. The cursive or 'Kutila' Oriya script originated from Brahmi and it combined the features of both southern Kalinga script and Nagari script of Gupta period."[60]

(c) Cultural tradition: Apart from great historical roots and distinct language, attention was also drawn to the unique Oriya cultural tradition which was inextricably linked with Oriya national deity Lord Jagannath. It was pointed out that Jagannath worship played a vital role in shaping Oriya cultural identity and influencing the customs, beliefs, practices and morals of the Oriyas. The social structure of the Oriya society was controlled by the "Mukti Mandap" situated in the holy precincts of Jagannath temple. The royal tradition of Orissa received its legitimacy from the authority of Lord Jagannath.[61] The impact of Jagannath cult on the artistic and literary life of Oriyas was also highlighted. The famous car festival (ratha yatra), the Odissi dance, the 'Goti pua' dance, the devotional songs and medieval literary writings depicting Jagannath as national hero were exalted to promote a sense of unity among the Oriyas from within and a sense of separateness from outside.

Towards end of the 19th century the language agitation engulfed all parts of British Orissa. The local Oriya newspapers played significant role in spreading the agitation. For example, 'Utkal Dipika', in one of its edition, noted that, "If Oriya is to be suppressed because it is spoken by a few millions of people, it might also be urged that Dutch, or Danish or Portuguese be obliterated also."[62] It also maintained that the deprivation of the Oriya people of their mother-tongue would amount to extinction of their cultural identity and cause for extreme backwardness of the region. Subsequently, in a meeting held under the auspices of the 'Utkal Sabha' chaired by M.S. Das, it was decided to send petitions to the Government of India and British Parliament demanding quick restoration of Oriya in Sambalpur and establishment of distinct status of Oriya in Orissa division.[63]

Around this time, the H.G. Cook report on Orissa was submitted. In his report, Cook supported the cause of Oriya people and described the political dismemberment of Orissa as administratively unsound and morally unjust. He argued for the extension of the boundaries of Orissa division so as to include the outlying Oriya-tracts such as Sambalpur and its feudatory states, Ganjam and Midnapore.[64] Encouraged by this, some leading persons of Sambalpur met Andrew Fraser, the then Chief Commissioner of C.P., and informed him of their desire to be integrated with Orissa division. They argued that, "if it was thought administratively inconvenient to have Oriya as the language of the Oriya-speaking district in a predominantly Hindi-speaking province, they would prefer to be transferred to Orissa division where Oriya was the recognised language."[65] They further stressed that Sambalpur belonged to Orissa on the basis of geographical contiguity, linguistic affinity and historical antecedent and therefore the transfer of Sambalpur would cause no problem either to the people or to the government. The Chief Commissioner of C.P. accepted the proposal and urged the Government of India to transfer Sambalpur to the Orissa division of Bengal presidency.[66] However, the Government of India did not think it appropriate to transfer Sambalpur to Orissa division at that time, though it restored Oriya in Sambalpur from 1 January 1903.[67]The anti-Oriya campaign of the Bengalis in Orissa division also died down slowly. The government of Bengal established the separate status of Oriya as a medium of instruction and discouraged the special status of Bengali in the schools of Orissa division.[68]

In sum, it can be argued that by the end of 19th century a genuine national sentiment incorporating a desire for maintaining a separate identity slowly emerged among the Oriya people under British rule. The impact of English education and new socio-economic opportunity in general and the collective sentiment shown during the successful language agitation in particular brought awareness among the enlightened Oriyas to think in terms of a culturally autonomous Oriya nation.

3. Utkal Union Conference and the Movement for United Orissa

From the experience of the language agitation the Oriyas realised that the political dismemberment of their homeland was the root-cause of the problem faced by them. The Oriyas believed that their survival as a distinct nationality could only be possible by effectively bringing the scattered British Oriya territories together under one administration, preferably a separate administration where they could preserve, protect and promote their language and culture. This very consciousness of protecting Oriya identity in a separate provincial unit gave birth to the united Orissa movement which began roughly from 1903.

Every national movement needs to be institutionalised so as to achieve the desired goals. The Oriyas till the beginning of 20th century not only lacked a national forum representing their community, but they also lacked a systematic and coordinated approach to pursue their goal. After the formation of Indian National Congress in 1885, Madhusudan Das, the chief architect of united Orissa movement, and other leaders of 'Utkal Sabha' decided to join the Congress to gain adequate support for the Oriya cause. But soon disiilusioned with the Congress attitude towards provincial national aspiration, M.S. Das and his followers parted with the Congress in 1901 and subsequently formed the Utkal Union Conference (hereafter UUC) on 25 October 1903 at Cuttack.[69] With the formation of UUC, the much needed national organisation of the Oriyas came into being, and with that the systematic political campaign for unification of Oriya territories began incessantly.

The UUC was a broad-based Oriya organisation and it identified itself with the interests of the Oriyas only. The non-Oriyas who had settled in Orissa centuries ago and those who identified themselves with the interests of the land were also allowed to participate in its activities. The main objectives of the UUC were: (a) to foster the feeling of oneness among the entire Oriya population; (b) to work for the improvement of the economic condition of the Oriyas and to spread education among them; (c) to safeguard the interest of the Oriyas against outsiders; and above all, (d) to work for the unification of Oriya-speaking tracts with a view to make it a separate province.[70] To achieve these objectives, the UUC basically adopted a policy of constitutional agitation through protest, petition and prayer. M.S. Das strongly believed that the Oriya problem could be resolved only with the blessing of the British government. This moderate tone of the UUC initially attracted some Oriya princes who formed a major power block in Orissa next only to the British.

The first meeting of the UUC was held on 30 December 1903 at Cuttack under the presidentship of the ruler of Mayurbhanj state. It was resolved there to send a memorial to the Viceroy of India demanding the transfer of the Oriya-speaking areas of Midnapur and Singhbhum from Bengal, Sambalpur from C.P., and Ganjam and Vizagpatnam agency from Madras to the Orissa division of Bengal Presidency on the basis of linguistic affinity and geographic contiguity.[71] In the following years the UUC met annually at various places in British Orissa.

Within a short period the UUC spread its branches throughout Orissa and recruited paid volunteers to spread the nationalist ideals among the masses. Steps were also taken to open Oriya schools in the outlying Oriya tracts. Memorials were submitted to both the imperial government and the provincial governments of Bengal, C.P. and Madras about the use of Oriya as a court language and as a medium of instruction in schools and universities in their respective regions. The memorials, however, mainly highlighted the demand for integrating all the Oriya-speaking areas under a single homogeneous administrative unit.[72]

In addition to its campaign for united Orissa, the UUC also took keen interest in promotion of cottage and village industries in Orissa. M.S. Das, for example, himself promoted the tannery and silver filigree works in Cuttack. In 1905 he established the famous 'Utkal Tanner' at Cuttack.[73] Also he motivated the villagers to take to spinning and to employ better means of cultivation.[74] Through these activities, M.S. Das intended to revive the lost glories of the great Oriya nationality. His stress on economic prosperity of Orissa was aimed at regenerating a spirit of self-awareness and self-pride among the Oriya people.

In the meantime, the Government of India was deeply thinking about reorganising the boundaries of Bengal. The idea of transferring Sambalpur to Orissa division and of placing both parts of Orissa (Oriya princely states and British Orissa) together under one government was also mooted. The scheme in this regard was spelt out in the Risley Circular of 3 December 1903 which contained the proposal for partition of Bengal and the amalgamation of all the Oriya areas under Bengal administration so as to relieve the provinces of the burden arising out of a variety of languages spoken in their territories.[75] The Circular added, "nowhere are there drawbacks more conspicuous than among the Oriya-speaking people distributed over different provinces and thus a constant source of anxiety to the Government and the people and hence in dealing with a question of this kind the true criterion of territorial redistribution should be sought not in race but in language."[76]

The Risley Circular evoked mixed reaction from different quarters. The Bengalis rejected outright any proposal for division of Bengal. The C.P. Government favoured the transfer of Sambalpur and five Oriya feudatory states of Sonepur, Patna, Kalahandi, Bamra and Rairakhol to Orissa division.[77] The Madras government, however, strongly objected to parting with the Oriya-speaking district of Ganjam and the Vizagpatnam agency tract on the ground that the Telugus formed a significant minority in those areas.[78] Protesting against the Risley circular, the Telugus argued that the proposed scheme would amount to separation of a section of Telugus from the rest. But the Oriya people whole-heartedly welcomed the idea of uniting their areas under Bengal administration.

Incidentally, the decision to partition Bengal turned into an all-India issue and the Congress all over India opposed this move unequivocally. The Congress at its Madras session in 1903 passed a resolution opposing the proposed scheme of partition of Bengal and the transfer of Oriya-speaking areas from Madras.[79] But ultimately Bengal was partitioned in 1905 and Sambalpur along with nine feudatory states were transferred to Orissa division of Bengal province. The Oriya-speaking tracts of Ganjam and Vizag in Madras were left untouched.[80] With the transfer of nine princely states the number rose to twenty-six under Orissa division.

The Oriya leaders considered the transfer of the Oriya areas to Orissa division as a first step towards realisation of united Orissa. At the same time, they expressed strong dissatisfaction over the exclusion of Ganjam and Vizag agency tract from the unification scheme.[81] The UUC in its successive annual sessions reiterated the demand for the inclusion of Ganjam and other such Oriya areas in Orissa division.[82]

At this juncture, a group of English-educated Oriya youth, popularly known as the 'Satyabadi' group, emerged on the scene and with its keen participation the Oriya national movement spearheaded by UUC became more and more active. The group was organised in 1909 by the famous Oriya leader Gopabandhu Das at Satyabadi national High School near Puri. The group worked under the aegis of UUC and largely followed M.S. Das's policy of appeasement towards the British. But gradually the group wielded much influence and began to dominate the functioning of UUC. The domination of UUC by 'Satyabadi' group estranged the Oriya princes from the Oriya national struggle.[83]

In the mean time, the agitation for the reunion of Bengal gathered momentum. Besides, the people of Bihar also clamoured for their separate province. All these developments exerted considerable pressure and ultimately the government carried out another territorial reorganisation. The partition of Bengal was annulled and a new province of Bihar and Orissa was created in 1912.[84] As regards the new province, it was maintained that the people of Bihar had very little in common with the Bengalis. Similarly, the reunion of Bengal was favoured on the ground that the Bengalis spoke a distinct language, followed a common culture and possessed a definite territory. Unfortunately, however, a similar line of argument was not advocated in favour of the Oriyas who not only spoke a distinct language but also had very little in common with both the Bengalis and the people of Bihar. Even, the Oriya-speaking tracts of Ganjam and Vizag from Madras were not included in the newly formed province of Bihar and Orissa.[85] This dissatisfied the Oriya leaders and hence they continued to press for their earlier demand.

The Montague-Chelmsford Commission, which visited India to initiate constitutional reforms, supported the national aspiration of the Oriya people. But while recommending for the unification of Oriya-speaking areas, the commission ruled out in principle the division of provinces on the basis of language.[86] It stated that any change in the territorial boundary of a province should be made with due regard to the legislative council of the province. This raised serious doubts in the minds of the Oriyas because they were in minority in respective provincial councils. Hence, the UUC in its 1918 session pleaded that amalgamation of Oriya areas should either precede or accompany the proposed reforms. The amalgamation issue was then taken up for discussion in imperial and provincial councils from time to time.

But at this time, the 'Satyabadi' group of Oriya nationalists vigorously tried to bring Oriya nationalism under the rubric of Indian nationalism. Led by Gopabandhu Das, this group espoused the cause of broader Indian nationalism and actively supported the Congress struggle against British colonialism in India. Unlike the UUC leader M.S. Das, the young Gopabandhu Das followed a different line of thinking. His philosophy was much influenced by the concepts of 'Swadeshi' and 'Swaraj' cherished by the Indian National Congress. M.S. Das, however, followed a policy of exclusion from the Congress in his conviction that the Oriya issue could be resolved only with the blessing of the British. This understanding of M.S. Das was shaped partly because of the indifferent attitude of Congress towards Oriya cause. All that he wanted was to integrate the Oriyas together under one administration so that they could assert their distinct identity in multicultural India.[87] Gopabandhu, however, depricated the loyalist approach of M.S. Das and inspired the Oriyas to join the mainstream Indian nationalism. He pointed out that the right to internal self-determination for the Oriyas was unthinkable without complete independence of India.[88]

Presiding over the 14th session of UUC at Cuttack in 1919 Gopabandhu appealed the members to make UUC a branch of Congress.[89] With a delegation of thirty-five he attended the Congress session at Nagpur in 1920.[90] It was in this session the issue of formation of provincial Congress committee on linguist basis was resolved and Orissa (then Utkal) was taken as a provincial unit.[91]

On his return from Nagpur, Gopabandhu attended the 16th session of UUC held at Chakradharpur in Singhbum in 1920. Speaking extensively on Congress ideals at this session, Gopabandhu urged the Oriya nationalists to assign more value to freedom of India.[92] He also persuaded the leaders to embrace the ideals of non-cooperation enunciated by Gandhiji to fight against the British.[93] He professed that the national aspiration of the Oriyas could only be met through active participation in the struggle for broader national identity. The UUC moderates, however, opposed the idea of merging UUC with the Congress and expressed their unwillingness to participate in the non-cooperation movement. They largely endorsed the policy of cooperation with the British for fulfilment of their demand. Having failed to prevail upon the UUC, Gopabandhu founded the Utkal Provincial Congress Committee in 1920 and with his followers actively participated in non-cooperation movement.[94]

Thus in 1920s two forms of political mobilisations were seen in British Orissa. One, led by the Utkal Congress Committee, cherished the ideals of broader Indian nationalism, and the other, led by the UUC moderates, solely fought for the unification of British administered Oriya areas. Slowly, the UUC lost ground to the Congress as most of its members deserted it and joined the non-cooperation movement.[95] The government of Bihar and Orissa took stern measures and put most of the leaders including Gopabandhu Das behind the bars.[96] With Gopabandhu in jail and the suspension of non-cooperation movement at the all-India level, the Congress movement in Orissa slowly receded.

The weakening of Congress movement paved the way for the resurgence of the united Orissa movement. The revival of the UUC at Berhampur in 1923 rejuvenated the movement further.[97]

In the following years both the UUC and the provincial Congress worked for the amalgamation of Oriya areas, though their policies on the issue differed considerably. The Congress pursued the goal of amalgamation within the framework of Indian freedom; while the UUC emphasised integration of the Oriya territories in British India.[98]

Meanwhile, the UUC leaders sent several delegations and resolutions to the provincial and imperial governments regarding unification of Oriya areas. Resolutions for unification were also tabled in the legislative councils of the province of Bihar and Orissa and Madras province.[99] In view of the persistent demand, the Government of India finally instructed the respective provincial governments to ascertain relevant facts. The government of Bihar and Orissa ruled out the transfer of Singhbhum as a majority in the area opposed integration with Orissa. The Madras government categorically rejected the inclusion of Ganjam and Vizag with Orissa. The government of Bengal reported that the Oriyas of Midnapur did not intend to join as they were naturalised in the process. The C.P. government agreed to transfer the Oriya-speaking area of Kharirar.[100]

After reviewing the situation, the Government of India noted that since in Singhbhum and Midnapur the Oriyas were in minority except for some pockets, these areas would not be transferred to Orissa. The whole attention then centred on the Oriya tracts in Madras province. To study the question of amalgamation of these areas with Orissa, the Government of India appointed the Phillip-Duff enquiry committee in 1924. The committee found that there was a genuine longstanding desire on the part of the Oriya people of Madras province for integration with Orissa. It, therefore, recommended for the transfer of Jeypore, Koraput, Navrangpur in Vizagpatnam agency and the whole district of Ganjam from Madras to Orissa division.[101]

The government of Madras denounced the report as utterly misleading and against the local Telugu sentiment. The government of Bihar and Orissa also raised the issue of financial imbalance and administration inconvenience in the case of inclusion of the Oriya territories from Madras in the Orissa division of Bihar and Orissa province. The unfavourable attitude of Bihar and Orissa government prompted the Oriya leaders to strongly demand for separate Orissa province. They demanded for both amalgamation and separation. However, in the debates of the house of the legislative assembly of Bihar and Orissa, the Oriya leaders were divided on the issue of the future administration of Orissa. One group, led by Nilakantha Das, supported the idea of amalgamation with a sub-province status under Bihar and Orissa province; the other group, led by Bhubanananda Das, pressed for unification with a distinct provincial status. Gradually, the latter view gained ground.[102]

Finally, the matter was referred to the Simon Commission which visited India in 1928 to examine the functioning of the constitutional reforms promulgated by the Government of India Act of 1919. The Simon Commission was boycotted all over India; the Congress in Orissa, led by H.K. Mahtab, also boycotted the commission. But the UUC leaders cooperated with Simon Commission and placed before it their grievances. The friendly gesture of UUC towards the commission was criticised in various quarters.[103] The Simon Commission observed that, "the province of Bihar and Orissa is the most artificial and defective of all the provinces and comprised areas which widely differed in physical features, racial traits, linguistic and cultural traditions."[104] Regarding the Oriya areas of Madras the Simon Commission appointed a sub-committee under C.R. Atlee to study the problem in greater detail.[105] The sub-committee recommended for the creation of a separate Oriya province, but it excluded Jeypore and Singhbhum from the proposed province.[106]

In the meantime, the Orissa Congress under H.K. Mahtab joined the civil disobedience movement launched by Gandhiji. H.K. Mahtab and his followers observed salt satyagraha at Inchudi near Balasore.[107] The UUC moderates strongly criticised the involvement of Orissa Congress in civil disobedience movement which according to them was detrimental to the Oriya cause.[108] After the end of civil disobedience movement the Orissa Congress once again joined hands with UUC moderates and worked out a combined strategy to fight for the Oriya cause. An all-party conference (known as United Orissa Conference) was convened at Cuttack in 1931 and it was decided that people belonging to all shades of opinion should work for the creation of a separate Orissa province.[109] Thereafter, the Provincial Congress Committee passed a resolution asking the AICC to deal with the Oriya issue sympathetically.[110] Subsequently, the chief of Parlakhemidi went to London to attend the Round Table Conference and there he presented a memorandum regarding the formation of separate Orissa province.

Finally, the Government of India appointed the S.P. O'donnel Committee to look into the reorganisation of boundaries and examine the administrative and financial viability of the proposed Orissa province.[111] The O'donnel committee visited several places, reviewed the claims of various people and organisations including UUC and on the basis of linguistic affinity, geographical contiguity, administrative and financial viability demarcated the boundaries for the proposed Orissa province. In its report of 1932 the committee recommended that the new province would include the Orissa division, Khariar and Padampur estates of C.P. and some parts of Ganjam and Vizagpatnam agency from Madras. Some areas of C.P. and some parts of Ganjam district remained outside the proposed boundary line.[112]

The Oriya leaders opposed the decision of the boundary committee as it did not include all the Oriya territories they had claimed for.[113] The 'white paper' announced that the province would include the areas proposed by the boundary committee with the exception of Jeypore in Vizag agency and Parlakhemidi in Ganjam district. Widespread protests were launched throughout Orissa against this decision. The case was then referred to the Joint Select Committee which in turn recommended for the inclusion of Jeypore and Parlakhemidi in the new province. Finally, the separate province of Orissa comprising six British administered districts of Balasore, Cuttack, Puri, Ganjam, Sambalpur and Koraput came into being on 1 April 1936 vide the Government of India (Constitution of Orissa) Order, 1936. It covered an area of 32,695 square miles with a population of 8,043,681.[114]

With the formation of separate Orissa province the long cherished dream of the Oriyas became a reality and with that the first phase of Oriya nationalism came to an end. The Oriya experience brings out some serious sociological implications of nationalism in multi-national context. It points out that when a nation/nationality is artificially divided and assigned to different administrative units, the national sentiment may crystallise into nationalism. This will aggravate if the administrative arrangement leads to economic exploitation and cultural stigmatisation of the victim-nationals. Here the distinction between the oppressor and the oppressed in terms of racial/cultural assimilation gets blurred.

From the Oriya point of view both the British and the Bengalis were perceived as enemies. But in this perception, while the British were a common enemy at the all India level, co-operation with the rest of the Indian nations/nationalities was called for giving birth to political nationalism. On the other hand, the Bengalis were viewed as internal colonisers sapping the vitality of Oriya nationalism. In this context, cultural nationalism crystallised in the Oriya-speaking land. In the case of Orissa, the two nationalisms ran simultaneously calling for selective co-operation with British in the context of Oriya nationalism, and necessary co-operation with Bengalis in the context of Indian nationalism.

It may, however, be noted that the Oriya territories comprising the princely states were not included in the Orissa province of 1936. The Oriyas had to wait for another phase of struggle to get these princely states integrated with the Orissa province. The following chapter deals with the manner in which the movements for integration of Orissa princely states were launched and successfully carried out to meet the goal of united Orissa.

Notes and References

1. For details see M.N. Das, "Ancient and Medieval Empires and Kingdoms" in his (ed.), *Sidelights on History and Culture of Orissa*, Vidyapuri, Cuttack, 1977, pp. 86-103; N.K. Sahu, *Odiya Jatira Itihas* (Oriya), Orissa State Bureau of Textbook Preparation and Production, Bhubaneshwar, 1977, p. 7; H.K. Mahtab, *History of Orissa: Part-I*, Cuttack, 1959, pp.1-7.
2. See N.K. Sahu, *History of Orissa*, Vol.I, Cuttack, 1964, pp.347-52; A.C. Mittal, *An Early History of Orissa*, Banaras, 1962, pp.323-33.

3. For details, see N.K. Sahu, *History of Orissa*, op. cit., p.148; R.D. Banerjee, *History of Orissa*, Vol.I, Cuttack, 1925, pp.1-28; H.K. Mahtab, op. cit., p.6; P. Acharya, *Studies in Orissan History, Archaeology and Archives*, Cuttack, 1969, p.163. Also see P. Acharya, "The Antiquity of the Words 'Odissa' and 'Odiya'," in *Orissa Historical Research Journal*, Vol. 2, No.364, 1953, pp.56-58. According to P. Acharya the modern anglicised name "Orissa" has been derived from the word 'Odradesa' through derivatives like Odravisya-oddivisa-odvisa-odissa-oresa, etc.
4. P. Mukherjee, *The History of the Gajapati Kings of Orissa*, Cuttack, 1981, pp.23-38.
5. A. Sterling, *An Account: Geographical, Statistical and Historical of Orissa Proper or Cuttack*, London, 1846, p.32.
6. B.C. Roy, *Orissa under the Marathas*, Allahabad, 1960, p.3.
7. For details on British occupation of Orissa see K.M. Patra, *Orissa Under the East India Company*, New Delhi, 1971, pp.4-10; H.K. Mahtab, *History of Orissa*, Part-II, Cuttack, 1959, pp.431-36.
8. K.M. Patra, op. cit., p.4.
9. Mahatab, op. cit.
10. *Ibid.*; also see S.P. Das, *Sambalpur Itihas* (Oriya), Sambalpur, 1969, pp. 304-33.
11. K.M. Patra, *op. cit.*, p.10.
12. *Ibid.*, Chapter I.
13. G. Toynbee, *A Sketch of the History of Orissa, 1803-1828*, Calcutta, 1928, pp. 26-27.
14. "Coweries" are little white glossy shells used as currency for petty transactions in ancient and medieval Orissa. See, S.C. De, "Cowry Currency in Orissa", in *Orissa Historical Research Journal*, Vol.I, No. 2, 1952, pp.10-21.
15. Manorama Mohapatra, "General Economic Condition of Orissa: 1803-1818", *Orissa Historical Research Journal*, Vol.I, No.2, 1952, pp.171-75.
16. K.C. Jena, "Economic Life of the Oriya People During the British Period" in M.N. Das (ed.), *Sidelights*, *op. cit.*, pp.189-217.
17. *Ibid.*
18. P.K. Mishra, *Political Unrest in Orissa in the 19th Century*, Calcutta, 1983; P. Mukherjee, *History of Orissa in 19th Century*, Cuttack, 1964, pp.26-29.

19. P. Mukherjee, "Employment of the People of Orissa in the 19th Century", *Orissa Historical Research Journal*, Vol. 3, 1959, pp.110-17.
20. See James Peggs, *History of the Baptist Mission*, Cuttack, 1859, pp.156-57.
21. K.M. Patra, *op. cit.*, p.35.
22. N. Samantray, *Odiya Sahityara Itihas: 1803-1920* (History of Oriya literature), Cuttack, 1964, pp.54-56.
23. See *General Report on Public Instruction in the lower province of Bengal, 1857-58*, p.111; Also see K.M. Patra, *op. cit.*, pp. 321-22.
24. C.F. Buckland, *Bengal under the Lieutenant Governors*, Vol.I, Calcutta, 1902. See especially his minutes on Orissa famine, pp.329-92; Nibedita Mohanty, *Oriya Nationalism*, Manohar, New Delhi, 1982, pp.15-18.
25. P. Mukherjee, "Orissa Famine of 1866", *Orissa Historical Research Journal*, Vol. 4, pp. 57-64.
26. Buckland, *op. cit.*, p.386.
27. See *British Parliamentary Papers*, Vol.LLII, 1868, cited in N. Mohanty, *op. cit.*, p.18.
28. *Utkal Dipika* (Oriya daily), 5 January 1867, 9 March 1867.
29. See *General Report of Public Instruction, 1868-69*, p.121, cited in S.C. Patra, *Formation of the Province of Orissa*, Punthi Pustak, Calcutta, 1979, p.72.
30. *Utkal Dipika*, 8 February 1868.
31. P. Mukherjee, "Promotion of Education in Orissa by T.E. Ravenshaw", *Orissa Historical Research Journal*, Vol. XIV, No. 2, pp.21-32.
32. J.N. Diwedy, *The British Policy for the Popularisation of Education among Women in Orissa*, Orissa Historical Congress Proceedings, Bhubaneswar, 1979, pp.79-82.
33. Tapas K. Chakravarti, "Social Content of Oriya literature of the late 19th Century" in B.S. Das, *Life and Culture in Orissa*, Calcutta, 1984, pp.132-78.
34. *Ibid.*
35. P. Mukherjee, *History of Orissa, op. cit.*, pp. 415-16
36. *Ibid.*
37. S. Patnaik, "Orissa in 1866", *Orissa Historical Research Journal*, Vol.IX, 1960, pp.70-75; Also see James Peggs, *op. cit.*, p.238

38. See for a list of these newspapers and presses that appeared in the period between 1866-1900, N. Samantray, *op. cit.*, pp.175-80.
39. K.M. Patra, *Orissa State Legislature and Freedom Struggle: 1912-47*, ICHR, New Delhi, 1979, p.6.
40. *Utkal Dipika*, 25 April 1868.
41. K.M. Patra, "Growth of Social Consciousness in Orissa in 19th Century", *Proceedings of the Indian Historical Records Commission*, Madras, 1970, Vol.II,, p.151.
42. N. Mohanty, *op. cit.*, p.26.
43. See S.C. Patra, *op. cit.*, Chap.IV.
44. *Report of the Educational Council: 1848-49*, pp. 336-7, cited in S.C. Patra, *op. cit.*, p.117.
45. See, *Journal of Asiatic Society of Bengal Proceedings*, Vol.XXIX, 1970, Part-I, pp.201-2.
46. P. Patnaik, *Odiya Sahitya* (Oriya literature), Cuttack, 1968, p.418.
47. *Utkal Dipika*, 26 March 1870.
48. P. Mukherjee, "Commissioners of Orissa, T.E. Ravenshaw", *Orissa Historical Research Journal*, Vol. XII, No.1, pp. 21-29.
49. *Utkal Dipika*, 23 January 1895.
50. Quoted in P. Mukherjee, *History of Orissa, op. cit.*, p. 413.
51. *Sambalpur Hitaisini*(Oriya daily), 23 January 1895.
52. *Ibid.*, 6 February 1895.
53. *Ibid.*, also see *Utkal Dipika*, 23 February 1895.
54. For details, see S.C. Patra, *op. cit.*, pp. 132-33.
55. See for details on Orissan historical tradition, M.N. Das, *Sidelights, op. cit.*, pp.87-122.
56. M.M. Chakravarti, "The language and literatures of Orissa", *Journal of Asiatic Society of Bengal*, 1898, Vol. LXVI, Part I, p. 339. Also see P. Mukherjee, *History of Gajapati, op. cit.*, pp.11-12.
57. See, *Journal of Asiatic Society of Bengal Proceedings*, Vol.XXIX, Part I, 1870, p.204.
58. John Beams, *A Comparative Grammar of the Modern Aryan Languages of India*, London, 1872; Also see his, "The Indigenous Literature of Orissa", *Indian Antiquity*, Vol.I, 1872, pp.79-80. In recent times S.K. Chatterjee, the noted linguist, also, offered a similar viewpoint about Oriya language in his, "The Language and the people of Orissa", *Indian Historical Quarterly*, Vol.XXIII, 1947,

p.337. In the words of S.K. Chatterjee, "Of the three speeches of Magadhi Apavramsa-Oriya, Bengali and Assamese-Oriya has preserved a great many archaic features in both grammar and pronounciation; and it may be said without any travesty of linguistic truth that Oriya is the oldest of the three sisters."

59. *Sambad Bahika* (Oriya daily), 1 November 1872.
60. L.S.S. O'Malley, *Bengal District Gazetteers: Puri*, Calcutta, 1921, p. 75.
61. J.N. Das, "Jagannath and Oriya Nationalism" in A. Eschman, H. Kulke and G.C. Tripathy (eds.), *The Cult of Jagannath and the Regional Tradition of Orissa*, New Delhi, 1978, pp. 359-74. Also see, H. Kulke, "Jagannath as the State Deity under the Gajapatis of Orissa", in Eschman, et. al. (eds.), *op. cit.*, pp.199-208.
62. *Utkal Dipika*, 23 February 1895.
63. *Ibid.*, 11 May 1895.
64. For details on Cook's report, see N. Mohanty, *op. cit.*, pp. 34-35.
65. Two Bachelors of Arts, *The Oriya Movement*, Aska 1919, p. 25.
66. *Ibid.*
67. *Utkal Dipika*, 1 January 1903.
68. *Sambad Bahika*, 16 February 1899.
69. See *The Oriya movement, op. cit.* And S.N. Das, *Desaprana Madhusudan* (Oriya), Cuttack, 1971, p.186. This national conference of the Oriyas was preceded by the Ganjam national conference which was constituted at Rambha by a group of enlighted Oriyas.
70. See *Utkal Dipika* (Oriya daily), 2 January 1904. Also see M.N. Das, *Utkal Gaurav Madhusudan* (Oriya), Utkal University, 1952, pp. 52-53.
71. H.K. Mahtab, *History of Freedom Movement in Orissa*, Vol.I, Bhubaneswar, 1957, pp.133-4.
72. For details on the activities of the UUC, see Nibedita Mohanty, *Oriya Nationalism, op. cit.*, pp. 54-67.
73. See A.K. Mishra, "Madhusudan and the Growth of Economic Nationalism in Orissa", *Orissa Historical Congress Proceedings*, Bhubaneswar, 1979, pp. 90-95.
74. *Ibid*
75. For details on Risley Circular see *Two Bachelors*, Appendix-D, *op. cit.*, pp. 312-18.

76. *Ibid.*, p.315.
77. *Two Bachelors*, op. cit., p.54.
78. See, *Report of the Indian Statutory Commission*, Vol. IV, 1930, p.536. Also see K.V.N. Rao, *Emergence of Andhra Pradesh*, Bombay, 1973, p.13.
79. *Indian Statutory Commission, op. cit.*, p.537.
80. *The Oriya Movement, op. cit.*, p.38.
81. *Ibid.*
82. *Ibid.*
83. See N. Mohanty, *op. cit.*, p.73 and P.K. Mishra, *op. cit.*, p.19.
84. *Indian Statutory Commission, op. cit.*, App.-IV, p.582.
85. *Utkal Dipika*, 2 March 1912.
86. See *Report on the Constitutional Reforms*, Calcutta, 1928, pp.157-58.
87. See S.B. Das, *Life of Madhusudan Das as seen by many Eyes*, Cuttack, 1962, p.18; R.N. Rath, Late Utkalmani Gopabandhu Das, Cuttack, 1964, P.33.
88. Baikoli Mohapatra, *Odiya Andolanara Itihas* (History of Oriya Movement), Cuttack, 1976, p.170.
89. *Who's Who of Freedom Workers in Orissa*, Govt. of Orissa, Cuttack, 1967, p.63.
90. *Utkal Dipika*, 4 September 1920.
91. See B. Pattabhi Sitaramaya, *The History of the Indian National Congress, 1885-1935*, Vol.I, Bombay, 1946, p.209. Prior to this period the delegates from Orissa to AICC were considered as representatives of Bengal and hence had no distinct identity of their own.
92. *Utkal Dipika*, 8 January 1921; *Smaj*, 7 January 1921.
93. *Samaj*, 7 January 1921.
94. H.K. Mahtab, *History of Orissa*, Cuttack, 1962, p.504.
95. *Samaj* (Oriya daily), 30 April 1921, 21 May 1921, 6 February 1922.
96. *Samaj*, 26 June 1922.
97. See N. Mohanty, *op. cit.*, pp.106-7.
98. *Utkal Dipika*, 5 July 1924; *Samaj*, 24 March 1923.
99. See, P.K. Mishra, *op. cit.*, p.119.
100. See, *Indian Statutory Commission, op. cit.*, pp.542-46.
101. Quoted in P.K. Mishra, *op. cit.*, p.159.

102. *Proceedings of the Legislative Council, Bihar and Orissa*, Vol.I, 1927, pp. 546-54.
103. *Utkal Dipika*, 3 March 1928.
104. See *Indian Statutory Commission*, Vol.I, 1930, p. 68.
105. *Indian Statutory Commission*, Vol.II, p. 49.
106. *Ibid.*, p.56.
107. *Prajatantra* (Oriya daily), 7 April 1930, 14 April 1930, 28 April 1930.
108. *Utkal Dipika*, 8 April 1931.
109. *Samaj*, 6 May 1931; *Utkal Dipika*, 16 May 1931.
110. *Samaj*, 15 May 1931.
111. See, Report of the Orissa Boundary Committee, Vol.I, Govt. of India, Delhi, 1932, p. 2.
112. *Ibid.*, pp. 2-34.
113. *Utkal Dipika*, 4 June 1932.
114. Quoted in J.N. Mohapatra, *Orissa in 1936-37 to1938-39*, Govt. of Orissa, Cuttack, 1941, p. 3.

5

National Movement in Princely Orissa and the Consolidation of Oriya Nationalism

It is noted in the previous chapter that nationalism in British Orissa arose due to the domination of the cultural outsiders, especially the Bengalis, over the local Oriya people. The formation of separate Orissa province in 1936 partly brought an end to this domination. But princely Orissa still remained under the clutch of the tyrannical native rule. It was due to popular struggle that princely Orissa was finally extricated from oppressive native rule and subsequently integrated with the province of Orissa. The rise of popular struggle in princely Orissa thus marked the second phase of Oriya nationalism. This chapter deals with the forces which led to the rise of popular struggle in princely Orissa.

1. Princely States of Orissa

The princely states of Orissa consisted of a group of twenty-six semi-independent territories. These states lay in the north-western and central parts of present day Orissa. They were bounded on the north by the erstwhile districts of Ranchi, Singhbhum and Midnapur; on the east by the districts of Cuttack, Balasore and Puri of Bengal Presidency; on the south by the districts of Ganjam and Vizag of Madras Presidency; and on the west by the district of Raipur in Central Provinces and the district of Sambalpur in Bengal Presidency. These states covered an area of 28,125 square miles.[1]

The origins of Orissa princely states date back to the process of indigenous state formation in India.[2] These states enjoyed semi-independent status under different regimes. But after the fall of the Orissa Empire in 1568, these states became virtually independent. But under the Mughal and Maratha rule these states acquired a distinct political status. As mentioned earlier, the Mughals divided Orissa into 'Mughalbandi' and 'Garhjats' divisions. The 'Garhjats', consisting of the princely states, remained as semi-independent territories under Mughal power. But under the Marathas the 'Garhjats' were left in the hands of Oriya princes who paid fixed annual tributes to the Marathas.

The Orissa states were thus already separated from the coastal areas (i.e. Mughalbandi) before the advent of the British on Oriya soil. The British accentuated the process of separation further when they conquered coastal Orissa in 1803. The British conquest of coastal Orissa in 1803 was soon followed by the submission of several princely states. As many as 19 Oriya states, adjacent to coastal plains, accepted British sovereignty and agreed to pay fixed annual tributes. They entered into treaty engagements with the colonial power and enjoyed British protection and military support.[3] These states were identified as Cuttack group of feudatory states and they were attached to the Orissa division of Bengal presidency. But later the number of these states was reduced to 17 as 'Banki' and 'Angul' lapsed into British Orissa in 1840 and 1847 respectively.[4]

In 1804 the British conquered the state of Sambalpur and its five dependencies comprising Patna, Sonepur, Bamra, Kalahandi and Rairakhol. Two years later these territories were restored to the Marathas. But finally in 1818 Sambalpur and its dependencies came under British occupation and they were placed under Chhotanagpur division. Subsequently in 1849 Sambalpur lapsed into British territory. In 1861 the district of Sambalpur and the Sambalpur group of states were placed under the Central

Provinces till they were finally transferred to Orissa division in 1905.[5] Around this time, four more Oriya-speaking states, known as Chhotanagpur group of states, were transferred to Orissa division. Thus, by 1905 the Orissa division of Bengal Presidency contained 26 Oriya princely states[6] and four British administered districts of Balasore, Cuttack, Puri and Sambalpur. As a result of these political arrangements the Oriya population in princely states remained politically disunited, territorially divided and culturally fragmented.

2. Colonial Rule and Princely Orissa

The British adopted a policy of non-interference towards Orissa princely states. The policy of non-interference aimed at: (a) obtaining fixed annual revenue; (b) maintaining the states as buffer zones; and (c) securing loyalty of the princes.[7] As per the agreements, the princes were granted freedom in their internal administration. They ruled in their respective territories as subordinate allies under British paramountcy. The policy of non-interference envisaged the right to interfere in political matters, cases of criminal offence, capital punishment, misrule, abuse of power and suppression of uprising and disturbances. To look into these affairs, the office of superintendent was created and the Commissioner of Cuttack was entrusted with the powers of superintendent for Cuttack group of states.[8] The Sambalpur and Chhotanagpur group of states were similarly made responsible to the commissioners in their respective administration.[9]

Initially, some superintendents tried for extension of Bengal regulations to Cuttack group of states. But the imperial power at Bengal rejected the proposals on the grounds of political expediency.[10] When all the 26 Oriya-speaking states were brought together under Orissa division, the British appointed a political agent to manage the affairs of both Chhatisgarh and Orissa states. Later a separate political agency for Orissa group of states was created.[11] The political agency required the chiefs to refrain from injustice and oppression and promote good administration.

(i) Pattern of Administration

As noted earlier, the Orissa states maintained their political autonomy under different paramount powers ranging from the native Oriya regime to Mughals, Marathas and finally the British rule. This political privilege helped the princes to unleash a reign of terror, oppression and exploitation in their states. Although the British exercised political control over the chiefs,[12] the absence of codified British laws in the states, made the chiefs assume enormous despotic powers over matters related to administration of civil justice, collection of land revenue, imposition of taxes and grant of civil liberties.

Excepting a few, in most of the states the personal rule of the chiefs guided the basic norms of administration, appointment, transfer and mode of payment of revenue and taxes.[13] As a result nepotism, corruption and malpractices continued unabated. The people were deprived of basic civil liberties, freedom of speech and expression. Right to information was severely curtailed. Peaceful meetings, circulation of newspapers and formation of associations were banned. Detention without trial, deportation and confiscation of properties were widespread.[14]

In addition, the poor peasants were subjected to the inhuman and cruel practice of performing 'bethi' and 'begari' (free and forced labour) on various occasions. Several public utility services such as construction of roads, barrages, tanks, etc., were undertaken using unpaid and forced labour. Royal buildings and houses for government officials were constructed on 'bethi'.[15] Apart from this, several other anti-people feudal claims like 'Rasad' (free ration), 'Magan' (contributions to royal weddings) and 'Bheti' (tributes) were widely prevalent in all states.[16]

The system of land revenue administration too was exploitative. While in neighbouring British Orissa land settlements were systematically made following sound land revenue principles, no such well-defined revenue laws existed in the princely states. In these states land settlements were made more frequently and often arbitrarily. The settlement officials, who were brought especially from Bengal and coastal Orissa, had poor knowledge about the agrarian situation in the states. The arbitrary short-term settlements thus resulted in over assessment of land revenue.[17] Further, assessment of land revenue was done regardless of the productive capacity of land and actual income from agriculture.

Ramdhyani, the special officer deputed to study land tenure in Orissa states, aptly pointed out: "Such a state of affairs allowed the rulers full scope to do what was financially advantageous to them.... Settlements were, in a fact, regarded as a means to augment revenue."[18]

Moreover, the peasants did not enjoy tenancy rights over the land they cultivated. No properly codified tenancy laws existed in the states. The right of occupancy remained with the cultivators as long as they paid their rents. Non-payment of land revenue amounted to ejection of peasants at will.[19] The village headmen, assisted by the tyrannical state police, often resorted to coercive and corrupt methods of collecting land revenue. In addition to high land revenue, various kinds of cess were also levied on the peasants.

People were also made to pay different kinds of illegal taxes such as road tax, grazing tax, forest tax, house tax, sales tax, plough tax, excise tax, etc. Further, the states established monopolies over essential articles like salt, oil, beetle leaf, coconut and a number of forest products like lac, cocoons, kendu leafs and hides and skins. Most of the states rarely maintained any annual budget. A large share of state revenue was spent on the comforts of the royal family and kin.[20]

On the whole, the grim agrarian situation, absence of industries, excessive land revenue, illegal taxation, state monopolies and above all the oppressive feudal claims and practices resulted in growing impoverishment of states people in general and the peasantry in particular.

(ii) Socio-economic measures

In the first half of 19th century the colonial administration did practically nothing to ameliorate the socio-economic conditions of the people of Orissa states. However, in the second half of 19th century the colonial attitude changed from non-interference to practical interference in developmental matters. The whole of India, including the princely areas, came under British Crown in 1858. Under the new political setup, the British authorities took active interest in the socio-economic well-being of the states people. The changed political situation also compelled the Oriya princes to look after the basic needs of their subjects. Because of these combined efforts, princely Orissa made satisfactory progress in the fields of education, transport and communication.

As mentioned earlier, after 1854 the British took some steps to spread English and vernacular education in both British and princely Orissa.[21] But as compared to British Orissa, the progress of education in the states was very low. The colonial policy of non-interference was partly responsible for the slow growth of education in the states. Moreover, the participation of missionaries in the spread of education was restricted to British Orissa only. Hence, in the area of education princely Orissa remained far behind British Orissa.

But considerable progress in education in Orissa states was seen in the early decades of 20th century. In 1911-12, altogether three English High Schools (located in the states of Bamra, Dhenkanal and Mayurbhanj), 20 English Middle Schools, six Vernacular Middle Schools, 280 upper primary and 1430 lower primary schools existed in Orissa states.[22] By 1931-32 the number of English High Schools rose to 10, English Middle Schools to 30 and Vernacular Middle Schools to 18.[23] Besides, steady progress in primary education was also recorded. By 1931 the number of upper primary schools rose to 360 and lower primary schools to 1630.[24]

The steady progress in education, especially primary education, was partly attributed to government's grant-in-aids and partly to the attention of the rulers. In some states primary education was made compulsory. Steps were also taken to establish night schools for daily labourers and special schools for backward classes. In 1941 altogether 56 special schools for backward classes were functioning.[25] Female education also received serious attention. As a result, the percentage of literacy rose from 2.7% in 1901 to 8.8% in 1947.[26]

Although primary and secondary education progressed somewhat satisfactorily, collegiate and technical education was highly neglected. Rajendra College, the only college in princely Orissa, was established in 1944 at Bolangir in Patna state.[27]

The development of education made indelible impact on the overall socio-political situation in Orissa states. It led to the growth of a group of politically conscious educated middle class. This enlightened section in later years provided effective leadership to the people in their fight against the oppressive rulers.

Apart from education, communication received a great deal of attention in early parts of 20th century. The chiefs encouraged construction of roads to improve the level of administration in their states. Rail communication was introduced in states around this time. The Bengal-Nagpur railway, opened in coastal Orissa in 1905, was linked to Talcher Coal Field railway in 1927.[28] The Vijainagaram-Raipur rail link also passed through the states of Kalahandi and Patna.[29] The spread of modern education, on one hand, and the expansion of communication network, on the other, accelerated the pace of interaction among the people and opened up new horizons of political aspirations for them.

3.Movement in Princely Orissa and Spread of Oriya Nationalism

(i) Awakening in Orissa states

The ruthless administration of Oriya princes and their oppressive feudal practices evoked strong reaction from the people in different times. During latter half of 19th century and early parts of 20th century several uprisings occurred in many Orissa states. For example, in 1862 peasants revolted against the ruler of Baud. Keonjhar witnessed two tribal uprisings in 1868 and 1891 respectively. Disturbances occurred in Mayurbhanj in 1866, in Dasapalla in 1890 and in Nayagarh in 1893.[30]

As many as five peasant uprisings broke out in Bamra between 1908-1928. In 1922 the peasants of Dhenkanal revolted against the ruler; and in Talcher three uprisings were seen between 1911 and 1933.[31] All these minor uprisings were easily stamped out by the princes with the active help of the British troops.

It is important to note that these uprisings were basically directed against local agrarian exploitation and ruthless feudal oppression. They were sporadic in nature and limited in scope.

Besides, they lacked effective leadership and mass appeal. As redress of agrarian grievances was the main concern of these local agitations, the concept of Oriya identity, the desire for united Orissa and the right to cultural and political self-determination did not figure in the minds of the agitators. These nationalistic ideals caught the attention of people in Orissa states during periods of popular movements in the late 1930s and early 1940s.

It may be noted that the All-India States People's Conference, the brainchild of Indian National Congress, was formed in 1927 to ensure responsible government and constitutional rights for the states people.[32] The Congress party in its Nagpur session in 1920, and later in Lahore session in 1929 resolved to support the states people in their fight for responsible government.[33] Around this time, the enlightened section[34] from Orissa states realised that unless the Oriyas of princely areas were brought together under a common platform the desired objective of responsible government and integration of Orissa states with British Orissa province could not be achieved. With this objective in mind, the Orissa States Peoples' Conference (hereafter OSPC) was formed in 1931 under the aegis of All-India States Peoples' Conference.[35] But soon the organisation became inactive.

The formation of British Orissa province, however, rekindled new hopes and OSPC was revived with the launch of its second session at Cuttack in 1937 under the presidentship of Pattabhi Sitaramaya.[36] Sarangdhar Das acted as its general secretary and its headquarters was permanently located at Cuttack. Mainly Congress workers from Orissa province assumed its leadership.

The OSPC in its second session resolved to secure responsible governments and civil rights for the people of princely Orissa. Further, OSPC appointed a committee to enquire into the injustice in Orissa states.[37] The birth of OSPC led to the formation of Prajamandals (Peoples' Associations) in almost every princely state. Although the Prajamandals were virtually led by Congressmen, the local people cutting across class lines joined them in large numbers.[38] The Prajamandals provided the necessary strength to demand for responsible government, socio-economic reforms, occupancy rights, civil liberties and abolition of forced labour and extortions.[39] The situation turned favourable as a popular Congress Ministry, headed by Biswanath Das, assumed office in Orissa province in 1937. The Ministry wholeheartedly extended moral support to the peoples' cause.

(ii) Movements in Orissa states

As noted above, the Prajamandals were organised to secure responsible governments for princely states of Orissa. But the rulers of these states neither recognised the Prajamandals nor fulfilled the just demands of the people. Rather, they resorted to repressive measures. As a result, widespread mobilisations, popularly known as the Prajamandal movements, flared up in almost all the states. The local press played a vital role in mobilising the people in an organised way. The Oriya dailies and weeklies like the 'Samaj', 'Prajatantra', 'Deshakatha' and the socialist mouthpiece 'Krushak' projected Prajamandal activities in high spirit and gave wide coverage to atrocities perpetuated by the princes. Periodicals like 'Garhjat Basini', 'Sanatan Dharma' and 'Sambalpur Hiteisini' published from the states of Talcher, Patna and Bamra respectively contributed further to the awakening of the people.[40]

These popular movements occurred in three phases spanning over nearly a decade from 1938 to 1947. Interestingly, the movements assumed intense form in the states adjacent to Orissa province. In Sambalpur group of states the agitations evoked low-key response.[41]

(a) First phase of struggle (1938-39): In its first phase Prajamandal movements took virulent forms in the states of Nilgiri, Talcher, Dhenkanal, Ranpur and Nayagarh. The first upsurge came in Nilgiri, a tiny state borderning the erstwhile Balasore district. Here the Prajamandal activists held public meetings to mobilise the people. Under the leadership of K.C. Mohanty and Banamali Das the people demanded recognition of elementary civic rights, agrarian reforms and abolition of forced labour. The ruler resorted to strong repressive measures to put down the struggle.[42] As the situation worsened, H.K. Mahatab, a notable Congress leader, held negotiations with the political agent and finally the ruler agreed to concede certain demands.[43] Sarangdhar Das, the Secretary of

OSPC, urged the people to emulate the Nilgiri example. Soon the movements spread to other states.

In Talcher and Dhenkanal people's agitation assumed serious proportions. Inspired by Nilgiri experience, the Talcher Prajamandal, under the leadership of Pabitra Mohan Pradhan, secretly mobilised the people and on 6th September 1938 a public meeting was held at Kosala in Angul where a list of demands was prepared.[44] The list of demands inter alia included the right to form associations, abolition of feudal practices (i.e. bethi, begari, etc.) and modification of tenancy and forest laws.[45] The ruler did not pay any heed to these demands. Instead, the Prajamandal was declared unlawful and repressive measures were promulgated. The people resisted state action by offering satyagraha. The villagers who refused to render forced labour were brutally tortured and their houses were raided and burnt down. The state police opened fire on the people and killed two persons and injured many more.[46]

Gradually, the situation worsened and thousands of people left Talcher and took shelter in refugee camps in Angul in British Orissa.[47] The massive exodus of people drew the attention of prominent Congress leaders including Gandhiji. In January 1939, N.G. Ranga, C.F. Andrews and Agatha Harisson, lady member of British Parliament, visited the camps and presented details of people's sufferings which were horrifying. The Congress government in Orissa also extended moral and material support to the refugees.[48] In the meantime efforts were made for a negotiated settlement. Finally, the ruler of Talcher yielded to pressure from British administration and agreed to concede some of the demands.[49]

In Dhenkanal, popular protest started towards end of 1938. Here, the Prajamandal, led by H.M. Pattnaik demanded responsible government and removal of feudal practices like 'bethi', 'begari', 'Magan' and 'rasad'. To arouse public consciousness, the leaders distributed leaflets containing legitimate demands. Also, two periodicals, namely, 'Ranbheri' and 'Hushiar' were brought out to spread the objectives of the movement.[50]

But the autocratic ruler of Dhenkanal adopted brutal measures to curb the movement. The state police resorted to indiscriminate firing and killed several persons. Men and women were trampled over by elephants and horses. In protest against the repressive measures the Congress leaders like N.K. Chaudhary, S.D. Das, H.K. Mahtab offered civil resistance and organised public meetings to boost up people's morale.[51]

As the people began to agitate, the ruler deployed armed policemen and requisitioned 200 British troops to put the state under a virtual seize, leading to a reign of terror. The state Prajamandal was declared illegal and the socialist paper 'Krushak' was banned. Local Prajamandal workers were arrested, their houses were burnt down and properties confiscated.[52] Thousands of people left Dhenkanal in protest and settled in refugee camps in British Orissa. As the stories of the movement reached far and wide, the ruler of Dhenkanal agreed to grant some concessions.[53] The people however remained unsatisfied as their major demand for responsible government was not conceded.

In the meantime, the agitation spread to other princely states of Ranpur, Nayagarh, Athgarh, Hindol, Pal-lahara, Sonepur, Bonai, Dasapalla and Keonjhar.[54] In every case the state ruler made all efforts to suppress the movement mercilessly. The ruthless suppression at last led to a violent incident in Ranpur state in January 1939. Here the agitated people gathered at the palace and demanded for the release of their Prajamandal leaders. To pacify the people, Major R.L. Bezzelgette, the Political Agent of Orissa states, rushed to the spot and started negotiations with the ruler. But unfortunately, the situation turned violent and the irate crowd killed Bezzelgette on the spot.[55]

The killing of Political Agent was widely condemned. The Congress urged the people to show restraint and refrain from violence to make their agitation successful. After the incident the British repressive machinery acted in full swing. Martial law was imposed and the military police almost seized the state.[56]

Meanwhile, the report of the States Enquiry Committee suggested some remedial measures which included: abrogation of sanads (rights) granted to chiefs, treating the chiefs as zamindars, civil liberties to the people, creation of permanent judiciary and finally transfer of the supervisory power from the

Resident to provincial government of Orissa.[57] A copy of the report was submitted to the then Viceroy Lord Linlithgow who visited Orissa in August 1939. The Viceroy remarked, "there is as such no geographical boundary between two parts of Orissa; the people of Orissa province and princely Orissa are closely intertwined in various ways."[58] But before anything substantial could be done the Second World War broke out and with that the first phase of people's agitation ended abruptly.

(b) Second phase of struggle (1940-44): The second phase of Prajamandal movement roughly coincided with the Quit India movement of 1942. Prior to this period, limited Prajamandal activities were launched as most of the top line leaders were detained under Defense of India Rules during Second World War. Some leaders, who escaped arrest, continued the agitation from underground. But the Quit India movement gave the necessary spark and soon Prajamandal agitations started with greater vigour than before. Once again, the states of Talcher and Dhenkanal came into the limelight. In these states, armed agitations were reported at few places. Another noticeable feature was that the movement this time turned more anti-British in character.[59] The British Government was accused of being at the roof of all evils.

By the end of 1939 some administrative reforms in the form of 'Praja Sabha', 'Praja Parishad' and 'Byabastha Parishad', were introduced in some states.[60] The people, however, perceived these measures as camouflage designs to suppress the movement and deny their just demands. As a result, in some states, notably Dhenkanal, Talcher and Nilgiri people's movement escalated vigorously.

In the Talcher state, Prajamandal was revived by Kalindi Pradhan[61] in the absence of Pabitra Mohan Pradhan, who was arrested under Defense of India Rules. Soon Pabitra Mohan Pradhan escaped from jail and organised an open revolt against the ruler. At his instance, a parallel government consisting of workers and labourers was constituted and soon the entire state excepting the headquarters came under the grip of the parallel government.[62] Thereafter, the agitators decided to capture the palace of the ruler in Talcher town. Several thousands people armed with crude weapons gathered near the palace on 7th September 1942 and staged an open confrontation to destroy the vestige of autocratic rule.[63] The situation turned so serious that the administration with the help of British military forces had resorted to aerial bombing and machine-gunning to disperse the agitators. The people retreated with some casualties. Thus by use of brutal force the authorities at last succeeded in establishing their control over the state.[64]

In Dhenkanal the sham 'Praja Parishad' set up by the ruler did not satisfy the people. At this juncture, Baisnab Patnaik, a revolutionary Prajamandal leader, appeared on the scene and being inspired by Quit India movement he motivated the people to capture power and establish a popular government in the state. With armed squad of 19 persons he attacked several police stations and brought Mudhi (now Kamakshyanagar) under his control. He established popular rule in the area for nearly two weeks.[65] The paramount military force recaptured the area and a special task force was constituted to nab Baisnab Patnaik. In spite of strenuous efforts the task force failed to catch him although other members of his group faced rigorous sentences.[66] Nevertheless, underground activities still continued in both Dhenkanal and Talcher. The two leaders, Baisnab Patnaik and Pabitra Mohan Pradhan, absconded and started guerrilla warfare which continued till 1946.

The impact of Quit India was felt in Nayagarh also. Sensing danger the state ruler put all the leaders behind bars. Such an action on the part of the ruler deteriorated the situation and people in large number took out procession and attacked police stations and offices. In the clashes between the people and armed police, one person was killed and several others were wounded. The police atrocities could not, however, prevent the agitation from escalating. Clashes between the people and the joint police force were also reported from Nilgiri state.[67]

Agitation also spread to Mayurbhanj state in this period. The enlightened section of Mayurbhanj formed 'Pargana Samitis' (Village Committees) in 1939 to undertake various rural reconstructive measures. The basic objective of these samitis was to improve the socio-economic standard of the people and make them politically conscious for popular government. To check the growing popularity of 'Pargana Samitis', the ruler established 'Praja Sabhas' (Peoples' Councils) at five places including the state capital Baripada.[68]

Unfortunately, the Praja Sabha could not win the favour of people as most of its membes were nominated by the ruler. At this stage the Pargana Samiti workers became more active for responsible government and subsequently the Mayurbhanj Prajamandal was born in 1942 under the leadership of Sarat Chandra Das. The Prajamandal, besides being involved in rural reconstruction, organised series of protest rallies and demonstration during Quit India movement. Public meetings were held, excise shops were picketed and weekly markets were boycotted as mark of protests.[69]

(c) Third phase of struggle (1945-47): The third phase of Prajamandal agitation began after Second World War. In this phase, the movement came closer towards the broad ideals of Oriya nationalism. The desire for the unification of Orissa princely states with Orissa province figured prominently in course of the agitation. In most of the instances, the Prajamandal workers shifted from the primary demand of having responsible government in their respective states to achieving the goal of united Orissa.

In view of the volatile political situation in India after the war period, the rulers of Orissa princely states adopted some statutory provisions guaranteeing rule of law and security of persons and properties in their territories. Efforts were made to eliminate free and forced labour.[70] These reforms, however, fell far short of the expectations of the people. In a bid to capture power and establish self-rule, the Prajamandals renewed their agitation in most of the states. This time the mobilisation for self-rule aimed at achieving the goal of integrated and united Orissa. In their efforts the Prajamandals received tremendous support from the people and government of Orissa province. Besides, the student community, local press and the workers unions rendered tremendous support to the cause of the states people.

For example, in the Students' Conference on 10 February 1946 at Cuttack it was resolved to demand the release of all

Prajamandal workers, recognition of civil liberties and amalgamation of smaller Orissa states with Orissa province.[71] The Orissa State Workers Conference, held at Cuttack in 1946, severely criticised the action of Oriya rulers, especially the ruler of Patna state, in obstructing the amalgamation plan.[72] H.K. Mahtab, the then Premier of Orissa province, remarked at the Students' Conference: "there is no legal, moral or historic justification for the retention of the Orissa states as separate entities."[73]

In the meantime the Prajamandal movement spread far and wide. In nearly every state the people clamoured for freedom and self-rule. For example, in Dhenkanal the Prajamandal reiterated its demand for responsible government and intensified its struggle to achieve that goal.[74] In a meeting on 9 June 1946, under the Chairmanship of Baisnab Patnaik, the Dhenkanal Prajamandal resolved to submit a 50-point charter of demands to the ruler. Among other things, the memorandum highlighted the desire of the people to bring Dhenkanal under a "unit comprising of Orissa states, British Orissa province and other outlying Oriya-speaking areas."[75] Also it was stressed upon to consider a responsible government for Dhenkanal during the interim period.[76]

In smaller states like Baramba, Narsinghpur, etc., the people challenged the feudal authorities and in several thousands they gathered to capture the palace in their respective states.[77] In Sambalpur group of states (i.e. Patna, Sonepur, Bamra, Kalahandi and Rairahkhol), the people who showed hitherto little interest in Prajamandal agitation became more active to secure their legitimate demands.

The peoples' organisations in Sambalpur group of states were formed around 1945. In Patna, for example, the 'Krushak Dal', formed in September 1945, represented Prajamandal activities for all practical purposes and worked towards securing civil liberties for the people.[78] At this juncture, the Patna ruler decided to set up a constituent assembly to win the confidence of the people. But the assembly failed to achieve the desired objectives. In a meeting on 23 February 1947 the 'Krushak Dal' resolved to start no-rent campaign and non-cooperation with the state officials.[79] Thereafter, the ruler considered installing a cabinet comprising of two members from 'Krushak Dal' and some nominated members.[80] This scheme also failed in meeting the demands of the people.

The Prajamandal activities in Kalahandi were taken up by a local tribal organisation called the 'Adivasi Sevamandal'. Except for carrying out some political propaganda, the organisation did not launch any vigorous struggle against the ruler.[81] In Sonepur and Gangpur, however, the Prajamandals indulged in serious agitation for the demand of popular government and civil rights.[82]

In the meantime, the political situation in Orissa princely states took a dramatic turn as the states of Eastern States Agency (which was formed in 1933) opted to form a federal union of Eastern States comprising of 14 Chhatisgarh states and 25 Orissa states.[83] Consequently, the Eastern States Union (ESU) came into being on 1 August 1947.[84] This measure was taken by the rulers precisely because of the declaration by British administration to restore sovereignty to the rulers on the occasion of India's independence. The lead role in the formation of ESU was played by the rulers of Patna, Kalahandi and Saraikella. This clever design of some Oriya princes was viewed in different quarters as a tactical move to jeopardise the efforts for integration of Orissa states with Orissa province. The leaders of several political parties in British Orissa and the states Prajamandal leaders categorically opposed the formation of ESU. For example, S.N. Dwivedy, the secretary of Utkal Pradesh Congress Committee urged all Congressmen in Orissa to fight for the immediate integration of the 26 princely states with the province of Orissa.[85] Similarly, the Orissa and Chhatisgarh States Regional Council, which met at Cuttack on 10 August 1947, passed resolution condemning the ESU and demanded the inclusion of Orissa states in the Orissa province on the basis of linguistic-cultural affinity.[86]

Soon after independence, peoples' agitation in Orissa princely states was intensified and in nearly every state the people gave ultimatum to grant full responsible government within a specified date. Such a move was clearly evident in Ranpur, Talcher, Dhenkanal, Keonjhar, Mayurbhanj, Patna, Bamra and Narsingpur. In Talcher, the famous Prajamandal leader Pabitra Mohan Pradhan organised around 20,000 volunteers and demanded the immediate merger of the state in Orissa province.[87] The Prajamandals of Dhenakal and Patna declared to take over the administration unless their demand for self-governance was fulfilled by December 1947. Meanwhile, the situation in Nilgiri became so serious that the government of Orissa finally intervened and took over the state on 14 November 1947.[88] But in Mayurbhanj the Prajamandal succeeded in establishing a responsible government in the state on 9 December 1947 under the premiership of S.C. Das.[89] Gradually, the Prajamandal movements petered out as the preparation for the merger of princely states of Orissa began by the close of 1947.

4. Integration of the Princely States of Orissa

The efforts for merger of Orissa states formed a part of the larger scheme for integration of Indian states with the Dominion of India. The integration of Orissa states, which came into effect from 1 January 1948, was not an isolated event. Evidently, the merger of Orissa states was the result of the decade-long struggles in these states.

In the course of their agitation, the states people realised that the geographical limitation and economic non-viability of their respective states could not provide suitable grounds for survival of responsible governments. Hence, behind their manifest agitation the people had the latent motive of creating a situation whereby it became imperative on the part of the rulers to opt for merger of their states with Orissa province.

The Congress leadership in Orissa province seized this opportunity and took all necessary steps to motivate the people of Orissa states for integration. It may be noted that the Orissa government of 1937 extended all possible moral and material support to the people in their fight against the princes. On the eve of independence, the provincial Congress left no stone unturned to materialise the scheme of integration of princely Orissa for the larger interest of Oriya nationality.

For instance, H.K. Mahtab, premier of Orissa in 1946, pleaded before the Cabinet Mission that the Orissa princely states and Orissa province constituted two inseparable parts of the same Oriya nationality.[90] Mahtab tried to convince the Mission that both the parts of Orissa represent one economic, political, geographic, historical and linguistic unit and hence Orissa states should be merged with the province of Orissa on the basis of geographic contiguity, linguistic affinity and cultural homogeneity.[91] He reminded the Cabinet Mission that the Attlee Committee report envisaged that "Orissa states should ultimately have to become an integral part of the province".[92]

These early attempts at integration were not free from opposition. As expected, the Oriya princes rejected outright Mahtab's merger scheme when the latter sought their cooperation for the cause of greater Orissa. As noted earlier, the rulers of Orissa and Chhatisgarh states formed the Eastern States Union in 1947. The motive behind this move was to scuttle the process of integration and maintain their internal sovereignty in the proposed Indian union.

The strongest opposition to integration came from the rulers of Patna, Kalahandi and Sonepur, the key Sambalpur group of states. These rulers instigated their subjects and coaxed them to launch counter-mobilisation against the merger plan. Besides, they pursued vigorous mass propaganda through folk songs, dances and distribution of money to get public support in favour of ESU.[93] But Orissa Premier Mahtab categorically stressed that integration was the ultimate goal of the states people and that the Congress at the all-India level adopted the linguistic basis of provincial reorganisation in India.

At this critical juncture, the foundation stone of the multi-purpose Mahanadi river valley project was laid by the Governor of Orissa at Hirakud in Sambalpur district.[94] The princes who opposed integration, considered the project as a tactical move by the Congress to jeopardise the regional interest of Sambalpur and save coastal Orissa, especially Cuttack district from flood.

Thus, both pro- and anti-merger mobilisations were seen in Oriya homeland for integration of Orissa states. The pro-merger group consisting of Congress and Prajamandal leaders opposed balkanisation and lobbied for integration; but anti-merger group comprising the Oriya princes opposed integration mainly to retain their separate identity.

But the intervention by Government of India and the escalation of fresh agitation by Prajamandal workers paved the grounds for integration of Orissa states. The Herculean task fell on the shoulders of Sardar Patel who persuaded the Oriya princes to join the Orissa province.

Advocating strongly in favour of merger, Mahatab, in his memorandum to Sardar Patel, suggested at first a common administration for Orissa province and the 'B' and 'C' class states.[95] But when V.P. Menon, the secretary to Department of States, discussed the matter with Sardar Patel, the latter suggested to arrange for the integration of all 'A', 'B' and 'C' class of states.[96] Meanwhile, the Government of India had decided not to recognise ESU. The Government of India maintained that the ESU was homogeneous neither on ethnic and linguistic grounds nor compact on geographical terms. The only solution was to dissolve ESU and integrate the Oriya-speaking states with Orissa province and the Hindi-speaking states with the Central Provinces.[97]

To carry out the plan of merger, Patel arrived in Orissa on 13 December 1947 and the next day he met the rulers of 'B' and 'C' class states at Cuttack.[98] Patel made the rulers aware of the inevitable consequences of the rising currents of the people's agitation in their respective states. He made it very clear that for the smaller states there was no alternative to integration. He further observed:

> *...the problem of the province, however, which was holding up its legitimate right to progress, was the problem of a number of petty states – left as a legacy of British rule – which cut across the province and ruined its unity. Orissa as a federal unit could only thrive and progress if it was built as a contiguous whole and not turn asunder by multifarious jurisdiction and authorities which ruined its compactness.*[99]

He further remarked that the demands of the people of princely states for responsible government could only be met if the rulers transfer their powers to the responsible government of Orissa province. Without much resistance the rulers of 15 'B' and

'C' class states accepted the merger plan and signed the instrument of accession on the evening of 14th December 1947. In return these rulers were assured of Privy Purse and dynastic succession.[100]

The same day afternoon Patel held a separate meeting with the rulers of eleven 'A' class states.[101] In his opening remark Patel noted:

It was unfortunate... but everyone realised that the Orissa states were like ulcers on the body of Orissa province and they had to be either cured or eliminated. If the rulers listened to his advice they could be cured, otherwise, they might find themselves uprooted by the people.[102]

In a coercive gesture Patel clearly stated that the merger of Oriya-speaking states with Orissa province indicated the merger of 'A' class states too.[103] He advised the rulers to take part in the building of a wealthy united Orissa. But when the matter was discussed the ruler of Patna voiced his opposition to merger. Soon the rulers of Kalahandi, Sonepur and Saraikella took sides with him. The Patna ruler pointed out that the merger agreement did not tally with the talks he had with Patel at Delhi.[104]

As an alternative to merger, the Patna ruler suggested for a Union of States. But in the case of merger he demanded for some degree of local autonomy to states particularly in the areas of less important subjects.[105] To this V.P. Menon replied that integration appeared essential in the case of Orissa states and it would not be possible to distinguish between 'A', 'B' and 'C' class states. Menon also hinted that in the event of the rulers not signing the agreement, the Government of India in the prevailing circumstances would be compelled to take over the administration of their states.[106]

Finally, after lot of discussions, persuasions and amendments all the rulers of 'A' class states except Mayurbhanj agreed to merger and signed the merger agreement. The ruler of Mayurbhanj declined to make any commitment as a popular ministry, headed by S.C. Das, was functioning in his state at that time.[107] Thus, except Mayurbhanj, the remaining 25 princely states of Orissa were merged with the province of Orissa with effect from

1 January 1948.[108] Addressing the Orissa Legislative Assembly on the merger of states, Dr. A.N. Katzu, the Governor of Orissa, remarked that the integration of Oriya-speaking states led to the "re-emergence of Utkal of ancient days."[109]

It may be noted here that the 25 states merged with the province of Orissa included Saraikella and Kharswan, the two Orissa states of Chhotanagpur group. The merger of these two states was, however, resented by the local tribal inhabitants.[110] Considering the desire of the people, the Government of India ultimately handed over these two states to Bihar on 19 May 1948.[111]

Mayurbhanj retained its separate existence nearly for one year. In the meantime the Jharkhand activists motivated the local tribes in Mayurbhanj to agitate in favour of its inclusion in Bihar.[112] To avoid further deterioration of the situation the ruler of Mayurbhanj signed the instrument of merger on 17 October 1948 and the Government of India finally made over the state to Orissa province on 1 January 1949.[113] With the inclusion of Mayurbhanj finally 24 Oriya-speaking states came under the province of Orissa and thereby the long spell of feudal rule in princely Orissa came to an end.

5. Consolidation of Oriya Nationalism

It is clear that people's movements in princely Orissa led to its integration with the erstwhile province of Orissa. The unification of the two parts of Orissa resulted in the growth of modern Orissa as a linguistically homogeneous province in independent India.

With the integration of princely Orissa, Oriya nationalism reached its culminating point and achieved its long cherished objective of unifying the Oriya homeland under a single provincial roof. The inclusion of the princely areas resulted in the emergence of greater Orissa with its political boundary coinciding with the cultural boundary of Oriya homeland. The co-terminality between Oriya homeland and its political boundary paved the grounds for further consolidation and homogenisation of Oriya nationality. In fact, greater Orissa ensured the Oriya people the right to internal political self-determination and cultural self-preservation like several other distinct nationalities in India.

Oriya nationalism spread from British Orissa to princely Orissa in the wake of people's movements in the latter. But a closer look reveals that, the nationalisms seen in the two parts of Orissa differ in several ways notwithstanding the shared objective of united Orissa.

Firstly, in British Orissa the rise of nationalism was the outcome of the cultural domination of the outsiders over the Oriya people. Here, Oriya nationalism acquired a linguistic character and it stood for protection of Oriya language and culture on the one hand, and resisted attempted assimilation and cultural hegemony, on the other. Conversely, in princely Orissa nationalism took the shape of mass struggle against the anti-people feudal domination. It strongly opposed the feudal socio-economic oppression by Oriya rulers. It advocated democratic responsible governments for the people and in due course of time it showed the signs of integrationist nationalism.

Secondly, in British Orissa the elites and urban educated middle class played the vanguard role in the nationalist struggle. Whereas, in princely Orissa, nationalist struggle assumed popular character cutting across people from several class backgrounds. People from different classes collaborated in the struggle for responsible government and integration of Oriya territories.

Thirdly, nationalist struggle in princely Orissa showed anti-British stance on many occasions. But in British Orissa, the nationalists remained pro-British throughout their struggle. Finally, in British Orissa the Oriya nationalists adopted the constitutional means of petition, prayer and protest to secure the goal of united Orissa. In princely Orissa, however, the people largely resorted to violent mass protest, revolt and rebellion on many occasions to secure legitimate civic rights and integration with Orissa province.

Integration of princely states gave birth to reorganisation of districts in Orissa and consequently the number of districts rose to thirteen. In 1936 the Orissa province comprised six districts of Balasore, Cuttack, Puri, Ganjam, Sambalpur and Koraput. After integration seven new districts were carved out from the erstwhile princely states. While some smaller Cuttack group of states formed parts of the existing districts of Balasore, Cuttack and Puri; some bigger states constituted the new districts of Dhenkanal, Mayurbhanj and Keonjhar.

Of the Sambalpur group of states, two smaller states were merged with the district of Sambalpur; and the remaining states formed the new districts of Kalahandi, Bolangir and Phulbani. The district of Sundergarh was carved out of the two Chhotanagpur states of Gangpur and Bonai.

It is important to note that the reorganisation of districts after integration of princely states divided Orissa into two distinct regional units: western region and coastal belt. Gradually, regional consciousness began to appear in the western region as it continued to lag behind the coastal region in socio-economic, political and cultural sphere.

Notes and References

1. The princely states of Orissa were variously dubbed as 'Feudatory states', 'Feudatory estates', Tributary Mahals', 'Tributary states', 'Garjats', etc. These states comprised Athmalik, Athgarh, Bamara, Baramba, Baud, Bonai, Daspalla, Dhenkanal, Gangpur, Hindol, Kalahandi, Keonjhar, Khandapara, Mayurbhanj, Narasinghpur, Nayagarh, Nilgiri, Pal-Lahara, Patna, Rairakhol, Ranpur, Sonepur, Talcher, Tigiria, Saraikela and Kharswan. See L.E.B. Cobden Ramsay, "Feudatory States of Orissa", *Bengal Gazetteers*, Calcutta, 1913, Chap.I.
2. See *Epigraphica Indica*, Vol.XVIII, pp.328-34; Hermann Kulke, "Fragmentation and Segmentation vs Integration", *The State – Studies in History* (Special Issue), JNU, New Delhi.
3. C.U. Aitchison, *A Collection of Treaties, Engagements and Sanads relating to India and Neighbouring Countries*, Vol.I, Calcutta, 1909, pp.188-90; S.L. Maddox, *Final Report on the Survey and Settlement of the Province of Orissa, 1890-1900*, 1901, Vol. I, Calcutta, pp.409-10.
4. For details, see J.K. Samal, *Princely States of Orissa*, Allahabad, 1988, pp.16-18.
5. See L.E.B. Cobden-Ramsay, *op. cit.*, p.29; Also see selection from Nagpur Residency Records, Vol. I, p. 236, cited in Sadasib

Pradhan, *Agrarian and Political Movements: States of Orissa: 1931-1949*, Delhi, 1986.

6. See *Orissa Records: Sambalpur Papers*, ACC No.73S, Govt. of Bengal to Commissioner of Orissa division, Circular No.17, 17 November 1905. The 26 feudatory states were grouped into three categories: (a) the Cuttack group consisting of 17 feudatory states such as Athmalik, Athgarh, Baramba, Baud, Dasapalla, Dhenkanal, Hindol, Keonjhar, Khandapara, Mayurbhanj, Ranpur, Talcher, Tigiria; (b) the Sambalpur group consisting of five feudatory states such as Patna, Sonepur, Kalahandi, Bamra, Rairakhol; (c) the Chhotanagpur group comprising four feudatory states such as Gangpur, Bonai, Sareikella and Kharswan. On the classification of states, see S. Pati, *Democratic Movements in India*, Delhi, 1987, pp.14-22.
7. K.M. Patra, *Orissa under the East India Company*, New Delhi, 1971, Chap.III; W. Lee Warner, *The Protected Princes of India*, London, 1894, pp.56-88.
8. K.M. Patra, *op. cit.*, p.283.
9. L.E.B. Cobden-Ramsay, *op. cit.*, p.29.
10. For details, see J.K. Samal, *Princely States, op. cit.*, pp.8-18; S. Pati, *Democratic Movements*, *op. cit.*, pp.14-20.
11. C.U. Aitchison (ed.), *A Collection of Treaties, Engagements and Sannads relating to India and Neighbouring Countries*, Vol.II, Calcutta, 1931, p.321.
12. The British administration exercised political control over Orissa states through the political agent and periodical grant of Sannads. See for details, *The Feudatory and Tributary States of Orissa Division and the Rules Applicable to Them*, Part I, Calcutta, 1907, p.23.
13. See for details, *Report of the Orissa States Enquiry Committee*, Cuttack, 1939, pp.18-20.
14. *Ibid.*, p.19.
15. Commenting on the 'bethi' (forced unpaid labour) R.K. Ramdhyani, the special officer deputed to study the Land tenure system in Orissa and Chhatisgarh states, observed, "Labour is 'dirt-cheap' in this country and to insist on free and underpaid labour is the height of callousness". See R.K. Ramdhyani, *Report of the Land*

Tenure and the Revenue System of the Orissa and Chhatisgarh States, Vol.1, p.96.

16. *Report of Orissa States*, *op. cit.*, pp.56-63.
17. R.K. Ramdhyani, *Report on Land Tenures, op. cit.*, Vol.II, p.193.
18. *Ibid.*, Vol.II, p.193.
19. *Annual Report on the Administration of the Feudatory States of Orissa*, 1931-32, pp.156-58.
20. See *Report of Orissa States Enquiry Committee, op. cit.*, pp.10-11; Also see *Deskatha* (Oriya daily), 10 February 1931.
21. See L.E.B. Cobden-Ramsay, *op. cit.*, p.106.
22. *Ibid.*
23. *General Review of the Administration of the Feudatory States of Orissa, 1931-32*, p.158.
24. *Ibid.*, p.159.
25. *The Samaja* (Oriya daily), 5 July 1941.
26. General Review of Administration of Feudatory States of Orissa, 1946-47, p.173.
27. N. Senapati, *Orissa District Gazetteers*, Bolangir, Cuttack, 1971, p.213.
28. See J.K. Samal, *Princely States, op. cit.*, pp.174-75.
29. *Ibid.*
30. For details see R.N. Rath, *The Story of Freedom Movements in Orissa States*, Cuttack, 1964, pp.13-17.
31. *Ibid.*
32. A.N. Sundari, *Indian States Register and Directory*, Madras, 1929, pp.301-16.
33. N.N. Mitra (ed.), *The Indian Quarterly Register*, Vol.II, Calcutta, 1929, p.293.
34. This enlightened section comprised the english-educated Congress workers from Orissa states. Notable among them were Sarangdhar Das and Harmohan Patnaik of Dhenkanal, R.N. Rath from Athgarh, Kapileshwar Nanda from Patna, Pabitra Mohan Pradhan from Talcher, K.C. Mohanty and Gangadhar Mishra from Ranpur and Sarat Chandra Das from Mayurbhanj.
35. *The Prajatantra*(Oriya daily), 29 June 1931. Also see, Lalmohan Patnaik, Ressurected Orissa, Cuttack, 1941, p.329.
36. *Indian Annual Register*, Vol.I, 1937, p.356.

37. See *All India States People's Conference*, File No.127, p.95, Nehru Memorial Muserum Library, New Delhi; *Indian Annual Register*, Vol.I, p.358. This Committee is known as Orissa States Enquiry Committee. S.D. Das acted as its convenor, while Satish Chandra Bose, Balwantrai Mehta and Braj Sundar Das acted as its members.
38. See S. Pradhan, *op. cit.*, pp. 90-91.
39. *Orissa Records, Kalahandi Papers*, ACC No.4, Resident, Chhatisgarh Agency to Maharaja of Kalahandi, Proceedings of the Orissa States Peoples Conference, July 1938.
40. S. Pati, *op. cit.*, p.78.
41. This was partly because Sambalpur group of states remained outside the impact of Congress activities in British Orissa, and partly because, the Prajamandals were formed in the late 1940s.
42. See *Orissa Records, who's who compilation committee*, ACC No.38, p.28.
43. H.K. Mahtab, *Sadhanara Pathe* (Oriya), Cuttack, 1972, pp.185-87.
44. See S.C. De (ed.), *Diary of Political Events in Orissa, 1936-47*, Cuttack, 1964, p.20.
45. *History of Talcher Prajamandal* (ed.), 1950, Talcher Prajamandal Committee, p.17; Pabitra, Mohan Pradhan, "Freedom Struggle in the Ex-States of Orissa", *Orissa Review*, Vol. XXIIX, No.1, Bhubaneswar, 1972, p. 58.
46. See *Orissa States Enquiry Report, op. cit.*, p.111.
47. *The Statesman*, 12 January 1939.
48. See H.K. Mahtab, *Sadhanar Pathe, op. cit.*, p. 47.
49. See H.K. Mahtab, *Sadhamar Pathe, op. cit.*, pp.192-94.
50. *Desakatha* (Oriya daily), 31 August 1938; also see, *Who's who compilation, op. cit.*, pp. 33-34.
51. *Desakatha*, 15 October 1938.
52. All India States People's Conference, File No.127, *op. cit.*, p.239, 255.
53. *Ibid.*; also see *Who's who, op. cit.*, p.46.
54. For details on people's uprisings in these states, see S. Pradhan, *op. cit.*, pp.126-36.
55. H.K. Mahtab, *Sadhanar, op. cit.*, pp.194-200. Mahtab offered a graphic account of the killing in this autobiography.

56. *Ibid.*; *Orissa Records, Who's who*, ACC No.38, pp.37-8; Indian Annual Register, Vol.I, 1939, p.442.
57. See *Report of States' Enquiry, op. cit.*, pp. 58-60.
58. *The Samaj* (Oriya daily), 2 August 1939.
59. The anti-British nature of the movement was partly due to the anti-British stance of the broader national movement for Indian independence (which influenced the states people's movement to a great extent) and partly because of the unflinching support the British shown to the rulers in suppressing the movement ruthlessly. As a matter of fact, the prajamandal movement in this phase became more acute in the state bordering the coastal districts of British Orissa province. For example, Dhenkanal and Talcher were adjacent to Cuttack district.
60. See S. Pati, *op. cit.*, pp. 127-28.
61. *Orissa Records, who's who*, ACC No.30, p. 35.
62. *History of Talcher Prajamandal, op. cit.*, pp. 51-58.
63. *Ibid.*
64. *Ibid.*
65. *Orissa Records, Dhenkanal Papers*, ACC No.1026 S, Raja of Dhenakanl to Political Agent, Orissa States, D.O.No.404-P/42, 29 August 1942.
66. *Orissa District Gazetteer, Dhenkanal*, Bhubaneswar, 1972, pp.55-60.
67. See S.N. Patnaik, *Odissare Swadhinata Andolan (Oriya)*, Cuttack, 1972, Nilgiri Administration Report, 1943-44, pp. 35-36.
68. See, *Orissa District Gazetteer, Mayurbhanj*, Bhubaneswar, 1967, pp.7-21.
69. *Report on the Administration of Mayurbhanj, 1942-43*, p.6; Also see *Souvenir*, Orissal Historical Congress, Bhubaneswar, 1982, p. 4.
70. See, *Sambalpur Papers*, ACC No.1085S, Political Department, New Delhi to Resident, Eastern States, Calcutta, D.O. No.F.23-P(S), 146, 21 February 1956.
71. *Orissa Records, who's who compilation committee*, ACC No.50, pp.68-70; ACC No.10, pp. 82-83.
72. *Orissa Records, who's who*, ACC No.28, p.17.
73. *Ibid.*, p.12.

74. *Orissa Records, Dhenkanal Papers*, ACC, No.1026S, Petitions of Pravakar Rout and Ramachandra Patnaik, 20 March 1946 and 31 March 1946.
75. *Orissa Records, Dhenkanal Papers*, ACC No.1026S. Baisnab Charan Patnaik to Chief Minister, Dhenkanal; Political Agent, Orissa Feudatory States; Resident, Eastern States Agency, Calcutta, 21 June 1946.
76. *Ibid.*
77. *Orissa Records, Sambalpur Papers*, ACC No.966S, Ruling Chief of Baramba to Political Agent, D.O. No.1513/D-12(a), 27 June 1946.
78. *Orissa Records, who's who of Sambalpur, Sundargarh, Kalahandi and Bolangir-Patna districts*, Bhubaneswar, 1969; The Krushak Dal was affiliated to All India States People's Conference as a mark of solidarity to people's movement.
79. *Orissa Records, Sambalpur papers*, ACC No.1180S, Proceedings of the meeting of Krushak Dal, 7 March 1947.
80. *Ibid.*
81. *Orissa Records, who's who of Sambalpur, Kalahandi, op. cit.*, p.iv.
82. *Ibid.*
83. V.P. Menon, *The Transfer of Power in India*, Delhi, 1968, pp.266-68.
84. *Orissa Records, Sambalpur Papers*, ACC No.1189S, Minutes of the Rulers Conference held on 10-12 July 1947.
85. *Orissa Records, who's who, op. cit.*, ACC No.99, p.26.
86. *Ibid.*, p.47.
87. See, Pabitra Mohan Pradhan, *Mukti Pathe Sainika* (Autobiography in Oriya), Part II, Cuttack, 1979, p.9.
88. For details on Nilgir takeover see, V.P. Menon, *The Story of the Integration of the Indian States*, New Delhi, 1961, p.147; also see H.K. Mahtab, *Beginning of End*, Cuttack, 1972, p.27. The occupation of Nilgiri state was legalised as merger with effect from 1 January 1948.
89. *Extraordinary Mayurbhanj State Gazette*, 10 December 1947; *Orissa District Gazetteer, Mayurbhanj*, Bhubaneswar, 1972, pp.83-84.
90. *Proceedings of Orissa Legislative Assembly*, Vol.II, Cuttack, 1949, p.864.

91. H.K. Mahtab, *Beginning of the End*, Cuttack, 1972, p.17.
92. *Ibid.*
93. *Hirakhand Samachar* (Oriya weekly), 22 October 1946.
94. See, V.P. Menon, *op. cit.*, p.148.
95. *Ibid.*, p.149.
96. *Ibid.*
97. Orissa Records, Secretariat Papers (Home), File No.19-I/1948, "Note on the Eastern States Union"; Also see Mahtab, *Beginning, op. cit.*
98. For details on the meeting between Sardar Patel and the Rulers of A, B, C class states, see, *Orissa Records Sambalpur Papers*, ACC No.1161S, Minutes of the Meeting, 14 December 1947.
99. *Ibid.*
100. V.P. Menon, *op. cit.*, p.157.
101. *Sambalpur Papers, Minutes, op. cit.*; V.P. Menon, *op. cit.*, p.158; The eleven class 'A' states comprised Bamra, Boudh, Dhenkanal, Gangpur, Kalahandi, Keonjhar, Mayurbhanj, Nayagarh, Patna, Sonepur and Sareikella.
102. *Ibid.*, Menon, p.159.
103. *Ibid.*, Menon, p.160.
104. See H.K. Mahtab, *Beginning of the End, op. cit.*, p.29.
105. Orissa Records, *Sambalpur Papers, Minutes, op. cit.*
106. *Ibid.*
107. *Orissa District Gazetteer, Mayurbhanj, op. cit.*, p.83.
108. See, *Orissa Legislative Assembly Proceedings*, Vol.II, No.22, Cuttack, 1949, p.874.
109. See *Orissa Legislative Assembly Proceedings*, Vol.VI, 1947-48, p.81.
110. *Ibid.*, p.86.
111. Mahtab, *Beginning of the End, op. cit.*, p.32.
112. *Orissa District Gazetteers, Mayurbhanj, op. cit.*, p.83.
113. *Ibid.*

6

Rise and Growth of Regionalism in Orissa

Undoubtedly, the rise of Oriya nationalism led to the establishment of Orissa state in India. The Oriya language served as a unifying factor at the time of both formation of Orissa province in 1936 and integration of Orissa princely states in 1948-49. But soon after the emergence of united Orissa, the Oriya language ceased to be the unifying factor among the Oriya people. Instead, the Oriya people got divided on the basis of regional identities which in turn continued to dominate politics and society in Orissa ever since independence of India. Not only that, the rise of regional particularism has begun to undermine the spirit of Oriya nationalism.

As previously noted, following the merger of Oriya princely states with the erstwhile Orissa province two distinct regional units, namely, the western region and the coastal belt have been formed in the state of Orissa (see Map No.1). Originally, the coastal belt comprises the four advanced districts of Balasore, Cuttack, Ganjam and Puri and the western region consists of the five backward districts of Bolangir, Kalahandi, Phulbani, Sambalpur and Sundargarh. But as already mentioned (see Chap. 1), with the reorganisation of districts in Orissa in 1993 the number of districts has gone up to eleven in each region. The new districts have resulted from the division of the erstwhile districts. Except for the district of Sundargarh, the remaining districts in the coastal and the western region have been divided to give rise to the new districts. In the coastal region the erstwhile district of Balasore has been divided into two new districts of Balasore and Bhadrak; former Cuttack district has been divided into four districts of Cuttack, Jagatsinghpur, Jajpur and Kendrapara; the district of Ganjam has been divided into two districts of Ganjam and Gajapati and the district of Puri has been divided into three districts of Puri, Khurda and Nayagarh. Likewise, in the western region the district of Bolangir has been divided into two new districts of Bolangir and Sonepur; Kalahandi district has been divided to constitute two districts of Kalahandi and Nuapada; Phulbani has been divided into the districts of Kandhamal and Boudh and finally the Sambalpur district has been divided into four new districts of Sambalpur, Bargarh, Deogarh and Jharsuguda. But in the present study, as previously noted, the original framework of the erstwhile undivided district has been followed for the purposes of analysing the rise and growth of regionalism in Orissa state. These two regions of Orissa state differ in terms of geographical features, historical background, cultural practices, speech/dialectal variation, levels of socio-economic development and political-administrative power and control. Given these regional cleavages and disparities, the people of the relatively backward western region rose against the more developed coastal region. This chapter focuses on these regional cleavages and disparities which gave rise to regionalism in western Orissa.

1. Genesis of Regionalism

The articulation of regional consciousness in western Orissa originated since the times of merger of princely Orissa.[1] As already noted, on the eve of merger, the rulers of Patna, Kalahandi and Sonepur launched counter-mobilisation to resist merger and to form a separate political identity of their own.

It may be recalled that the Cabinet Mission observed with regard to Indian states that, 'all rights surrendered by the states to the paramount power would go back to them.'[2] Encouraged by this, R.N. Singh Deo, the ruler of Patna motivated other Oriya rulers to join the proposed Eastern states federation and thwart the merger plan.[3] In his letter to the then Viceroy of India, R.N. Singh Deo pointed out:

That the states federating the Eastern States Union are similar in size, resources, history, tradition and the administrative system with no danger of encroachment from or absorption or exploitation by any predominantly large unit in the group; ...on the other hand the dangers of grouping with Orissa province are: (a) danger of large unit like Orissa, encroaching upon the rights of smaller states unit; (b) dangers of political exploitation of states' people by the more politically conscious people of Orissa province; (c) danger of economic exploitation of the state by the province.[4]

Meanwhile, the then Orissa premier H.K. Mahtab made frantic political efforts to amalgamate the states on linguistic basis. Opposing Mahtab's move, the Patna ruler claimed that the linguistic basis of forming provincial units was not always feasible or justifiable. He argued that the linguistic principle was not observed in the formation of Hindi-speaking states in India. Taking cue from this, he rejected the question of common language as the basis for amalgamation of Orissa states.[5]

Meanwhile, the Kalahandi State Legislative Assembly in its first sitting on 12 August 1946 passed a resolution disapproving the idea of amalgamation of Orissa states.[6] The Patna ruler also pointed out that the natural division of Orissa into highlands (the area of the states) and coastal plains (the area of Orissa Province) favoured the formation of two distinct Oriya blocks. According to him, the coastal plains corresponding to the old Kalinga-Utkal Empire formed one compact Oriya block with different cultural tradition, historical experience and outlook. Similarly, the highlands covering the states formed another Oriya block with separate tradition, experience and dialectal affinity.[7] Hence, at the merger conference of 14 December 1947 the Patna ruler pressed for joining of Orissa states with Eastern States Union. The Government of India, however, strongly opted for merging Oriya-speaking states with Orissa. As a last resort then, the rulers of Patna, Kalahandi and Sonepur insisted on some form of local autonomy. They alleged that in the absence of local autonomy, power would be totally concentrated in the politically more advanced coastal people, i.e. the 'Katakias' and the Sambalpur states would be completely deprived.[8]

Map No. 1

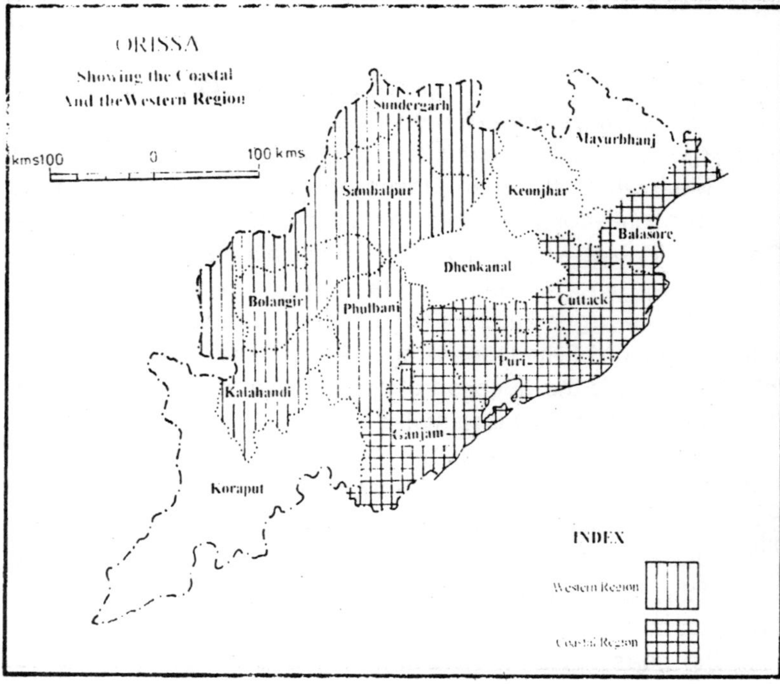

But as these demands were not entertained, these rulers of Sambalpur states spearheaded the Mahakoshal movement. It was claimed that Sambalpur district along with Sambalpur group of states constituted the erstwhile 'Koshal' or 'Hirakhand' kingdom of ancient and medieval times.[9] Further, the historical background and the socio-cultural affinities, in general, and the Sambalpuri speech, in particular, bound the people of the Sambalpur-Koshal tract together in a common bond and set them apart from the coastal tract of Orissa. Hence, the rulers maintained that a separate Koshal province should be formed for the Oriyas of Koshal-Sambalpur territory on the grounds of common culture and history.[10] Later, Angul and Khondmals were added to demand a Mahakoshal (i.e. greater Koshal) province.

It may be noted here that the idea of Koshal province at this stage was based on Oriya regional identity and not on separate linguistic identity. It also follows that the demand for Koshal was aimed at two things: (a) to block the process of merger; and (b) to establish the leadership of Sambalpuri people in Koshal region.

However, with the merger of Orissa states the hopes for Koshal province were buried. Immediately, anti-merger agitation broke out in some key Sambalpur states such as Patna, Kalahandi and Bonai. The agitators distributed leaflets favouring the Eastern States Union and condemning the act of merger. Pro-union and anti-Congress slogans were raised at the behest of the ruling chiefs. Even, newspapers like 'Patna Dipika' and 'Hirakhand Samachar' supported anti-merger move and stressed on regional particularism.[11] The Government of Orissa took precautionary measures to prevent any untoward happenings.[12]

It follows that the anti-merger resistance marked the beginning of regionalism in Orissa. The pro-merger lobby was identified with coastal region and the anti-merger move was identified with western region. The anti-merger groups opted for bifurcation of Orissa. They favoured the formation of two Oriya-speaking provincial units on the basis of regional geography, history, common culture and common perception.

Close on the heels of the anti-merger resistance came the agitation against the construction of the Hirakud dam. Again, the local chiefs and the land owning class of the western region played a pivotal role in this agitation. As a post-war plan the foundation stone of the multi-purpose Mahanadi river valley project was laid down by the then Governor of Orissa at Hirakud in Sambalpur district in March 1946.[13] The Hirakud dam project in Sambalpur created the largest man-made water reservoir in the world. But at the same time it led to the submerging of a vast tract of land inhabited by backward people of the western region. The project also involved large-scale displacement and evacuation of people. As many as 247 villages covering an area of 1.7 lakhs acres of land were submerged and nearly one lakh people were displaced.[14]

On the whole, the Hirakud dam project was viewed as a symbol of modernisation and industrialisation for the western region in particular and Orissa in general. But the people of western Orissa region perceived the construction of the dam as a part of a larger scheme intended to prevent the coastal Orissa districts from the misery of recurring floods.[15] To the poor villagers the project meant disaster and disappointment as they had to leave their ancestral lands. The prospects of rehabilitation and resettlement seemed to them a very poor compensation in lieu of what they lost. The affected people thus launched a strong agitation against the dam project. The discontented ruling chiefs, local land owning castes (the gountias), some disgruntled local Congressmen and retired government servants joined the agitation. They used the regional card to motivate and mobilise the people.[16] L.N. Mishra, a prominent Congress leader of Sambalpur, stated in the Orissa Legislative Assembly that:

The project for the dam was chalked out in darkness... In the teeth of opposition of the people, who are going to be landless and homeless, the project is going to be pursued... that a flourishing tract should be submerged on account of a dubious project whose merits are not discussed sufficiently well.[17]

Another Congressman, Bodhram Dubey, organised the people in their fight against the proposed dam. The state government reacted sharply and orders were issued to Bodhram Dubey to abstain from mobilisation activities.[18] The agitators maintained that construction of the dam was against the interest of the people of the region. They insisted that instead of displacing the people from the proposed dam site, the people in the flood affected areas of coastal region should be displaced.

A series of meetings were organised following the inauguration of the dam. The affected people carried out procession and offered resistance when notification for acquisition of land was served in September 1946. An anti-dam committee also passed resolution to oppose the construction and take steps to separate Sambalpur from Orissa.[19] The rulers of erstwhile Sambalpur group of states, who offered stiff resistance to merger of Orissa princely states with the Orissa province, seized this opportunity and goaded the local people to protect their regional interest. Two local newspapers, the 'Hirakhand Samachar' and 'Patna Dipika' carried extensive campaign for arousing regional sentiment. The Orissa government was dubbed as 'Kataki Sarakar' (government of the Cuttack region) and the Congress leaders were seen as 'Kataki' leaders (leaders of coastal Orissa).[20]

As regards the Mahanadi valley Hirakud dam project the government of Orissa was given the responsibility of payment of compensation, evacuation and rehabilitation. The policy of government in respect of compensation was to give land in exchange of land and that too well ahead of actual submergence. The compensation in kind or cash was supposed to be on equitable and generous terms.[21] But the people felt utterly disappointed regarding compensation and rehabilitation. The Hirakud dam displacement and rehabilitation problems thus provided a crucial ground for the origins of regionalism in Orissa.

Another significant factor for origins of regionalism was the emergence of the political party called Ganatantra Parishad. After the merger of princely states, the ex-rulers faced a new political equation. The integration of states reduced them to a status of commoners devoid of real political powers and privilege. The loss of power motivated them to launch a regional political party. A few Congress dissidents and disgruntled Prajamandal activists of the region joined hands with the rulers. Through their collective effort a new political party called the 'Koshalotkala Praja Parishad' was born in 1948 under the leadership of R.N. Singh Deo with headquarters at Bolangir.[22] In 1950, it was rechristened as the Ganatantra Parishad (GP). Within a short time, the Ganatantra Parishad spread throughout the ex-state areas. But its leadership largely fell in the hands of R.N. Singh Deo and P.K. Deo, the ex-rulers of Patna and Kalahandi respectively.[23]

The rise of Ganatantra Parishad accentuated regional animosity further. Following merger the people of ex-states suffered serious socio-economic hardships. In addition, the new bureaucratic administration in place of the personal rule of the native princes caused practical inconveniences to the affected people.[24] The Ganatantra Parishad articulated some of these grievances and it fought with the government for their redress. Right from the beginning, the Ganatantra Parishad adopted an anti-Congress posture. It filled the minds of the local people with the impression that Congress leadership was dominated by the coastal people, and that the Congress leadership was biased towards coastal Orissa.

As regards Hirakud dam, the Gantantra Parishad accused the state government of making half-hearted effort in payment of compensation.[25] The Ganatantra Parishad leaders criticised the land acquisition Act which empowered a single officer to exercise wide discretion in payment of compensation. They also reported about the massive bungling and irregularities in compensation payment.[26] On the whole the Ganatantra Parishad viewed the Hirakud dam construction as a ploy by the then Congress leadership of Orissa state to protect the interests of the people of the coastal region at the cost of the interests of the people of the western region. Going by this logic, the Ganatantra Parishad justified the anti-Hirakud dam agitation by the affected people of the western region.

Displacement of people at the time of Rourkela Steel Plant construction also contributed to the rise of regionalism in the western Orissa region. The construction of Rourkela Steel Plant in the Sundargarh district of western Orissa involved large-scale demolitions and displacement of several tribal and non-tribal villages. Being the main opposition party at that time, the Gnatantra Parishad staged hunger strike outside the Assembly to protect against the ill-treatment given to the people displaced by the Rourkela demolitions.[27] Also, the opposition put several adjournment motions to discuss the Rourkela problem, but those were disallowed. Finally, the Congress Ministry yielded to opposition demand and agreed to stop demolitions until an enquiry was held. The government also invited the opposition leader, R.N. Singh Deo, to attend the enquiry.[28]

Apart from the above, some other miscellaneous factors were also responsible for the rise of regionalism. For example, the rise in the price of rice caused acute economic hardship to western people. Further, people's perception and attitude did not change in the new administrative set up. Though merger of Orissa princely states put and end to feudal rule, yet the attitude of suspicion and contempt could not be eliminated. For example, in pre-merger period the princes mostly recruited officials from the coastal Orissa districts for settlement of land revenue as well as for administrative services. As the subordinate officials were very oppressive, the local people developed a deep-seated feeling of hatred and hostility towards the coastal Orissa people in general.[29] Every person hailing from coastal Orissa was dubbed with contempt as 'Katakia', although the term literally means a dweller of Cuttack district. The sudden transformation of the administrative machinery also created considerable stress and strain among the local people of the western region. The administrators, who were sent by the provincial government, descended in the western region like conquerors and each one of them seemed to feel that he was a little 'Maharaja'.[30] Thus, in the perception of the people of the western Orissa region, the administrators from coastal area appeared as exploiters and oppressors and the provincial government as perpetrators of exploitation and oppression.[31]

2. Factors Accounting for the Growth of Regionalism

It is clear from the above analysis that anti-merger resistance, Hirakud agitation, emergence of Ganatantra Parishad, Rourkela agitation and above all the attitudinal conflicts have contributed to the origins of regionalism in Orissa. In this section some of the core factors which accounted for the growth of this regional tension have been discussed.

(A) Major Regional Cleavages

Post-merger Orissa reveals striking regional cleavages. The two principal regions, i.e., western Orissa and the coastal Orissa exhibit natural differences in terms of history, culture and linguistic/ dialectal affiliation.

(i) Historical cleavages

Historically, coastal Orissa is associated with the Utkal-Kalinga empires and western Orissa is identified with the Koshal kingdom. The historical record which these empires/kingdoms left behind and the nostalgic sentiment they create in recent times contributed to the growth of sharp regional divide between these two conspicuous regions of Orissa state.

The political history of western Orissa underwent many changes since time immemorial. In ancient time western Orissa was known as Koshal which was a distinct part of 'Dakishin Koshal'. Reference to the location and antiquity of Koshal country has been found in various writings and inscriptions. For example, the Valmiki Ramayana mentioned about two countries, namely, 'Uttar' (north) and 'Dakshin' (south) Koshal. Mention of south Koshal is also found in the Allahabad inscriptions of Samudragupta.[32]

Mazumdar noted that, 'Sambalpur with its feudatory states formed in ancient times a part of Dakshin Koshal and the hilly country lying between Kalinga and Dakshin Koshal was the Odraland, while Utkal as a separate country lies to the north of Odra'.[33] During the reigns of Emperor Kharvela, Koshal formed a part of his empire which extended over the whole Oriya land. After Kharvela, Koshal country was ruled by the Somavanshi Guptas till 11th century. The inscriptions of the Somavanshi kings show that Sambalpur tract was included in the Koshal Desh in 9th century and was not considered then in any way connected with either Kalinga or Odra or Utkal Desh.[34]

In 7th century the Somavanshis shifted their capital from Sonepur (now in western Orissa) to Puri. After the Somavanshis, the Koshal land disintegrated into smaller states. The imperial Ganga dynasty of Kalinga extended their suzerainty over these states for quite some time. The reunion of Koshal states occurred during the Chauhan rule. The Kokshal kingdom of the Chauhan dynasty (1355 AD-1821 AD) comprised a group of 18 smaller states popularly known as the 'Atharagarh' (Eighteen Forts) confederacy.[35] These states were first held in subordination to the most powerful Chauhan ruler, the Maharaja of Patna, who afterwards yielded supremacy to the Maharaja of Sambalpur.[36] Under the imperial Gajapati kings of Orissa these Chauhan rulers of Koshal states enjoyed semi-independent status. After the fall of the last Gajapati king Mukund Dev in 1568, these states became fully independent.[37]

The core of Koshal, i.e., Patna state once consisted of eight forts known as Athmalik. Ramai Deo, the exemplary Chauhan ruler united these eight forts and founded the powerful Patna state. In 16th century Sambalpur emerged as the most powerful among Koshal states. The ruler of Sambalpur belonged to Patna-Chauhan family. The Koshal unity under Patna-Sambalpur supremacy was broken when the 'Atharagarh' Koshal confederacy fell into the British hands in 1818 following the third Anglo-Maratha war.[38] Thus through the vicissitudes of times the Koshal tract was disintegrated and reunited several times over.

In comparison to western Orissa, the history of coastal Orissa is well recognised. The glories of Utkal-Kalinga empires of the ancient and medieval times are fairly well-known. The kingdom of Kalinga existed as a famous independent state even during the powerful Nanda and Maurya dynasties of the Magadh Empire. Under the legendary Oriya Emperor Mahameghavahan Kharvela, Kalinga emerged into a prominent empire and extended far and wide (see Chapter 4).

After Kharavela, dynasties like Sailodbhavas, Bhaumakaras, Somovanshis, Gangas and Gajapatis ruled the Kalinga Empire. The famous Ganga ruler Chodaganga Dev united Kalinga, Utkal and Koshal to form one Oriya country. The graet Gajapati King Kapilendra Dev held sway over the Kalinga, Utkal and Koshal kingdoms for a pretty long time.[39] The famous Orissan Empire of the Gajapatis disintegrated in the16th century.

The historical cleavages between the two regions became more pronounced during the Mughal, Maratha and finally the British rule over Orissa. Under the Mughals the Koshal states of western Orissa remained in the 'Garhjat' division; while the coastal parts of Orissa comprised the 'Mughalbandi' division. The Marathas treated the eighteen Koshal states as tributaries and placed them in the Chhatisgarh province of the Bhonsla of Nagpur.

The political map of Koshal went through many changes during the British rule. The British first took possession of the Koshal confederacy in 1804, but returned it to the Marathas as a conciliatory gesture. But following the third Maratha war in 1818 all the Koshal states including Sambalpur came under British paramount power.[40] As mentioned earlier, the British took over coastal Orissa in 1803 and placed it under their direct administration. The Orissa princely states including the Koshal-Sambalpur group were ruled separately in the 'Garhjat' division under the British paramount power.

The British broke Koshal confederacy and treated these smaller states as separate entities. These smaller states were first placed in the newly created Southwest Frontier Agency, and then they were placed under the Chhotanagpur division. In 1849 Sambalpur was annexed and it was ruled as a British administered district. The district of Sambalpur along with other smaller Koshal states was placed in the Central Provinces in 1862.[41] In 1905, Sambalpur district and seven Koshal states were transferred to Orissa division of Bengal Presidency. Finally in 1936 Sambalpur became a part of Orissa province and the Koshal states were merged with Orissa province in 1948.

The above appraisal shows that both coastal and western Orissa have long historical traditions and on account of their placement under different regimes and administrative units the two regions acquired distinct historical personality.

(ii) Cultural cleavages

The culture of western Orissa differs significantly from that of the coastal Orissa districts. Popularly, western Orissa culture is known as the 'Sambalpuri' culture; while the culture of coastal Orissa is dubbed as 'Oriya' or 'Kataki' culture.

For one thing, the cultural diversity in Orissa resulted to a large extent from her vivisection especially under the Mughals, the Marathas and the British regimes. The geographical proximity of western Orissa to the Chhatisgarh region and the placement of Sambalpur area under Central Provinces in British time produced indelible effect on western Orissa culture. Another distinguishing factor which caused cultural diversity in Orissa is the presence of a sizeable tribal population. Out of the 62 tribes living in Orissa, quite a large number is found in western Orissa. Indigenous tribes like Gond, Khond, Kol, Oraon, Ho, Munda, Kissan, Binjhal, Bhuiyan, Bariha, Bhumij, etc. constitute important segments of western

Orissa population. Their cultural practices heavily influenced the speech pattern, food habits, belief, custom, tradition, dance, drama, song, music, fairs and festivals of western Orissa. In contrast the coastal districts of Balasore, Cuttack, Puri and Ganjam have a sparse tribal population which is less than 6% of the population of the state.[42]

In fact, the western Orissa or 'Sambalpuri' culture has grown out of the fusion of Aryan elements with tribal cultural practices, which occurred in the periods of state formation under different dynasties, especially the Chauhan dynasty.[43] Basically this culture contains folk elements which are drawn from both tribal and caste-Hindu cultural matrices.[44] The twin process of sanskritisation and tribalisation mainly contributed to the evolution of this culture.

Many folk songs like entertainment songs, play songs, ritual songs, work songs and customary songs, are noticed in the western region. Entertainment songs like 'Rasarkeli', 'Sajani', 'Jaiphula', 'Nialimalli' and 'Dalkhai' are quite famous in the region.[45] These songs render a typical ambience to the western Orissa 'Sambalpuri' culture. The folk musical instruments like 'Muhuri', 'Dhol', 'Nishan' and 'Ghumura' accompany these folk songs and dances. Conversely, the 'Odissi' dance, a famous classical dance of Orissa, originated from the coastal Orissa region. The 'Odissi' dance songs, the devotional songs like 'Janana' and the traditional songs like the 'Chhanda' and 'Chautisa' are associated with the coastal Orissa people to a great extent.

As far as festivals are concerned, some typical festivals like 'Nuakhai', 'Puspuni', 'Karamasani', 'Puajitia' and 'Bhaijitia' are exclusively observed in western Orissa and with which the coastal people are not at all acquainted. In western Orissa the 'Nuakhai' is observed as a harvest festival when the new grains of the paddy crop are cooked and offered to the deities. In coastal Orissa region this festival is observed as 'Navarna', but it is observed with different religious fervour and is confined to individual families. The 'Puspuni' festival in western Orissa symbolises the day of termination of old contracts and beginning of fresh contracts with share croppers. 'Bhaijitia' is a festival that women observe for the prosperity of their brothers.

The two famous regional festivals, 'Nuakhai' and 'Puspuni', are observed in western Orissa on a mass scale to assert 'Sambalpuri' cultural identity. Recently, some cultural associations and temple committees have endorsed the idea of celebrating the 'Nuakhai' festival as a common regional festival throughout western Orissa. Another famous regional festival depicting the wedding ceremony of Lord Shiva with Goddess Parvati is the 'Sitalsasthi' festival of western Orissa.[46]

The typical festivals of coastal Orissa like 'Raja', 'Prathama Astami', 'Kumar Purnima', 'Boita Bandana', 'Khudarkuni Osha', etc. are not observed by the people of western region of Orissa. 'Raja', a typical Oriya festival, is associated with worshipping the mother earth before tilling the soil for cultivation. 'Boita Bandana' is celebrated in remembrance of the maritime glory of ancient Kalinga Empire. Even the world famous Car Festival (Rath Yatra) of Lord Jagannath, which is celebrated mainly in Puri town and allover coastal Orissa, is observed in a very limited scale in the western Orissa region. In fact, a majority of festivals of the coastal Orissa are associated with Lord Jagannath, e.g. Rath yatra, Chandan yatra, Snana yatra, Jhulan yatra, Nava kalebar, etc.[47]

Yet another difference between the two regions exists in the form of worship. While 'sakti' worship (worship of feminine power) and 'tantra' tradition predominate in western region, the coastal people are more acquainted with different forms of Jagannath worship. That is, Vaishnavism and Saivism dominate the religious life in coastal Orissa. Among the temples of 'sakti' worship, the temple of Samaleswhari (a regional manifestation of Hindu Goddess Durga) occupies a central place in the hearts of the people of western region. Other manifestations of 'sakti' like Patneswari, Manikeswari and Sureswari are worshiped in different parts of western Orissa.[48]

It may also be noted that some caste groups and surnames commonly found in western Orissa are alien to the coastal Orissa districts. For example, castes like Gauntias, Agarias and surnames like Bohidar, Supakar, Pujari, etc. are not found in the coastal belt. Among the Brahmins in Orissa, the 'Jhadua' (Aranyaka) Brahmins are found mostly in the western region.

Apart from the above, both regions have some cultural specialties. For example, coastal Orissa is famous for its filigree, appliqué works and 'Khadi' prints. Similarly, western Orissa is widely known for its unique 'Sambalpuri saree', tie and dye weaving and floral motifs.[49]

But to the common perception of the coastal Orissa people the western Orissa Sambalpuri culture basically contains folk elements and therefore it is not a standard culture.

(iii) Linguistic cleavages

Although, Oriya language served as the basis of formation of Orissa state, yet the form of Oriya spoken in western Orissa differs from the standard Oriya spoken by the coastal Orissa people. The people of western Orissa speak 'Sambalpuri' as their mother-tongue. 'Sambalpuri' speech is usually regarded as a regional or colloquial variation of Oriya language. Nevertheless, Sambalpuri-Oriya speech is distinct in its own right, and it is easily distinguishable from coastal Oriya speech.[50]

The difference is noticed at the lexical and phonological levels. There are a number of 'Sambalpuri' words which are not intelligible to the coastal Oriya people. Interestingly, an average coastal Orissa person cannot speak 'Sambalpuri' speech; and an uneducated person from western Orissa cannot speak or understand the standard coastal Oriya speech.

Besides, 'Sambalpuri' speech was heavily influenced by Chhatisgarhi form of Hindi and a host of tribal dialects spoken in western Orissa. Notably, tribal dialects like Bhatri, Kissan and Kui affected 'Sambalpuri' speech to a great extent.[51]

Scholars on Oriya language generally treat 'Sambalpuri' speech as a dialect of Oriya language. They argue that 'Sambalpuri' speech has no autonomous structure and is akin to Oriya structurally. Some Oriya scholars even reject a distinct language status for 'Sambalpuri' speech because it does not have a script of its own.[52]

The linguistic cleavage is reflected in the perception of the common people in both the regions. The Oriya language spoken by the coastal Orissa people is referred to as 'Kataki speech' by the western Orissa people. On the other hand, average coastal Orissa people regard the 'Sambalpuri' speech as an 'adivasi' (tribal) language, and even some consider it as a dialect of Oriya language. Be it as it may, 'Sambalpuri' speech provides a sense of solidarity to the people of western Orissa and defines a line of separation from the coastal Oriyas.

(B) Regional Socio-Economic Disparities

As is well-known, disparities in the levels of regional socio-economic development have historically played a significant role in accentuating regional aspiration. More often than not, regional developmental disparities act as the critical factors in the growth of regionalism. Socio-economic underdevelopment of a particular region motivates people to rise against the people of the socio-economically advanced region. Compared to the coastal districts, the western districts of Orissa experienced long spell of feudal rule. Except Sambalpur, the remaining four districts of western Orissa, viz., Bolangir, Kalahandi, Phulbani and Sundargarh formerly constituted the territories of princely states of Orissa and were not under direct British administration. On the other hand, the four coastal districts of Balasore, Cuttack, Puri and Ganjam constituted British administered territories. This historical accident turned the tide in favour of coastal region.

The onset of developmental measures unleashed by the British in the coastal districts brought significant improvement in irrigation, communication and education. Conversely, the long spell of feudal rule left western Orissa agriculturally impoverished, economically backward and educationally poor. This uneven pace of development surfaced in the form of regional imbalance soon after the merger of states. In the post-independent period though the situation improved, yet the level of socio-economic development in western Orissa remains comparatively low vis-à-vis coastal Orissa. In this section the extent of regional socio-economic disparities existing between coastal and western regions of Orissa has been analysed to find out the socio-economic factors giving rise to regionalism in western Orissa.

The analysis is based on data obtained from secondary sources such as census reports, economic surveys, statistical abstracts, etc., over three decades, i.e. 1971-2001, a period which has witnessed significant development as a result of the planned development beginning from the early 1950s. It may be noted that in the early decades of independence developmental disparities in socio-economic terms existed between the two regions. But the people of western Orissa began to respond to these regional disparities around the late 1970s and early 1980s, that is, the time when articulation of regionalism began to appear in western Orissa region. Precisely, therefore, the data from 1971 to 2001 have been analysed to explain the regional socio-economic disparities. While the two regions are compared to find out regional disparities based on selected socio-economic indicators, care has also been taken to examine the intra-regional differences within the region concerned by a reference to district level data.

It may be noted here that for the purpose of analysing the regional socio-economic disparities for the period from 1971 to 2001 the original framework of the undivided district of Orissa state has been selected. The data on regional socio-economic disparities from 1971 to 1991 have been presented for the erstwhile undivided districts; but the socio-economic data based on 2001 census for the new Orissa districts formed after 1993 have been combined for the analysis of regional disparities for the erstwhile undivided districts of the two concerned regions. For example, to show the 2001 census data for the undivided district of Balasore, the 2001 census data of the new districts of Balasore and Bhadrak have been combined. It may be recalled that these two new districts have been created from the erstwhile district of Balasore. Similarly, the 2001 census data for the new districts of Cuttack, Jagatsinghpur, Jajpur and Kendrapara have been combined for the undivided district of Cuttack; the data for the new districts of Ganjam and Gajapati have been combined for the undivided district of Ganjam and for undivided Puri district the 2001 census data of Puri, Khurda and Nayagarh have been combined. Likewise, in the western region except for the district of Sundargarh (which has not been divided), the 2001 census data have been combined for the remaining districts in the following manner: for undivided Bolangir district the data of the new districts of Bolangir and Sonepur have been combined; for erstwhile Kalahandi district the data of the new districts of Kalahandi and Nuapada have been combined; for the former Pulabani district the data of the new districts of Boudh and Kandhamal have been combined and finally for the undivided district of Sambalpur the data of the new districts of Sambalpur, Bargarh, Deogarh and Jharsuguda have been combined.

In order to examine the socio-economic disparities in these two regions of Orissa as many as seven factors have been considered. They are: (a) demographic and geographic disparities; (b) agricultural development; (c) employment and occupational situation; (d) infrastructural amenities; (e) education; (f) healthcare; and (g) urbanisation. The disparities both at the district and regional level have been analysed.

While looking for the possible disparities in the above mentioned factors, and their improvement/deterioration over the years between coastal and western regions, one is supposed to know whether there has been a conscious effort by the authorities (government) to discriminate against any region or not. This can be explained by the per capita public expenditure on different sectors of social and economic development allocated to the respective district/regions. As the classified expenditures are not available in the government documents at the district level, the idea of using major input indicators for the analysis has been dropped. Instead, we have selected a set of socio-economic indicators which may indirectly show government allocation of resources to different regions. One may infer from these indicators the amount of input coming in from the government for socio-economic development of a particular district or region. Thus most of them could be considered roughly as input indicators such as number of persons dependent on a school/hospital or a post-office/bank.

(i) Geographical and demographic disparities

Geographically Orissa is divided into four distinct physical regions: (i) the Coastal Plains, (ii) the Central Table-Land, (iii) the Eastern Ghats and (iv) the Northern Plateau.

Table-VI.1

Geographical Area and Population of Coastal and Western Orissa

District/Region	*Total Geographical Area in sq. km.*	*% to Total Geographical Area of State*	*Total Population*			
			1971	*1981*	*1991*	*2001*
1. Balasore	6311	4.05	1830504	2242808	2796321	3358257
2. Cuttack	11142	7.15	3827678	4628800	5508307	6325069
3. Ganjam	12531	8.04	2293808	2669899	3143120	3679472
4. Puri	10182	6.53	2340859	2921045	3570192	4244593
Coastal Region	40166	25.79	10292849	12472552	15017940	17607391
5. Bolangir	8913	5.72	1263657	1459113	1703755	1879029
6. Kalahandi	11772	7.56	1163839	1339192	1591984	1866184
7. Phulbani	10119	6.49	621675	717280	858553	1021573
8. Sambalpur	17506	11.24	1844894	2280976	2688395	3065773
9. Sundargarh	9712	6.23	1030758	1337871	1568442	1830673
Western Region	·58022	37.26	5924827	7134432	8411127	9663232
All Orissa	155707	100	21944615	26370271	31659736	36804660

Source: Statistical Abstract of Orissa, 1981, 1991 and 2005, Govt. of Orissa, Directorate of Economics and Statistics, Bhubaneswar.

Table-VI.2

Demographic Disparities between Coastal and Western Orissa Districts

District/ Region	1971		1981		1991		2001	
	% to Total Population of State	Density of Population per sq. km.	% to Total Population of State	Density of Population per sq. km	% to Total Population of State	Density of Population per sq.km.	% to Total Population of State	Density of Population per sq. km.
1. Balasore	8.34	290	8.54	356	8.83	443	9.12	532
2. Cuttack	17.44	343	17.55	415	17.39	494	17.18	570
3. Ganjam	10.45	183	10.12	213	9.92	251	9.99	253
4. Puri	10.66	229	11.07	286	11.27	350	11.53	440
Coastal Region	46.90	256	47.29	310	47.43	373	47.82	448
5. Bolangir	5.75	141	5.53	163	4.95	191	5.10	217
6. Kalahandi	5.30	98	5.07	113	5.02	135	5.07	153
7. Phulbani	2.83	61	2.72	70	2.71	84	2.77	101
8. Sambalpur	8.40	105	8.64	130	8.49	153	8.32	177
9. Sundargarh	4.69	106	5.07	137	4.95	161	4.87	188
Western Region	26.99	102	27.05	123	26.56	144	26.53	167
All Orissa	100	140	100	169	100	203	100	236

Source: Census of India 1971: (Orissa: series-16), Census of India 1981: (Orissa: series-16), Census of India 1991: (Orissa: series-19) and Census of India 2001: (Orissa: series-22), Census Directorate, Bhubaneswar, Orissa.

The coastal plains stretch over the districts of Balasore, Cuttack, Puri and a part of Ganjam. This region has been highly fertile and prosperous and is well suited for intensive cultivation. The central table-land covers a number of erosion plains and river basins. The districts of Sambalpur, Bolangir and Kalahandi come under this region. This area is partly hilly and thickly forested. The districts of Phulbani, Koraput and a part of Ganjam fall in the eastern ghat region. The northern plateau covers the districts of Sundargarh, Keonjhar, Mayurbhanj and Dhenkanal. The western region is abundant in oilseeds, tobacco, salt, teak and kendu leaves, etc., whereas rice and jute are mainly grown in the coastal belt.

Differences existing in the geographic environment and demographic features are important factors which directly or indirectly induce socio-economic disparities between regions.

As evident from Tables-VI.1 and VI.2 the western region has a larger geographical area, but supports much less population compared to coastal region. Moreover, the density of population in the coastal region is much higher than the western region and the state as whole. This shows that the pressure of population is much larger in the coastal belt compared to the western region. This situation is but natural considering the agricultural potential and development in these two broad regions. While the coastal region (CR) is agriculturally much developed due to its deltaic plains, the hilly and highland terrain in the western region (WR) hinder full-scale agricultural development in the absence of modern agricultural technology and farming methods. Nevertheless, the pressure of population in these two regions is vastly different as evident from the indicator of population density (see Table-VI.2).

The intra-regional disparity in density is much less in the coastal region as compared to the western region. This indicates uniformly high population pressure in the former, whereas in the latter the pressure of population seems to be localised. The relative difference in population density, both inter-regional and intra-regional, is maintained over time.

An analysis of growth rate (Table-VI.3) of population suggests less disparity between the two regions during the period 1971-81.

But the difference increases in the subsequent decades. On an average the coastal region is experiencing higher population growth than the western region, while the inter-district differences remain marginal.

Table-VI.3
Decadal Growth Rate of Population

District/Region	*1971-81*	*1981-91*	*1991-01*
1. Balasore	+23.07	+24.13	+20.09
2. Cuttack	+20.93	+18.89	+14.82
3. Ganjam	+24.29	+22.22	+17.06
4. Puri	+16.40	+17.72	+18.88
Coastal Region	+21.29	+20.74	+17.24
5. Bolangir	+15.47	+16.77	+10.28
6. Kalahandi	+15.47	+16.77	+17.22
7. Phulbani	+15.38	+19.70	+18.98
8. Sambalpur	+23.64	+17.86	+14.03
9. Sundargarh	+29.79	+17.23	+16.34
Western Region	+19.95	+17.68	+14.88
All Orissa	+20.17	+19.50	+16.25

Source: Computed from Census of India 1981, 1991 and 2001 (Orissa series).

Thus in terms of demographic size the coastal region holds a predominant position, which has serious implications in the context of political power and domination. The western region on the other hand on account of its smaller size in terms of population feels dominated and neglected. This may have created 'minority psyche' among the people of the western region, within the all-Orissa context.

A characteristic feature of Orissa state is the large concentration of the Scheduled Castes (SCs) and the Scheduled Tribes (STs) in its population. As per 2001 census the SCs and STs constitute 38.66 per cent of the total population of Orissa, of which 22.13 per cent are STs and 16.53 per cent are SCs. The tribal population of Orissa is nearly 10.4 per cent of the total tribal population of India.

Table-VI.4

Percentage of Scheduled Caste (SC) and Scheduled Tribe (ST) Population

District/ Region	*1971*		*1981*		*1991*		*2001*	
	% of SC Popu	*% of ST Popu*	*% of SC Popu*	*% of ST Popu*	*% of SC Popu*	*% of ST Popu*	*% of SC Popu*	*% of ST Popu*
1. Balasore	18.51	7.06	17.95	6.85	20.20	6.93	19.89	7.55
2. Cuttack	18.06	2.99	17.67	3.13	20.40	3.30	20.71	3.24
3. Ganjam	15.92	9.91	15.03	9.48	16.67	9.44	17.00	9.63
4. Puri	13.53	3.70	12.93	3.46	15.53	3.56	15.30	3.53
Coastal Region	16.50	5.91	15.98	5.73	18.20	5.80	18.47	5.48
5. Bolangir	16.49	19.72	15.65	19.22	17.30	18.59	18.74	17.48
6. Kalahandi	17.11	29.26	16.76	30.28	15.94	31.11	16.94	31.68
7. Phulbani	18.98	40.31	18.56	38.94	18.85	37.55	18.71	37.52
8. Sambalpur	15.61	28.13	15.35	27.21	17.47	27.53	17.91	27.24
9. Sundargarh	8.02	53.40	8.53	51.26	8.80	50.90	8.62	50.19
Western Region	15.24	34.16	14.97	33.38	15.67	33.13	16.13	32.34
All Orissa	15.09	23.11	14.66	22.43	16.20	22.21	16.53	22.13

Source: Computed from Census of India 1971, 1981, 1991 and 2001 (Orissa series)

The SC population is more or less uniform in both regions (see Table-VI.4). However, the difference in the ST population account for crucial reasons for regional imbalance. Moreover, tribalism may add to the regional consciousness of a particular region. In western region there is a greater concentration of STs and the inter-district variation is low. This indicates a nearly uniform distribution of ST population in the western region; and this is true of all the census years mentioned in the table. As per the 2001 census the district of Sundargarh in the western region has the largest concentration of STs, i.e. 50.19 per cent followed by Phulbani, Kalahandi and Sambalpur with 37.52 per cent, 31.68 per cent and 27.24 per cent respectively.

Since the Scheduled Castes and the Scheduled Tribes together constitute the bulk of the backward sections of the people, their distribution in these two regions reveals a significant dimension of regional poverty and disparities in Orissa. It is evident from the Table-VI.4 that the western region as a whole contains much larger (nearly 50%) deprived segments consisting of SCs and STs. Such a proportion is uniformly low in the coastal region. The district of Cuttack has the lowest percentage of STs, i.e, 3.24 per cent, followed by Puri district with 3.53 per cent of ST population. Even the share of SC and ST population as per 2001 census is much smaller in the coastal region (i.e. 23.95%) than the western region (i.e. 48.47%) and the all-Orissa (i.e. 38.66%) averages.

(ii) Agricultural development

In the area of agricultural development one of the key indicators is the percentage of work force engaged in agricultural activities (see Table-VI.5). The disparities in the proportion of workforce absorbed by the agricultural sector are hardly noticeable between the two regions at least in the early period of independence, i.e. up to 1971. But by 2001 the disparities are conspicuous.

The average percentage of agricultural workers in these two regions is almost similar, i.e. 76 per cent in the coastal region and 77 per cent in the western region in 1971. By 1981 the figures are 72 per cent and 75 per cent respectively; whereas in 1991

Table-VI.5
Percentage of Agricultural Workers (Cultivators+Agricultural Labourers) to total Main Workers

District/Region	*1971*	*1981*	*1991*	*2001*
1. Balasore	84.52	79.20	75.72	67.35
2. Cuttack	74.36	68.35	64.18	55.34
3. Ganjam	73.54	74.59	74.36	70.59
4. Puri	72.16	67.56	60.66	50.94
Coastal Region	76.14	72.42	68.59	61.05
5. Bolangir	82.89	81.67	80.60	74.17
6. Kalahandi	85.66	86.09	84.85	80.16
7. Phulbani	84.10	82.54	83.28	73.74
8. Sambalpur	75.57	72.95	72.10	63.17
9. Sundargarh	59.95	55.95	57.09	59.38
Western Region	77.63	75.84	75.59	70.18
All Orissa	77.44	74.65	73.06	64.77

Source: Computed from Census of India 1971, 1981, 1991 and 2001 (Orissa series).

agricultural workers account for over 68 per cent in the coastal region and about 76 per cent in the western region and in 2001 the coastal region has 61 per cent and the western region has little over 70 per cent of such workers. The changes over time in the proportion of such workers sufficiently indicate growing disparities in the economic development of the two regions as declining proportion of agricultural workers in the coastal region definitely indicates structural transformation in the economy by way of redistribution of the work force into the non-agricultural sectors (i.e., into the secondary and tertiary sectors) of the economy, whereas such a transformation is conspicuous by its absence in the western region.

The intra-regional variation in the western region is also significant as a single district, viz., Sundargarh has the lowest proportion of agricultural workers among all the districts of both the regions. If one excludes this district, the dependence on agriculture in the remaining district of western region is much higher, i.e. nearly 80 per cent.

This understanding is further sharpened when one examines the disparities in agricultural development in terms of agricultural/ cropping intensity (i.e. how many times a land is used for cultivation). The agricultural intensity shows wide disparities and more so such disparities are increasing over time and space. While the intensity index for the coastal region and western region was 128 per cent and 120 per cent respectively in 1971, they are 162 per cent and 134 per cent respectively in 1991 and 164 and 145 respectively in 2001 (see Table-VI.6). Since intensive cultivation depends upon a variety of factors like irrigation, climate, topography, agricultural technology and diversification in cropping pattern, a low level of agricultural intensity in the western region indicates an overall low agricultural development. It also affects agricultural productivity. The intra-regional variations are also substantial in the western region, whereas it is comparatively low in the coastal region (Table-VI.6).

Table-VI.6
Agricultural Intensity (% of Net Sown Area to Gross Cropped Area)

District/Region	*1971*	*1981*	*1991*	*2001*
1. Balasore	114	135	139	144
2. Cuttack	142	176	170	184
3. Ganjam	102	170	176	166
4. Puri	141	172	160	164
Coastal Region	128	165	162	164
5. Bolangir	120	132	137	142
6. Kalahandi	125	150	135	160
7. Phulbani	115	145	144	157
8. Sambalpur	120	130	130	139
9. Sundargarh	110	124	129	128
Western Region	120	136	134	145
All Orissa	120	142	144	152

Source: Computed from Statistical Abstract of Orissa, 1981, 1991 and 2005, Govt. of Orissa, Directorate of Economics and Statistics, Bhubaneswar

In the case of irrigation too the western region, except for the Sambalpur district, lags far behind the coastal region. While the Gross Irrigated Area in 2001 is 47 per cent in the coastal region, the share of the western region is merely 24 per cent for the same year. The intra-regional difference shows much better and uniform development in irrigation in all the districts of coastal region in sharp contrast to the situation in western region (see Table-VI.7).

Table-VI.7
Percentage of Gross Irrigated Area to Gross Cropped Area

District/Region	*1971*	*1981*	*1991*	*2003*
1. Balasore	38	28	37	38
2. Cuttack	38	29	42	55
3. Ganjam	63	31	33	40
4. Puri	52	38	54	55
Coastal Region	44	30	41	47
5. Bolangir	24	18	30	23
6. Kalahandi	8	6	12	27
7. Phulbani	7	10	18	20
8. Sambalpur	36	28	39	33
9. Sundargarh	10	8	20	17
Western Region	32	16	25	24
All Orissa	36	49	32	33

Source: Computed from Census of India, 1971, 1981, 1991 and Statistical Abstract of Orissa, 2005

So far as fertiliser use is concerned (see Table-VI.8) the inter-regional difference is not very substantial, whereas intra-regional difference, in the western region particularly, is quite significant. For example, in the western region the district of Sambalpur uses fertiliser more than two times of the regional average; but the districts of Phulbani, Kalahandi and Sundargarh use fertiliser ranging from one-fifth to almost half of the extent of fertiliser use in the region as a whole during the period from 1971 to 2001. Of course, in 2001 Balasore district in the coastal region registered the highest consumption of fertiliser, i.e., 86.58 kilograms per hectare, while Kalahandi showed marked improvement in fertiliser use, i.e., 36.47 kilograms per hectare for the same year. This intra-regional difference in fertiliser use in the western region, therefore, indicates a general lack of agricultural development in the region as a whole excepting some areas, and this shows widespread disparities in contrast to the coastal region where the intra-regional difference is minimum.

Table-VI.8
Fertiliser Use in k.g. Per Hectare

District/Region	*1971*	*1981*	*1991*	*2001*
1. Balasore	13.21	8.78	26.64	86.58
2. Cuttack	15.10	13.26	21.85	43.31
3. Ganjam	11.44	10.52	37.21	43.41
4. Puri	25.66	13.35	34.63	41.30
Coastal Region	15.67	11.88	30.01	53.65
5. Bolangir	12.42	9.10	16.11	30.23
6. Kalahandi	2.50	5.43	15.42	36.47
7. Phulbani	4.97	2.73	5.47	12.13
8. Sambalpur	21.08	21.93	54.18	78.97
9. Sundargarh	5.90	6.26	17.34	24.00
Western Region	11.09	10.72	21.62	36.36
All Orissa	11.10	8.73	21.71	41.00

Source: Govt. of Orissa, Statistical Abstract of Orissa, 1981, 1991 and 2005, Directorate of Economics and Statistics, Bhubaneswar.

(iii) Employment and occupation

Regional disparities in the sphere of employment and occupation may be understood with reference to a few indicators such as the workers' participation rate, male participation rate and workers in registered factories.

If one examines the general work participation (Table-Vi.9) rate, it is clear that the coastal region as a whole absorbs much less proportion of the workforce in gainful activity compared to the western region. This is true of the entire period of investigation

Table-VI.9
Percentage of Main Workers to total Population

District/Region	*1971*	*1981*	*1991*	*2001*
1. Balasore	26.98	27.58	26.79	23.34
2. Cuttack	27.49	27.61	26.48	23.39
3. Ganjam	32.54	34.83	36.64	27.17
4. Puri	29.07	29.15	28.83	24.74
Coastal Region	29.02	29.76	29.68	24.66
5. Bolangir	33.59	35.08	35.19	26.87
6. Kalahandi	32.73	36.02	37.61	27.52
7. Phulbani	35.29	39.45	38.69	27.59
8. Sambalpur	35.53	36.53	36.84	28.32
9. Sundargarh	31.45	32.48	32.42	26.23
Western Region	33.71	35.91	36.15	27.31
All Orissa	31.92	32.82	32.70	26.05

Source: Computed from Statistical Abstract of Orissa, 1981, 1991 and 2005

from 1971 to 2001. A relatively higher work participation in the western region does not necessarily show a healthy economy in the region because in the evolution of the economy a lower proportion of the population should be engaged in work. In this context, it may be thus interpreted that smaller proportion of workers in the coastal region is indicative of a better state of economy as lesser proportion of workforce is in a position to support larger dependency.

On the other hand, a relatively higher participation rate in the western region may indicate that more people have to work in order to support themselves economically. The situation remains by and large same when the percentage of male main workers is considered for both the regions (see Table-VI.10).

In the case of workers engaged in registered factories, regional disparities seem to be more intra-regional rather than inter-regional in nature. It is evident from the Table-VI.11 that a slightly higher proportion of such workers in the western region compared to the coastal region is largely due to a very high percentage of such workers only in one district of western region, i.e. Sundargarh, while the rest of the western region districts have very few such workers. On the other hand the coastal region has less of disparities across the districts, though the case of Puri district is an exception to the generally low industrial growth in the region as a whole. This may be attributed to the presence of the industrial belt in and around Bhubaneswar, the capital city of the state of Orissa.

Table-VI.10
Male Main Workforce Participation Rate

District/Region	*1971 (%)*	*1981 (%)*	*1991 (%)*	*2001(%)*
1. Balasore	51	50	52	42
2. Cuttack	51	50	52	45
3. Ganjam	48	51	53	41
4. Puri	58	53	54	44
Coastal Region	52	51	52	43
5. Bolangir	60	58	61	45
6. Kalahandi	60	60	63	46
7. Phulbani	59	59	62	44
8. Sambalpur	61	57	63	45
9. Sundargarh	55	53	61	42
Western Region	59	57	62	45
All Orissa	55	54	57	43

Source: Computed from Census of India 1971, 1981, 1991 and 2001 (Orissa series)

The case of industrial development in Orissa is highly uneven. Not only that, industrial development in Orissa also shows an island character. This appears to be true of the western region where a single district i.e. Sundargarh containing the Rourkela Steel Plant and some ancillary factories account for the entire industrial population. Viewed in this context, it may be concluded that the entire western region is industrially much more backward than the coastal region which is at least agriculturally more advanced.

Table-VI.11
Percentage of Workers in Registered Factories to Main Workers

District/Region	*1971*	*1981*	*1991*	*2001*
1. Balasore	0.23	0.38	0.61	1.20
2. Cuttack	1.17	1.29	1.40	1.01
3. Ganjam	0.30	0.33	0.35	0.27
4. Puri	2.90	2.43	5.30	4.62
Coastal Region	1.03	1.22	1.91	1.77
5 Bolangir	0.16	0.20	0.50	0.46
6 Kalahandi	0.10	0.14	0.17	0.35
7 Phulbani	0.02	0.03	0.04	0.05
8 Sambalpur	1.38	1.80	1.70	1.71
9 Sundargarh	4.90	6.62	7.66	8.25
Western Region	1.31	1.75	2.01	2.16
All Orissa	0.89	0.99	1.77	1.75

Source: Census of India 1971, 1981, 1991 and 2001 (Orissa series).

(iv) Education

One of the most important considerations with regard to regional disparities pertains to the sphere of social development and provision of social amenities particularly in the sectors of education and health. These issues acquire more significance in a developing country like India because the state through successive governments has taken a greater responsibility in providing these two basic amenities considered to be essential for social transformation and development.

As far as the literacy rate, one of the key indicators of social development, is concerned, it is clearly evident from the Table-VI.12 that the western region lags far behind its counterpart in the coastal districts. The disparities are extremely remarkable both across as well as within the regions. For example, though Sambalpur and Sundargarh districts in the western region register a higher literacy rate of around 66 per cent and 65 per cent respectively in 2001, which is little higher than the state average, the proportion falls far below the state average in 1991. However, this was not so in the earlier decade, i.e., 1971-81. The remaining three districts in the western region show an extremely low level of literacy in all the years compared to the state average till 1991, but the situation in these districts has drastically improved in 2001 although the figures still remain lower than the state average. The coastal region on the other hand, except for the district of Ganjam, records a much better response to literacy in all the years. The district of Puri with 76.02 per cent of literates records the highest percentage of literacy in the region as well as the state followed by Cuttack with 75.99 per cent and Balasore with 72.21 per cent in 2001.

Table-VI.12
Literacy Rate: Percentage of Literate Population to the Total Population

District/Region	*1971*	*1981*	*1991*	*2001*
1. Balasore	33.71	42.07	48.70	72.21
2. Cuttack	36.42	45.42	53.36	75.99
3. Ganjam	24.40	31.31	36.61	51.10
4. Puri	35.34	45.50	54.34	76.02
Coastal Region	32.45	41.07	48.25	68.83
5. Bolangir	19.90	25.63	33.08	59.27
6. Kalahandi	13.80	19.42	25.31	43.97
7. Phulbani	19.70	27.02	31.73	55.20
8. Sambalpur	27.10	33.83	41.52	65.56
9. Sundargarh	26.40	36.16	44.42	64.86
Western Region	18.60	28.16	30.15	57.77
All Orissa	23.18	34.23	49.10	63.08

Source: Computed from the Statistical Abstract of Orissa, 1981, 1991 and 2005.

The responses to literacy and the consequent literacy rate may be due to a number of factors ranging from personal choice to social, cultural and economic values. It may be stressed here, as many studies reveal, that provision of adequate educational infrastructure plays a vital role in influencing the literacy rate. Since this provision of providing the infrastructure is largely in the hands of state government, disparities in this sphere would at least indicate some kind of discrimination and lack of proper planning.

Table-VI.13

Educational Institutions per One Lakh Population

District/ Region	*1971*			*1981*			*1991*			*2001*		
	Primary	*Seco-ndary*	*Graduate & above*	*Primary*	*Seco-ndary*	*Graduate & above*	*Primary*	*Seco-ndary*	*Graduate & above*	*Primary*	*Seco-ndary*	*Graduate & above*
Balasore	125	11.4	0.43	104	11.8	0.39	97	16.0	1.25	91	23.7	2.11
Cuttack	123	11.4	0.47	104	12.0	0.45	100	14.3	1.57	99	22.5	2.38
Ganjam	117	6.0	0.47	118	5.8	0.41	106	7.3	1.04	105	15.0	1.63
Puri	106	8.4	0.55	121	7.8	0.47	124	11.3	1.45	83	16.3	1.83
Coastal Region	118	9.3	0.48	112	9.4	0.43	107	12.2	1.35	96	19.3	2.04
Bolangir	136	6.1	0.47	158	5.6	0.41	144	6.9	0.64	144	18.7	2.23
Kalahandi	127	3.6	0.08	140	4.7	0.07	129	5.7	0.50	130	19.1	1.71
Phulbani	201	4.3	0.16	222	4.8	0.13	206	5.7	0.69	206	13.9	1.46
Sambalpur	124	6.1	0.59	114	6.2	0.56	109	8.4	0.92	113	17.7	1.76
Sundargarh	134	6.5	0.58	112	8.2	0.44	111	8.6	1.08	112	16.9	1.74
Western Region	144	5.3	0.37	145	5.9	0.32	139	7.06	0.76	141	17.6	1.81
All Orissa	130	6.80	0.37	131	7.4	0.34	122	9.50	0.95	115	18.5	1.89

Source: Computed from the Census of India, 1971, 1981, 1991 and 2001 (Orissa Series)

Ironically, provision of educational institutions at the primary level is much better in the western region than in the coastal region. This is of course not true in the area of the secondary and graduate levels of educational institutions. Expectedly, the coastal region is better served by educational institutions above secondary and college levels. The Table-VI.13 reveals that the difference in the level of secondary and college level educational institutions between the two regions are significant in 1991 as compared to the figures of the previous decades represented by 1981 and 1971 as well as the successive period represented by 2001. The western region has made considerable progress in the area of secondary and college level educational institutions by the year 2001.

It is also clear from the above Table-VI.13 that, at least in terms of infrastructure at the primary level, the western region is not at disadvantage though this has not translated itself into a better response to literacy. This contradiction can be attributed to the history of education as well as the existing socio-cultural and economic realities. The coastal region has had a long history of education due to British influence, whereas in the tribal and backward castes dominated western region the spread of education/literacy was thwarted by the vested interests of the erstwhile feudal chiefs.

In the matter of university education, out of the five universities of the state, four are located in coastal region and only one is situated at Sambalpur in western region. Besides, the Engineering Colleges at Burla and Rourkela and the Engineering Schools at Jharsuguda and Rourkela in the western region are considered as colonies of the people of the coastal region.

(v) Health care

In the area of health care provisions, i.e., medical infrastructural facilities, there exist some disparities between the two regions during the period from 1971 to 1981, especially in the case of some districts of the western region (see Table-VI.14). For example, up to 1981 the districts of Bolangir, Kalahandi and Phulbani were relatively poorly served by hospitals/dispensaries such as district hospital, medical college hospital, primary health centers, community health centers, mobile medical units and dispensaries. The inter-district variation during this period is marginal in this sector.

But after 1991 the situation has improved drastically for all the districts in both the regions. Even the districts of the western region were better served by medical institutions per one lakh population in 1991 and 2003 than the districts of the coastal region. While the districts of Kalahandi, Phulbani and Sambalpur record 4.55, 7.04 and 4.56 medical institutions respectively per one lakh population in 2003, the districts of Cuttack, Ganjam and Puri record 3.96, 4.10 and 4.61 medical institutions respectively for the same year, despite the fact that two big medical institutions of the state—one at Cuttack city and the other at Berhampur town—are located in the coastal region.

Table-VI.14
Hospitals/Health Centers/Dispensaries per one Lakh Population

District/Region	*1971*	*1981*	*1991*	*2003*
1. Balasore	2.40	2.04	4.32	4.34
2. Cuttack	2.42	1.77	4.06	3.96
3. Ganjam	2.39	2.35	4.16	4.10
4. Puri	2.94	2.43	4.59	4.61
Coastal Region	2.53	2.14	4.28	4.25
5. Bolangir	1.58	1.64	4.16	4.52
6. Kalahandi	1.37	1.71	5.15	4.55
7. Phulbani	1.93	1.95	7.68	7.04
8. Sambalpur	2.76	2.63	4.64	4.56
9. Sundargarh	2.71	2.84	4.71	4.47
Western Region	2.07	2.15	5.26	5.02
All Orissa	2.33	2.34	4.75	4.62

Source: Computed from the Statistical Abstract of Orissa 1981, 1991 and 2005

As far as number of doctors per one lakh population is concerned, the disparities between the two regions reveal different pictures at different points of time. The Table-VI.15 clearly shows that there existed wide gap in the availability of doctors in the two regions up to 1991. While about 5 doctors were available per one lakh of population in the coastal region in 1991, the ratio is as low as 3 doctors in the western region in the same year. But in 2001, while the coastal region was served by nearly 13 doctors per lakh population, the western region was served by almost 15 doctors per lakh population. This shows that the situation in the western region has improved in 2001. One reason of this high doctor-population ratio in the western region may be due to the low level of population in the western region than its coastal counterpart. Interestingly, there is very little intra-regional variation in either the coastal or the western region, meaning thereby the doctor-population ratio in both the regions is more or less the same.

Table-VI.15
Number of Doctors per one Lakh Population

District/Region	*1971*	*1981*	*1991*	*2001*
1. Balasore	3.74	4.09	5.57	8.36
2. Cuttack	6.28	6.49	6.91	14.24
3. Ganjam	4.02	4.43	4.62	16.03
4. Puri	3.42	3.85	4.85	12.32
Coastal Region	4.36	4.71	5.48	12.73
5. Bolangir	2.21	2.46	3.84	11.97
6. Kalahandi	1.37	1.56	2.07	12.11
7. Phulbani	2.23	2.26	3.27	18.11
8. Sambalpur	2.74	2.78	3.28	19.57
9. Sundargarh	2.03	2.09	3.57	12.02
Western Region	2.11	2.23	3.20	14.75
All Orissa	2.78	3.19	4.02	13.37

Source: Statistical Abstract of Orissa, 1981, 1991 and 2005; Govt. of Orissa, Health and Family Welfare Dept., Bhubaneswar.

An examination of the availability of hospital beds reveals more or less a similar picture as that of availability of doctors (see Table-VI.16). While up to 1991 the availability of hospital-beds per one lakh population was little better in the coastal region than the western region, in 2003 the western region records a slightly better

Table-VI.16
Number of Hospital Beds per One Lakh Population

District/Region	*1971*	*1981*	*1991*	*2003*
1. Balasore	31	25	26	23
2. Cuttack	69	52	57	41
3. Ganjam	57	58	62	48
4. Puri	48	49	50	43
Coastal Region	51	46	47	39
5. Bolangir	20	23	27	32
6. Kalahandi	20	21	23	35
7. Phulbani	34	32	34	47
8. Sambalpur	66	64	72	53
9. Sundargarh	42	48	50	34
Western Region	36	37	41	41
All Orissa	43	44	46	38

Source: Computed from Statistical Abstract of Orissa, 1981, 1991 and 2005

hospital-bed-population ratio, i.e., 41 as against 39 in the coastal region. However, unlike the doctor-population ratio there is a great deal of intra-regional variation in the index of hospital beds per lakh population, especially in the western region. Importantly, Sambalpur where a medical college/hospital is located has a very high hospital bed-population ratio, while the districts of Bolangir, Kalahandi and Sundargarh in the western region have such a ratio lower than the regional and all-Orissa average. Likewise, in the coastal region, Balasore is more comparable to the districts of western region in the availability of hospital beds. On the whole, in 2001-03 the regional average of the western region in the areas of availability of different kinds of health care facilities, number of doctors and number of hospital beds per one lakh population remains better than the average of the coastal region. This clearly shows that the state government has taken effective measures to improve the situation of health care facilities in the western region which in turn has contributed positively in correcting the regional imbalance.

(vi) Infrastructure

Another area in which the state government plays an exclusive role as far as financial allocations are concerned pertains to development of infrastructure which is essential for rapid pace of development and transformation. It is well known that road connectivity constitutes one of the most important indicators of infrastructure development. The levels of road connectivity in the coastal and the western region of Orissa show significant disparities. Due to geographical and historical reasons the coastal districts are better accessible as indicated by a higher road density per 100 sq. km. of area compared to the western region and the all-Orissa average (see Table-VI.17). In terms road density the district of Puri in the coastal region records the highest in 2001, i.e., 236.19 km. of road length per 100sq. km. of area, followed by Cuttack district with 164.62 km. and Ganjam district with 137.25 km. Whereas, in the western region except for the district of Phulbani the rest of the districts show better road density than the districts of Balasore and Ganjam in the coastal region. In 2001 the highest road density in the western region is shown by the district of Sambalpur with154.67 km per 100 sq. km of area, followed by the district of Kalahandi with 152.75 km and Bolangir with 144.31 km. per 100 sq km. of area. Nevertheless, the western region as whole accounts for lower degree of road connectivity, i. e., an average of 139.05 km. per 100 sq. km. of area compared to the coastal region average of 164.80 km per 100 sq. km. The indicator of road density here includes different types of roads such as national highways, express highways, state highways, district roads, panchayat samiti roads, gram panchayat roads, rural roads and the forest roads. That there have been little efforts to correct this regional imbalance in the last three decades is evident from the persistence of this imbalance between 1971 and 2001, although some districts of the western region have made quite significant progress in the period from 1991 to 2001.

It is interesting to note that the road density varies very little across the districts in both coastal and western regions. It is clear, then, that the development of road connectivity is uniformly lacking in the western region and there is little spatial variation within the

Table-VI.17
Road Length (in km.) per 100 square kilometers of Area

District/Region	*1971*	*1981*	*1991*	*2001*
1. Balasore	55.94	99.14	102.83	121.14
2. Cuttack	85.05	132.12	156.43	164.62
3. Ganjam	45.62	72.08	134.61	137.25
4. Puri	74.10	102.02	229.38	236.19
Coastal Region	65.17	100.68	159.69	164.80
5. Bolangir	33.38	66.84	132.93	144.31
6. Kalahandi	21.00	68.05	149.34	152.75
7. Phulbani	24.31	57.49	126.34	116.40
8. Sambalpur	42.66	74.05	144.94	154.67
9. Sundargarh	38.39	73.98	125.41	127.15
Western Region	31.94	68.82	137.28	139.05
All Orissa	43.40	76.32	133.12	136.56

Source: Computed from the Census of India 1971, 1981, 1991 and 2001 (Orissa series).

region. Like road, railway route connectivity constitutes another important dimension of infrastructure development. In the case of rail connectivity the disparities between the two regions are not substantial, although the coastal region is slightly better placed in terms of railway route length than the western region. The railway route length per 100 sq. km. of area in the coastal region in 2001 was 1.86 km. compared to the western region average of 1.58 km. and the state average of 1.47 km. per 100 sq. km. of area. In the coastal region there is no significant intra-regional variation, whereas in the western region the intra-regional variation is strikingly noticed. As per 2001 census the district of Phulbani in the western region has absolutely no railway route, while the remaining districts such as Bolangir, Kalahandi, Sambalpur and Sundargarh have 2.13 km., 0.59 km., 1.74 km. and 3.48 km. respectively of railway routes per 100 sq. km. of area.

The relatively better position of the district of Sundargarh in railway route length is due to the presence of Rourkela Steel Plant in that district. In the case of the coastal region the district of Cuttack occupies the first place with 2.54 km of railway route length per

100 sq. km. of area followed by the district of Balasore with 2.27 km., the district of Puri with 1.57 km. and the district of Ganjam with 1.08 km of railway routes as per 2001 census reports. As regards bank-population ratio even the districts of the coastal region are better served than the districts of the western region. In 2001 while there are nearly 8 branches of scheduled commercial banks per one lakh population in the coastal region, the western region is served by 6 such branches per one lakh population, which slightly less than the state average of 7 bank branches per lakh population. In the case of bank branches the intra-regional variation across the districts is not much in both the regions. In the coastal region the number of bank branches in the districts of Balasore and Puri is the highest, i.e., 8.25 branches in each, while the districts of Cuttack and Ganjam have 6.26 and 5.92 branches, respectively as per 2001 census. In the western region the district of Sambalpur has 6.72 bank branches per one lakh population followed by Sundargarh with 6.50, Kalahandi with 5.79, Phulbani with 5.68 and Bolangir with 5.06 number of bank branches as per the 2001 census.

Table-VI.18

Percentage of Villages Electrified to Total Number of Villages

District/Region	*1971*	*1981*	*1991*	*2003*
1. Balasore	3.83	51.31	68.30	88.55
2. Cuttack	6.68	64.35	76.02	95.65
3. Ganjam	8.04	43.62	55.60	68.60
4. Puri	7.51	58.92	70.21	88.53
Coastal Region	6.93	54.55	67.52	85.33
5. Bolangir	4.28	42.68	67.56	91.35
6. Kalahandi	0.44	18.66	46.16	72.25
7. Phulbani	0.55	14.05	33.13	54.95
8. Sambalpur	2.05	46.72	63.55	79.30
9. Sundargarh	1.92	54.41	56.12	89.80
Western Region	1.84	35.30	53.30	76.33
All Orissa	4.17	36.33	55.75	77.00

Source: Computed from Statistical Abstract of Orissa, 1981, 1991 and 2005

As far as rural electrification is concerned, the gap between the two regions was considerable in 1971 (see Table-VI.18). However, there is discernible trend in the reduction of this gap in the last two decades. Nevertheless, the western region as a whole remains less electrified compared to the coastal region districts. Up to 1991 the situation regarding rural electrification remains precarious in Kalahandi and Phulbani districts of western Orissa; while the remaining districts have on average more electrified villages than the all Orissa average. However, in 2003 rural electrification in the districts of the western region improved significantly with Bolangir having 91.35 per cent of villages electrified followed by Sundargarh having 89.80 per cent, Sambalpur with 79.30 and Kalahandi having 72.25 per cent villages electrified. The district of Phulbani in the western region showed the lowest parentage of villages electrified, i.e., 54.95 per cent. But as a matter of fact the rural electrification in the coastal region has always been higher than the state average.

Table-VI.19
Post-Offices per One Lakh Population

District/Region	*1971*	*1981*	*1991*	*2003*
1. Balasore	38.41	33.43	28.77	24.65
2. Cuttack	21.22	20.41	20.38	18.68
3. Ganjam	22.73	27.67	25.83	22.44
4. Puri	26.48	21.92	26.91	18.94
Coastal Region	27.17	25.89	25.48	21.70
5. Bolangir	23.62	22.24	19.23	20.38
6. Kalahandi	2[illegible].14	25.91	23.33	22.39
7. Phulbani	15.41	18.53	21.34	25.17
8. Sambalpur	23.91	22.84	21.56	19.40
9. Sundargarh	21.75	24.19	24.82	22.34
Western Region	20.91	22.57	22.07	21.58
All Orissa	24.04	25.15	24.54	22.21

Source: Computed from Statistical Abstract of Orissa, 1981, 1991 and 2005.

With regard to the availability of post offices per one lakh population, the gap between the two regions is not too wide to merit serious attention. The intra-regional variation too is not so significant. Notwithstanding this, better situation prevails in the coastal region (see Table-VI.19).

(vii) Urbanisation

In the case of urbanisation, which is often viewed as an indicator of development, the western region indeed seems to be more developed than the coastal region of Orissa (see Table-VI.20).

A closer examination, however, reveals that urbanisation is localised in a few pockets in the western region, especially in Sundargarh and Sambalpur districts. The pattern of urbanisation in the western region is such that its spatial impacts are of enclave character. Only one or two towns, particularly Rourkela and Sambalpur, account for much of the urban population while the remaining areas in the western region are vastly rural. A higher urban proportion in the western region is therefore highly misleading as intra-district variation is significant (see Table-VI.20). In coastal region, however, the spread of urbanisation is spatially more uniform. The level of urbanisation in the western region is only quantitative and thus reflects the underdevelopment of the region. But in 2001 the two regions held more or less same position as regards rate of urbanisation, while during this period the western region showed 16.34 per cent of urban population the average of the coastal region remained at 16.52 per cent which is little higher than the state average of 14.99 per cent.

Summing up the preceding analysis the following broad generalisations can be made:

(a) The geographical and historical differences between the two regions have been sustained till the recent times if the select indicators of geographic, demographic and socio-economic variables/features are taken into consideration. It appears that contrary to the stated objective of planned development the regional imbalances and disparities have only widened barring a few notable exceptions, particularly the provision of primary school, health care facilities and post-offices.

(b) Another significant observation that can be made on the basis of the foregoing data pertains to the intra-regional variation,

Table-VI.20
Rate of Urbanisation

District/ Region	*1971*		*1981*		*1991*		*2001*	
	Urban Popul	*% of Urban Popul.*	*Urban Popul*	*% of Urban Popul.*	*Urban Popul*	*% of Urban Popul.*	*Urban Popul*	*% of Urban Popul*
1. Balasore	100151	5.47	185963	8.25	263993	9.44	361439	10.76
2. Cuttack	305625	7.98	475995	10.28	678619	12.31	892696	14.11
3. Ganjam	259856	11.33	380389	14.25	470522	14.96	609247	16.55
4. Puri	229147	9.79	432079	14.79	706004	19.77	1046800	24.66
Coastal Region	894777	8.69	1474426	11.82	2119138	14.50	2910182	16.52
5. Bolangir	86665	6.86	133225	9.14	164250	9.64	194391	10.34
6. Kalahandi	56553	4.86	80541	6.01	103928	6.52	130257	6.97
7. Phulbani	19568	3.15	37761	5.26	51120	5.95	62119	6.08
8. Sambalpur	221771	12.02	353433	15.49	462608	17.20	563300	18.37
9. Sundargarh	239683	29.20	419333	30.60	525005	33.41	629194	34.36
Western Region	624238	10.53	1023993	14.35	1306911	15.53	1579261	16.34
All Orissa	1845395	8.41	3110287	11.79	4234983	13.37	5517238	14.99

Source: Census of India 1971, 1981, 1991 and 2001 (Orissa series).

particularly in the western region. It has been observed that in one or two districts of western region a slightly better socio-economic development is reported, while the remaining areas lag far behind. This is true of literacy, urbanisation, road density, irrigation, fertiliser use, workers in registered factories, etc.

It may be noted that rural Orissa is the epitome of India's poverty where nearly 56 per cent of the population live below the poverty line, a majority of whom belong to SCs and STs. The districts of Kalahandi, Phulbani and Bolangir in western Orissa contain a huge tribal and backward caste people who are poverty-ridden.

(c) It may also be concluded that the process of development in terms of its regional manifestation is highly spatially fragmented in the western region, while its manifestation is relatively more uniform in the coastal districts. This shows that the state efforts have induced more or less uneven development within the western region.

These conclusions have far-reaching implications for the growth of regionalism. For one thing, the objective conditions of socio-economic disparities created the subjective conditions which widened the antagonism between the two regions and paved the way for regional consciousness to grow among the people of western Orissa.

(C) Political Cleavages and Politics of Regionalism

Another critical factor which promoted regionalism in Orissa is the political cleavage. Politics in Orissa assumed new dimensions after merger of the princely states with Orissa province. The active participation of the ex-princes in Orissa politics, which led to formation of the regional political party called Ganatantra Parishad (GP), was a significant development in creating political cleavage and regional antagonism.[53]

Merger brought an end to princely rule, but the traditional loyalty of the people was not eroded. Rather, it re-surfaced in their electoral behaviour. The Congress, which tried to extend its support base in the ex-state areas, could not succeed in the western Orissa region due to the growing popularity of the regional political party the Ganatantra Parishad. The people of western Orissa region favoured Ganatantra Parishad as they were averse to Congress leadership because of its traditional linkage with coastal Orissa region ever since the days of the noted Oriya Congress leader Gopabandhu Das and his most popular nationalist organisation the 'satyabadi' school.

The affiliation of the Ganatantra Parishad with the historically, culturally and linguistically compact region of western Orissa and the natural identification of Orissa Congress leadership with the coastal region contributed to polarisation of politics along regional lines in the state of Orissa for a pretty long time.

In pre-independent times, the Orissa province experienced two elections – first in 1937 and the next in 1946. On both occasions, the Congress party secured majority in the 60-member Orissa Legislative Assembly[54] The people of Orissa princely states did not participate in these elections as they remained out of British Orissa. Following merger of Orissa princely states, the strength of the Legislative Assembly increased to 91 and subsequently it was raised to 140 at the time of the first general election in 1952. The Ganatantra Parishad, which emerged in western Orissa as a strong regional party since 1950, posed formidable opposition to Congress since the first general election till 1971.[55]

The people of the coastal region, which was formerly in British Orissa, were much more advanced in terms of political consciousness and participation compared to the people of western region, which formerly comprised seven Orissa princely states and the British administered district of Sambalpur. Further, the growth of urban-educated middle class and rise of Congress movement in coastal Orissa led to the growth of many distinguished political leaders in that region. Obviously, therefore, after the merger of Orissa princely states, the political leadership in the united province of Orissa was largely concentrated in the hands of the politically advanced coastal people. As a regional political party, the Ganatantra Parishad challenged this political domination of coastal Orissa and with a bid to share power competed with the Congress in several Assembly elections in Orissa state.

Several studies have reported about the Congress-Ganatantra Parishad tussle for political power. For example, K.V. Rao examined the competition between Ganatantra Parishad and the Congress to capture political power in Orissa between 1952 and 1961.[56] S.C. Das remarked that the Ganatantra Parishad has challenged the one-party dominance of Congress and regionalised the state politics in Orissa in three Assembly elections.[57] Mohanty and Mishra observed that Congress factionalism and personality-oriented regional politics of Ganatantra Parishad dominated electoral politics in Orissa from 1952 to 1974.[58]

In the first general election of 1952, the Ganatantra Parishad registered a tremendous success. In a house of 140, the Ganatantra Parishad secured 31 as against 67 of the Congress. With the help of the independents, the Congress formed the Government under the leadership of N.K. Chaudhary. Being the second largest party the Ganatantra Parishad assumed the role of the opposition. The victory of the Ganatantra Parishad mainly remained confined to its stronghold, i.e., western Orissa region. The anti-Hirakud agitation and the charismatic influence of R.N. Singh Deo and P.K. Deo, the ex-rulers of Patna and Kalahandi respectively, contributed to the political success of the Ganatantra Parishad. Its performance was very impressive in districts of western Orissa. Out of total 38 seats it secured 20, winning all the 9 seats from Bolangir, 5 from Sambalpur and 4 from Kalahandi (see Table-VI.21). The Congress secured 41 seats from its stronghold, the coastal districts.

In the second general election in 1957 the strong regional bias of the people of western Orissa was reflected more clearly. The Ganatantra Parishad improved its tally and bagged 51 seats. The Congress was able to secure only 56 seats. The Congress secured 42 out of the 66 seats from the coastal region of Orissa. In the five districts of the western region the Ganatantra Parishad secured 31 out of 38 seats, while the Congress drew blank in Bolangir, Phulbani and Sundargarh (see Table-VI.21). The minority government led by the Chief Minister H.K. Mahtab could not survive and finally the first Congress-Ganatantra Parishad coalition government was formed in May 1959.[59]

Table-VI.21

Region-wise Breakup of Seats won by Congress and Ganatantra Parishad (GP) in 1952 and 1957

District/ Region	*1952 General Election*			*1957 General Election*		
	Total Seats	*Congress*	*GP*	*Total Seats*	*Congress*	*GP*
1. Balasore	12	11	--	11	8	--
2. Cuttack	26	18	1	24	15	1
3. Ganjam	15	4	--	16	11	--
4. Puri	15	8	--	15	8	1
Coastal Region	68	41	1	66	42	2
5. Bolangir	9	--	9	9	--	9
6. Kalahandi	7	3	4	8	2	6
7. Phulbani	4	1	--	4	--	4
8. Sambalpur	13	6	5	12	2	9
9. Sundargarh	5	3	2	5	--	3
Western Region	38	13	20	38	4	31
Orissa	140	67	31	140	56	51

Source: State Election in India: Data Handbook on Vidhan Sabha Elections (1952-1985), Vol.3, East and North East.

In the mid-term poll of 1961 the Congress secured an absolute majority by winning 82 seats. The strength of GP however declined considerably, it secured only 37 seats which were 14 less than its strength in the previous Assembly.[60] Obviously, the Congress formed the government with Biju Patnaik as the Chief Minister. But Patnaik resigned in 1963 on account of corruption charges and subsequently Biren Mitra and thereafter Sadasiv Tripathy headed the government between 1963 and 1967.

The trends of the first three elections to Orissa Assembly suggest that the state was divided into well-defined spheres of regional influence with the coastal region voting for the Congress and the western region voting overwhelmingly for the Parishad. Because of this regional bipolar trend, the Congress and GP came to be identified with coastal and western Orissa respectively.

Prior to the fourth general election in India in 1967, two important changes occurred in Orissa politics. First, the Ganatantra Parishad merged with the Swatantra Party led by Rajgopalchari following the 1962 general elections.[61] Second, the dissident Congress leader H.K. Mahatab formed a regional political party called the Jana Congress (JC) in Orissa in 1966.

The Jana Congress made an electoral alliance with the Swatantra party (formerly Ganatantra Parishad) in Orissa and got the tacit support of the Praja Socialist Party (PSP) to fight the common enemy, the Congress.[62] The alliance secured as many as 75 seats with Swatantra party winning 49, Jan Congress 26 and PSP 21 in the 1967 Assembly election. The Congress won a meagre 31 seats. The Jana Congress won maximum seats from the coastal districts and thereby established its regional spread. The Swatantra maintained its traditional support base in western Orissa wining 29 out of the 39 seats from these districts (see Table-VI.22). The Swatantra-Jana Congress coalition government came to power with R.N. Singh Deo as the Chief Minister and P.M. Pradhan as the Deputy Chief Minister.[63]

The fourth Orissa Legislative Assembly elections were memorable in several respects. First, it provided the first non-Congress government in Orissa; second, it gave the first Chief Minister (R.N. Singh Deo) from western region of Orissa; third, it

Table-VI.22

Breakup of Seats won by Congress, Swatantra, Jana Congress and Utkal Congress in 1967 and 1971

District/Region	1967 General Election				1971 Mid-term Poll			
	Total Seats	Cong-ress	Swata-ntra	Jana Cong-ress	Total Seats	Cong-ress	Swata-ntra	Utkal Cong-ress
1. Balasore	11	1	1	4	11	4	--	4
2. Cuttack	24	2	--	8	24	8	2	11
3. Ganjam	15	9	1	--	15	7	2	4
4. Puri	15	5	1	5	15	7	1	3
Coastal Region	65	17	3	17	65	26	5	22
5. Bolangir	9	--	9	--	9	--	9	--
6. Kalahandi	8	2	6	--	8	--	7	--
7. Phulbani	4	--	3	1	4	1	3	--
8. Sambalpur	12	4	6	1	12	10	2	--
9. Sundargah	6	--	5	--	6	2	2	--
Western Region	39	7	29	1	39	13	23	--
All Orissa	140	31	49	26	140	47	36	33

Source: Same as Table-VI.21.

saw the first coalition between two regional parties having strong regional affiliation—Swatantra party identified with the western region and the Jana Congress with the coastal region of Orissa.

The mid-term polls for the fifth Orissa Assembly were held in 1971. In the meantime, following the Congress split at the all-India level in 1969, in Orissa Biju Patnaik formed a regional political party called the Utkal Congress (UC) in 1970 to protest against the authoritarian leadership of the then Congress President Indira Gandhi.[64] In the election the three major parties, viz. Congress (R), Swatantra and Utkal Congress secured 51, 36 and 33 seats respectively. Out of its total 36 seats, the Swatantra bagged 23 from the districts of the western region, while the Utkal Congress drew maximum support from the coastal region districts (see Table-VI.22).

After the elections, a Swatantra-Utkal Congress coalition government assumed power in Orissa under the leadership of the veteran Oriya leader Biswanath Das. But the Das Ministry collapsed soon following the decision of the Utkal Congress to join the Congress party. Thereafter, Nandini Satapathy headed the Congress Ministry from June 1972 till February 1974 when the mid-term elections for the Sixth Orissa Assembly were held. The same year the strength of the Orissa Legislative Assembly was raised from 140 to 147 seats. A significant aspect of this election was the formation of Pragati Party comprising three constituents, viz., Swatantra, Utkal Congress and Praja Socialist Party (PSP).[65] In terms of seats the Congress won 71, while the Swatantra, the Utkal Congress and the PSP secured 20, 35 and 2 respectively. The strength of the Swatantra party declined, but it captured 16 seats from western Orissa.[66]

From the electoral results in Orissa up to 1974, it is evident that the influence of the main political parties was regionalised. From 1952 to 1974, the Congress as well as its splinter groups, namely, the Jana Congress and Utkal Congress secured maximum seats from the four coastal districts of Cuttack, Balasore, Puri and Ganjam. By and large the people of the western Orissa region perceived the Congress and its breakaway groups, the Jana Congress and Utkal Congress, as coastal region parties. Hence, they always preferred the erstwhile Ganatantra Parishad (and later the Swatantra party) to the political parties supposedly associated with the people of the coastal region. These developments clearly show the politicisation of regional conflict and the articulation of regional identity through party politics in the state of Orissa. The three coalition governments formed in 1959, 1967 and 1971 respectively are quite significant in the context of the development of this regional divide in Orissa.

In 1977 the Janata Party[67] came to power in Orissa following the countrywide anti-Congress and pro-Janata wave. With this significant political development the identification of a region with a particular political party in Orissa state politics came to an end. In the 1977 election to the Orissa Legislative Assembly the Janata Party won 56 and 26 seats from the coastal districts and the western region respectively out of its total tally of 110 seats. The Congress managed only 26 seats in this assembly election.

However, from 1980 to 1989 Orissa came under the grip of Congress rule with Chief Minister J.B. Patnaik heading the government for two consecutive terms. In both 1980 and 1985 election to the Orissa State Assembly the Congress won 117 seats, while the Janata Party secured only 13 and 19 seats respectively. The Congress obtained 48 and 38 from the coastal belt and western Orissa respectively in 1980 assembly election. While in 1985 assembly election it won 55 from the coastal districts and 30 from the western Orissa districts. The Congress rule of 10 years is said to have accentuated the regional tension in Orissa significantly. As both coastal and western regions came under the clutch of a single political party, new political equations emerged in Orissa. Political polarisation along regional lines, which was formidable in earlier years, gave way to single-party dominance during this period of 10 years. This has eventually resulted in the complete domination of the coastal region and the total isolation of the western region in Orissa power politics and decision-making. Congress favouritism towards coastal Orissa gave rise to regional forces within the party and with that regionalism in Orissa scaled new heights. The situation continued unabated under the successive governments headed by Biju Patnaik from 1990 to 1995 and again by J. B. Patnaik from 1995 to 1999. The Janata Dal government under the Chief Ministership of Biju Patnaik created more regional problems than it solved. During the tenure of Biju Patnaik government from 1990 to 1995 the number of districts in Orissa rose from 13 to 30. This move by the Biju Patnaik government was viewed by many political activists in western Orissa as a clever design to scuttle the politics of regionalism in western Orissa region. It was alleged that the division of the erstwhile districts would ultimately divide the people of western Orissa and undermine their solidarity to a great extent. But as a matter of fact the division of the erstwhile districts in no way undermined regional identity consciousness in the western Orissa region, it only broadened the list of the districts included in the concerned region.

It is clear from the foregoing analysis that regional disparities and cleavages affected party politics in Orissa to a great extent which in turn helped in the perpetuation of regional identity and the articulation of regionalism in the western Orissa region. The greatest share in the articulation of regional aspiration and sentiment goes to the regional political party in western Orissa, the Ganatantra Parishad. By and large, the Ganatantra Parishad strictly followed a regional ideology for meeting its ends. Whether in opposition or in government, the Ganatantra Parishad during its existence always fought for greater attention to western Orissa in particular and the ex-state areas of Orissa in general. Even after the merger of Ganatantra Parishad with the Swatnatra party the regional issues figured prominently in its agenda. Both inside and outside the state Assembly, the Ganatantra Parishad pleaded for proper rehabilitation and adequate compensation for the people displaced by the construction of the Hirakud Dam and the Rourkela Steel Plant in western Orissa. It continuously alleged that proper and timely compensation was not paid to the displaced people.[68] It also demanded for the appointment of an enquiry committee to probe into the gross irregularities in connection with evacuation from the dam area.[69] In the case of Rourkela Steel Plant, the Ganatantra Parishad demanded for reservation of class III and IV jobs for the displaced people.[70]

The kendu-leaf issue also played a major role in stoking regionalism in western region of Orissa. The kendu-leaf trade dominated Orissa politics till 1974 when it was nationalised by the government. The kendu-leaf traders in Orissa usually acted as an active pressure-group and influenced the state electoral politics. More often than not, the opposition used the kendu-leaf issue to corner the party in power. It was on this issue the Swatantra-Jana Congress coalition government and the Swatantra-Utkal Congress coalition ministry in Orissa fell in 1971 and in 1972, respectively.[71]

Kendu leaf, a type of leaf used for bidi-making, is found in plenty in western Orissa, particularly in Sambalpur and Bolangir districts. Before merger of princely states of Orissa, long-term contracts were given for collection of kendu leaves. In 1961 the government of Orissa introduced monopoly over kendu-leaf trade. Due to favourable treatment of the government some traders from the coastal region made huge profits. The Ganatantra Parishad criticised the policy of state trading and demanded to end the government's monopoly over kendu-leaf trading. The Ganatantra Parishad and later the Swatantra always favoured free-trading in kendu-leaf to safeguard the regional interests. Even in 1971 the Swatantra party leaders opposed the move of the Utkal Congress for nationalisation of kendu-leaf trading.[72] Subsequently, the kendu-leaf trade was nationalised in 1974 despite strong opposition from the leaders of western region.[73]

So far as participation in government and decision-making is concerned, western Orissa always lagged behind the coastal region. The Office of Chief Minister has been mostly monopolised by the political leaders from the coastal region. Out of the 18 times the post of Chief Minister was held between 1952 and 2004, only two persons (i.e. R.N. Singh Deo and Hemanda Biswal) belonged to western Orissa region (see Table-VI.23). Naveen Patnaik, the son of the famous Oriya political leader Biju Patnaik of the coastal region, is elected for his second consecutive term and is still continuing as Chief Minister since April 2004. Further, barring few occasions, the western region has very poor representation in the Council of Ministers of the state. It was in the coalition ministries formed in 1959, 1967 and 1971 that the western region received a reasonably fair representation in the Council of Ministers.

Table-VI.23

The Chief Ministers of Orissa from 1952 to 2004

Sl. No.	*Name of Chief Ministers*	*Period in Office*
1.	Nabakrishna Chaudhary	20 Feb. 1952 – 19 Oct. 1956
2.	Harekrishna Mahatab	19 Oct. 1956 – 25 Feb. 1961
3.	Bijayananda Patnaik	23 June 1961 – 2 Oct. 1963
4.	Biren Mitra	2 Oct. 1963 – 21 Feb. 1965
5.	Sadasiba Tripathy	21 Feb. 1965 – 8 March 1967
6.	Rajendra Narayan Singh Deo	8 March 1967 – 9 Jan. 1971
7.	Biswanath Das	3 Apr. 1971 – 14 June 1972
8.	Nandini Satapathy	14 June 1972 – 3 March 1973
9.	Nandini Satapathy	6 March 1974 – 16 Dec. 1976
10.	Binayak Acharya	29 Dec. 1976 – 30 Apr. 1977
11.	Nilamani Routray	26 June 1977 – 17 Feb. 1980
12.	J. B. Patnaik	9 June 1980 – 7 Dec. 1989
13.	Hemananda Biswal	7 Dec. 1989 – 4 March 1990
14.	Biju Patnaik	5 March 1990 – 15 March 1995
15.	J. B. Patnaik	15 March 1995 – 17 Feb. 1999
16.	Giridhar Gamango	17 Feb. 1999 – 6 Dec. 1999
17.	Hemananda Biswal	6 Dec. 1999 – 5 March 2000
18.	Naveen Patnaik	5 March 2000 – 16 April 2004

Source: Secretariat of Orissa Legislative Assembly, Bhubaneswar.

From 1977 to 2000, one-party dominant system operated in Orissa. It was during this period the representation of western Orissa in the successive ministries was not very encouraging considering the tremendous support the Janata Party, the Janata Dal and the Congress received from western Orissa (see Table-VI.24). Also in terms of distribution of portfolios, except for the coalition periods, the relatively important portfolios like Home, Finance, Industry, Revenue, etc. had gone to the leaders from coastal Orissa. As a result, the intra-party tensions along regional lines continued to mar Orissa politics during this period. The political polarisation between the two regions continued even in the Ministry formed by Janata Dal party of Biju Patnaik in 1990. The representation of western Orissa in Biju Patnaik's government was not very satisfactory.

Table-VI.24

Representation of Coastal and Western Regions In the Council of Ministers of Orissa from 1952 to 2000

Year	*Coastal Region*	*Western Region*	*Total*
1952	8 (61.5%)	2 (15.3%)	13
1956	6 (66.6%)	2 (22.2%)	9
1957	9 (64.2%)	2 (14.2%)	14
1959 (coalition)	6 (54.5%)	4 (36.3%)	11
1961	5 (71.4%)	-	7
1963	8 (57.1%)	2 (14.2%)	14
1965	7 (50.0%)	3 (21.4%)	14
1967 (coalition)	4 (21.0%)	8 (42.1%)	19
1971 (coalition)	12 (46.1%)	6 (23.0%)	26
1972	8 (53.3%)	3 (20.0%)	15
1974	10 (55.5%)	4 (22.2%)	18
1976	8 (57.1%)	3 (21.4%)	14
1977	7 (46.6%)	3 (20.0%)	15
1980	12 (63.1%)	3 (15.7%)	19
1985	7 (43.7%)	5 (31.2%)	16
1989	9 (36.0%)	7 (28.0%)	25
1990	17 (45.9%)	9 (24.3%)	37
1995	14 (48.2%)	6 (20.6%)	29
2000	13 (52.0%)	4 (16.0%)	25

Source: Research and Reference Wing, Secretariat of Orissa Legislative Assembly, Bhubaneswar.

Even in the Orissa State Legislative Assembly the numerical strength of the coastal region establishes its political supremacy. In the 147-member Legislative Assembly, the four districts of the coastal region account for 69 (i.e. 46.93%) seats compared to the 40 (27.21%) seats allotted to the five western Orissa districts. The coastal region is geographically smaller but demographically larger than western Orissa. In terms of size, coastal Orissa accounts for

25.79 per cent of state's area, and in terms of population it constitutes 47.43 per cent of the state population. Whereas, the western region's percentage shares in size and population of the state are 37.26 per cent and 26.56 per cent respectively.[74] Naturally, therefore, the number of MLAs from the coastal districts exceeds that of the western region. This discrepancy in the number of seats in the Legislative Assembly gives a political upper hand to the coastal region which in turn leads to political domination of the coastal region over the western region in Orissa.

To sum up, it may be argued that certain objective conditions like compact geographical area, distinct history, common culture and a separate mother-tongue largely helped to create a strong sense of regional identity among the people of western Orissa notwithstanding the formation of an integrated and united Orissa state in independent India. In addition to this, their relatively backward socio-economic position in comparison to the people of coastal Orissa created a sense of material deprivation among them. The relative material deprivation in socio-economic terms coupled with the disaffection resulting from political disadvantage contributed immensely to the growth of regionalism among the people in western Orissa. The next chapter deals with the process of articulation and the emerging trends in the regional mobilisation seen in western Orissa.

Notes and References

1. Some people even trace the origins to 1905 when the Sambalpur district was merged with Orissa division of Bengal Presidency. It may be noted that, the merger of Orissa princely states in 1948 led to the unification of two conspicuous regions (i.e. British Orissa and Princely Orissa) with differential stages of socio-economic and political development. Some people even argue that integration of states laid the very foundation of regionalism in Orissa.
2. See V.P. Menon, *Transfer of Power in India*, Delhi, 1968, p.266.
3. The Eastern States Union came into being on 1 August 1947. It comprised 26 Oriya-speaking states and 14 Chhatisgarh states.

4. Letter from R.N. Singh Deo, Maharaja of Patna, to the Viceroy and Governor General of India, dated 30th June 1946, cited in Sadasib Pradhan, *Agrarian and Political Movements: States of Orissa: 1931-1949*, Inter-India Publications, New Delhi, 1984, p.194.
5. See, Koshali, *Whither Koshal*? Calcutta, 1946, p.37.
6. See, *Orissa Records, Kalahandi Papers*, ACC No.1064S, Proceedings of the Kalahandi Legislative Assembly, 12 August 1946.
7. See, *Whither Koshal, op. cit.*, p.38.
8. The people of Sambalpur area (i.e. present-day western Orissa) referred to the coastal Oriyas as 'Katakias' (i.e. the people belonging to the Cuttack area). The province of Orissa was then identified as the Cuttack region.
9. See, Koshal Sangha, *The Koshal Tract*, Bolangir, 1946, pp.1-4.
10. *Ibid*, p.27.
11. See, H.K. Mahatab, *Beginning of the End*, Cuttack, 1972, p.109.
12. *Orissa Records, Kalahandi Papers*, ACC No.335 Kal.
13. Later, Jawaharlal Nehru inaugurated the construction works of the Dam in 1948. See S. Supakar, *Itihasara Parihas* (Oriya), Sambalpur, 1988, pp.7-8.
14. *Ibid*, p.4.
15. Certainly, the Mahanadi Valley project was taken up to control flood situation in Orissa. But the project, inter alia, was also aimed at power generation, navigation, irrigation, soil conservation, etc.
16. The people were told that the project would be advantageous to the people of Cuttack and Puri districts in coastal Orissa. The ruler of Patna even used the anti-dam plank to mobilise the people in favour of Eastern States Union.
17. See *Orissa Legislative Assembly Proceedings*, Vol.II, 1946, pp.133-34.
18. *Orissa Legislative Asssembly Proceedings*, Vol.III, 1947, pp.147-48, cited in K.M. Patra, *Orissa Legislature and Freedom Struggle: 1912-1947*, ICHR, New Delhi, 1979, p.242.
19. In the debate that followed over the police action, the Orissa Premier Mahtab replied that anti-dam supporters wanted that the project should be abandoned and steps should be taken to

separate Sambalpur. See, *Orissa Legislative Assembly Proceedings*, Vol.IV, 1947, p.177.

20. See, *Hirakhand Samachar* (Oriya weekly), 22 October 1946.
21. *Hirakud Dam Project Report*, p.10, cited in Itihasara Parihasa, Suparkar, *op. cit.*, p.7.
22. See, *Report of the General Secretary*, Ganatantra Parishad, 1950, p.1; Also see F.G. Bailey, "Politics in Orissa: The Ganatantra Parishad", *Economic Weekly*, 24 October 1959, pp.1469-76.
23. See K.V. Rao, "Politics in Orissa – Social Ecology and Constitutional Compulsions", *Indian Journal of Political Science*, Vol.26, 1965, pp.101-10.
24. See F.G. Bailey, *op. cit.*, p.1471.
25. S. Supakar, *Sambalpur Budi Anchalara Lokankara Durdasha* (The Suffering of the People of Submerged Area of Sambalpur), Pamphlet released by GP, Cuttack, 1956, pp.2-4).
26. *Orissa Legislative Assembly Proceedings*, Vol.I, Part II, No.44, 1952, p.19.
27. See *The Samaj* (Oriya daily), 21 March 1959.
28. See F.G. Bailey, "Orissa Politics: Congress Loses Majority", *Econommic Weekly*, 29 August 1959, pp.1204-5.
29. F.G. Bailey, "Politics in Orissa: The Feudatory States", *Economic Weekly*, 19 September 1959, p.1299.
30. F.G. Bailey, "Parliamentary Government in Orissa – 1947-56", *Journal of Commonwealth Political Studies*, Vol.I, 1963, pp.112-22.
31. K.V. Rao, "The Pattern of Orissa Politics" in Iqbal Narain (ed.), *State Politics in India*, Meerut, 1967, pp.209-16.
32. See *The Koshal Tract*, Koshal Sangh, Bolangir, 1946, pp.1-14.
33. Mazumdar also said that Ptolemy in his work referred to Sambalpur as 'Sambalka' and river Mahanadi as 'Manada' which was famous for its diamonds. See B.C. Mazumdar, *Orissa in the Making*, Calcutta, 1925, p.27.
34. *The Koshal Tract, op. cit.*, p.10.
35. See the notes on the 'garjat' state of Patna by H.E. Impey, 1863, in N. Senapati and N.K. Sahu (ed.), *Gazetteers of Orissa, Bolangir*, Cuttack, 1968, pp.63-65. These 18 principalities were: Patna, Sambalpur, Sonepur, Bamra, Rairakhol, Bonai, Phuljhar, Gangpur,

Raigarh, Bargarh, Sakti, Baud, Athamalik, Sarangarh, Chandrapur, Khariar, Bindra-Nawagarh and Borasambar.

36. Koshal Tract, *op. cit.*, p.20.
37. See P. Mukherjee, *The History of the Gajapati Kings of Orissa*, Cuttack, 1981, pp.23-25.
38. L.E.B. Cobden-Ramsay, *Feudatory States of Orissa*, Calcutta, 1925, pp.26-27.
39. Mukherjee, *op. cit.*
40. These territories were finally ceded to the British in 1826. See S.P. Das, *Sambalpur Itihasa* (Oriya), Sambalpur, 1969, pp.304-8.
41. Cobden-Ramsay, *op. cit.*
42. See Govt. of India, *Census of India*, 1991.
43. S.P. Das, *op. cit.*, pp.240-44.
44. See N. Senapati and B. Mohanty (eds.), *Orissa District Gazetteers, Sambalpur*, Cuttack, 1971. The folk-tradition is handed down orally from one generation to another. Recently, efforts are made to standardise and popularise the western Orissa folk culture.
45. See M.K. Mishra, *Folk-songs of Kalahandi*, Mayur Publications, Bhubaneswar, 1989.
46. Senapati and Mohanty, *op. cit.*, p.112.
47. Direndranath Patnaik, *Festivals of Orissa*, Orissa Sahitya Academy, Bhubaneswar, 1982, p.48.
48. B. Baboo, for instance, attributes environmental factors to the growth of two different religious systems: coastal plains adhere to Jaganath worship and the western highland region follows Sakti worship. See B. Baboo, "Geography of Sakti Cult in the Sambalpur District of Orissa", *Folklore*, Vol.20 (9), pp.191-200.
49. Senapati and Mohanty, ODG, *op. cit.*, pp.2-3.
50. See Senapati and Mohanty, *op. cit.*, p.106, and Prayag Dutta Joshi, "Swatantra Koshali Bhasa", *Saptarshi* (Oriya), Vol.16(6-7, pp.26-42.
51. P.K. Padhee, "Sambalpuri O Bhatri", *Saptarshi*, Vol.14(4), pp.9-22; Also see B. Patel, "Bhasha: Sambalpuri O Kissan", *Saptarshi*, Vol.14(2), pp.1-5.
52. Senapati and Mohanty, *op. cit.*, p.107.
53. See F.G. Bailey, *Politics and Social Change: Orissa in 1959*, University of California Press, California, 1963.

54. The Congress won 36 and 47 seats in 1937 and 1946 respectively. See F.G. Bailey, "Politics in Orissa: Congress Loses Majority", *Economic Weekly*, 29 August 1959, p.1203.
55. The Ganatantra Parishad not only led to bipolarisation in politics but also gave rise to politics of regionalism in Orissa. For details, see Myron Weiner, *The Politics of Scarcity: Public Pressure and Political Response in India*, Bombay,1963, pp.19-20.
56. K.V. Rao, "Politics in Orissa", *op. cit.*, pp.101-10.
57. S.C. Dash, "Government and Politics in Orissa", *Indian Journal of Political Science*, Vol.26, 1965, pp.83-100.
58. M. Mohanty and L.N. Mishra, "Orissa: Politics of Political Stagnation" in Iqbal Narain (ed.), *State Politics in India*, Meerut, 1967, pp.240-61.
59. *The Samaj* (Oriya daily), 23 May 195.
60. Although the GP maintained its position in Bolangir, Kalahandi and Sundargarh, it lost a few seats to Congress in Sambalpur and Phulbani. Out of 38 seats of western Orissa it secured 23. See Govt. of Orissa, *Assembly-wise and District-wise Party Position in Orissa Assembly*, Secretariat of Orissa Legislative Assembly, Bhubaneswar, 1991.
61. For details on the rise of Swatantra Party, see H.L. Erdman, *The Swatantra Party and Indian Conservatism*, London, 1967, pp.115-7.
62. See *The Samaj*, 30 April 1966 and 1 May 1966 and 23 June 1966. Also see M. Mohanty and L.N. Mishra, *op. cit*.
63. See Amal Ray, "Sub-Regional Politics and Elections in Orissa", *Indian Journal of Political Science*, 1974, October-December, pp.340-42.
64. *The Statesman*, 11 April 1970.
65. Amal Ray, *op. cit*.
66. *Ibid*.
67. The Janata Party was formed by uniting Bharatiya Lok Dal, Congress (O) and the Socialist Party. Again, the Bhartiya Lok Dal came into being in 1974 by combining seven parties including the Swatantra, Utkal Congress and Sanyukta Socialist Party.
68. See *Orissa Legislative Assembly Proceedings*, Vol.II, Part II, No.56, 1955, 23 August, pp.34-36.

69. *Ibid.*
70. P.K. Deo, *My Humble Contributions, Gantantra Parishad, 1956-61*, Bawanipatna, 1961, p.65.
71. See *Report of the Sarjoo Prasad Enquiry Commission*, Govt. of Orissa, Home Deptt., 1972,pp.91-94.
72. *The Statesman*, 19 October 1971; *The Hindu*, 27 October 1971.
73. *The Hindustan Times*, 2 October 1974.
74. Govt. of India, *Census of India*, 2001.

7

Process of Regional Articulation and Mobilisation

In the foregoing chapter, it is noted that coastal and western Orissa differ in respect of history, culture and speech. In addition, there exist wide-range socio-economic disparities between the two regions. Given this regional imbalance, the relatively backward western region developed strong undercurrents of regional discontent. The growth of regional parties, the struggle for power and the incidence of political inequality and under-representation in successive ministries accentuated regional consciousness further and motivated the people of western Orissa to rise against their coastal counterpart.

So far as the process of regional articulation and mobilisation in western Orissa is concerned, two distinct trends are noticeable: (i) the 'autonomist' and (ii) the 'separatist'. The autonomists call for greater regional autonomy, preferential treatment and administrative and judicial decentralisation. The separatists, on the other hand, clamour for separate provincial statehood for western Orissa. This chapter examines these two trends of regional mobilisation in western Orissa.

1. Regional Aspiration: The Autonomist Trend

(i) Major Grievances

The regional issues have been raised by different bodies of western Orissa from time to time. Particularly, the Ganatantra

Parishad/Swatantra party played a stellar role in articulating regional demands in the 1950s and 1960s. Apart from taking up issues like Hirakud Dam and Rourkela rehabilitations, the GP/Swatantra also fought for greater developmental benefits to western Orissa. For example, P.K. Deo, the notable GP leader, introduced a bill in the Lok Sabha seeking amendment to the Article 371(2) of the Indian Constitution.[1] The proposed amendment called for proportionate distribution of developmental expenditure, educational and employment opportunities in different regions of Orissa. It also demanded the constitution of developmental councils for efficient utilisation of resources.

But towards the mid-seventies the influence of GP/Swatantra had declined and finally in 1977 it merged with Janata Party. In the meantime, another organisation called the 'Paschim Odissa Gana Samukshya' (Western Orissa People's Front) vigorously campaigned against regional injustice. The Western Orissa People's Front (hereafter WOPF) was formed in 1973 following the clashes among the students of V.S.S. Medical College in Sambalpur district. The Front mainly operated in the districts of Sambalpur, Bolangir, Kalahandi and Sundargarh. It basically protested against the discriminatory treatment in the fields of education, culture, industrialisation and employment.[2] The Front pledged to work for the removal of regional imbalance.

In a representation to the Governor of Orissa, the Front argued in favour of reservation of seats for the students of western Orissa in the Medical and Engineering Colleges at Burla, Sambalpur. It also demanded for appointment of local selection committees for the recruitment of 3rd and 4th grade employees.[3] Demands were also placed for opening up branches of key offices, a separate Board of Secondary Education, different course curriculums for primary and secondary levels based on local conditions, appointment of judges to Orissa High Court from western region etc.[4] In a memorandum to the Prime Minister the front leaders urged the Central Government to consider the 'Scheduled Areas' status for western region and constitution of a special development authority for the western districts along with formation of an advisory council for need-based development as the region is continuously neglected by the government of Orissa since the merger time.[5]

The Front criticised strongly the land ceiling imposed by the Orissa Land Reforms Act. It stated that the cultivable land in coastal plains is much more fertile than western region. Therefore, the ceiling limit in western area should be three times more than the plains.[6] The Western Orissa United Youths Front raised a few more regional demands which inter alia included: holding periodical sessions of Orissa Legislative Assembly and Orissa State Public Service Commission at Sambalpur; establishment of another steel plant at Bonai; reservation of 75 per cent of seats in Medical, Engineering and Government Training Colleges for the local students.[7]

The joint convener of WOPF in his representation to the Governor of Orissa pointed out that after merger the people of Sambalpur region are treated as second class citizens in Orissa. He further noted that most of the posts including the 4th grade are occupied by the coastal people. To check the growing neglect of the region he therefore pleaded for the introduction of 'Mulki rule' in western region.[8]

During the Janata rule from 1977 to 1980, regional aspiration was articulated at the intra-party level. Leaders representing regional interests were divided over the Land Reforms Act of 1977 which imposed ceiling on land holdings. To protest against this decision, the ruling party MLAs and MPs of the region held a conference at Bargarh in 1978 and urged the government to review the decision as the cultivable land in the coastal belt is more fertile compared to the western region. The following resolutions were passed in the conference:

(a) For the purpose of implementation of land reforms the term family should be redefined to treat every grown up son as a unit of the family. (b) To pay compensation at the market rate to the cultivators losing their land. (c) Classification of land in terms of productivity. (d) Special protection should be given to illiterate backward cultivators of the region to promote social justice. (e) To give priority to the region in matters relating to minor irrigation, health, electrification, sanitation and communication. (f) Expansion of educational institutions in the region. (g) Fifty per cent reservation of medical seats for the local students of the region. (h) Preference to western people in the matter of employment at the state secretariat. (i) To reserve the class III and IV jobs in western Orissa for the local people of the region.[9]

Another issue which caused tremendous resentment among the people of western region is the rehabilitation of the people displaced by the Rourkela Steel Plant. Led by the local M.P., Harihar Patel, the Rourkela Displaced Persons Welfare Committee submitted a memorandum to the President of India when he visited Rourkela to inaugurate the first blast furnace in 1959. Emphasising the misery and hardship of the people the memorandum highlighted that the construction of the steel plant led to acquisition of land and villages.[10] As many as 16,000 persons belonging to 3,300 families were displaced from their home and hearth. The assurances like 'land for land' and 'house for house' and adequate compensation for all land, trees and buildings were not fulfilled. The employable persons among the displaced were not given gainful employment. Out of the 16,000 persons only 4,000 were resettled. But lands for resettlement were given at distant forests which were not economically self-sufficient. As regards compensation, very negligible sum were paid and contrary to the assurance the displaced were not given sites for setting up business at Rourkela.[11] Even after three decades the persons displaced from Rourkela still complain about the injustice regarding compensation, rehabilitation and absorption of suitable displaced persons in various commensurate jobs in the steel plant. Protesting against the inattention, the Displaced Persons Welfare Committee launched agitation in 1992 and placed a charter of demands before the state government and the plant authorities. The demands include: (a) absorption of the dependents of displaced persons including non-matriculates and female candidates in Rourkela Steel Plant; (b) issue of certificate to displaced persons; (c) infrastructural development for all resettlement colonies and villages in and around Rourkela; (d) regularisation of unauthorised construction by displaced persons in the government land; (e) reservation of seats in technical institutions for displaced persons and local people; and (f) 75 per cent reservation for local inhabitants in local employment.[12]

The 'Nagra Mukti Samukshya', a Rourkela-based Welfare Organisation of the displaced people alleged that lands in excess were acquired and the surplus lands were sold off to different individuals and parties at higher costs.[13] The Adivasi and Harijan Youth Welfare Association of Rourkela in its memorandum to Orissa Chief Minister demanded for cent per cent reservation for ST and SC students in all the educational institutions in Sundargarh district; setting up of an Adivasi and Harijan Boys' Hostel in Rourkela; establishment of an Adivasi and Harijan College at Rourkela and above all appointment of displaced persons in Rourkela Steel Plant.[14]

Calling for appropriate government action, the 'Hirakhand Nagarika Parishad' of Sambalpur in its memorandum to the Orissa Governor highlighted some of the major problems facing the Sambalpur town in particular and western region in general. The memorandum contained the following demands such as (a) modernisation of the Hirakud canal system; (b) autonomous status for V.S.S. Medical College of Sambalpur; (c) expansion of Sambalpur district headquarters hospital and the medical facilities; (d) establishment of TV studio at Sambalpur; and (e) improvement of infrastructural facilities at G.M. College and University College of Engineering.[15]

Another issue which caught sufficient public attention and aroused tremendous regional discontent was the demand for the establishment of the programme production centre at the Television Centre in Sambalpur. It may be remembered that under the Satellite Instructional Television Experiment, television broadcasting in Orissa started at Sambalpur, Bolangir and Dhenkanal in 1978. Later, a studio for production of television programmes was created at Cuttack and the relay transmitter installed at Sambalpur telecast the programmes produced at Cuttack studio.[16] Unfortunately, the programmes produced at Cuttack studio did not reflect the culture, custom, tradition, educational and agricultural requirements of the western region. It created a contradiction in that the Sambalpur TV centre did not have its own production facilities.

In 1982 the Cuttack TV centre was established and with that the possibility of having a programme production centre at Sambalpur was closed down for ever. The Cuttack TV centre dominated television broadcasting and telecast in Orissa, while the Sambalpur centre was reduced to a relay centre. Because of the favourable treatment of the state government to the coastal region, the Union Information and Broadcasting Ministry paid no attention to the just demand of the people of western region. In the absence of a programme production studio, the aspiring artists of the region could not find a suitable medium to expose their rich cultural tradition. The regional network service telecast from the Cuttack centre mostly reflect the language, literature, culture, tradition, fairs, festivals and cropping pattern of the coastal region. In order to have an independent programme production centre at Sambalpur some activists therefore launched an agitation. For instance, on 4 September 1991, a group of activists of the Sambalpur Artist Forum led by Bhagabat Prasad Nanda, Suresh Pujari, Ashok Mishra, Benibhuj Sahu and Jadunandan Panda intruded into the office of the Assistant Station Engineer of Sambalpur TV centre and submitted a memorandum demanding a full-fledged programme production centre at Sambalpur.[17] Soon after that the agitators indulged in demonstration and picketing. They also burnt down the effigy of Ajit K. Panja, the then Union I&B Minister and attempted road blockade on national highway. The protestors prevented the members of the Sambalpur Kala Parishad from participating in cultural programme held at Cuttack.[18] They alleged that the government's decision to provide 15 minutes every week for telecast of Sambalpuri programmes is not enough to preserve, promote and propagate cultural heritage of western Orissa.

(ii) The Decentralisation Issue

There have been strong acts of protests and demonstrations demanding for establishment of a Circuit Court of Orissa High Court in western Orissa. The demand for the circuit sitting of the High Court is aimed at decentralisation of the judicial machinery. As the seat of Orissa High Court is located in the Cuttack city in coastal Orissa, the poor people of western region face enormous problems in securing legal justice and easy disposal of cases.

The demand for Circuit Court dates back to 1959. The Orissa High Court in its letter to the Government of Orissa observed:

Although the Law Commission is not in favour of the idea of setting up Benches at different centres of a state, the Court feels that in Orissa there is a case for having at least one circuit court preferably at Bolangir-Patna. This is very necessary for the purpose of enabling poor litigants of the merged areas especially of Bolangir, Kalahandi, Sonepur, Boudh and nearby areas to fight out their litigation.[19]

In 1961, the High Court again recommended the Government of India to start the Circuit Court on experimental basis for two years at Bolangir. Later in 1965 the people of Sambalpur strongly protested in favour of having the circuit court at Sambalpur town.

As regards the conflict over the question of location, the Orissa High Court made the following remark to the government of India:

The Court examined the question in connection with the proposal for the establishment of a Bench at Sambalpur and in Court's letter No.5042 dated the 6th October 1965 the special reasons for recommending the circuit sitting of the High Court at Bolangir prior to the merger and they have been deprived of this facility after the merger of these states.[20]

Thereafter, the Bar Association of Sambalpur intensified its struggle to have the sitting of High Court at Sambalpur and not Bolangir. In their effort, the lawyers of Sambalpur received tremendous support from leaders of various political parties, members of Parliament and the state legislature, representatives of social and welfare organisations, student unions, trade unions and above all the All Orissa Lawyers Association and the majority of the Bar Associations of the districts of western Orissa.[21] Even the Congress and the Janata Dal in their election manifesto in 1985 and 1990 respectively, promised the establishment of Circuit Court in the western region. As leader of the opposition, Biju Patnaik assured the President of the Sambalpur Bar Association for opening the Circuit Court.[22] To fulfil the commitment, Biju Patnaik after becoming Chief Minister in 1990 wrote to the Chief

Justice of the Orissa High Court for setting up of Circuit Court at Sambalpur.[23] The Chief Minister's action came in response to the representation submitted by a group of 26 MLAs from the western region.[24] The Chief Justice of Orissa High Court, however, refused to accede to the recommendation of Orissa government in this matter. The vested interests at Cuttack Bar Association strongly opposed the idea of opening Circuit Court at Sambalpur.

In protest against the decision of Orissa High Court, the Lawyers boycotted the courts at Sambalpur. Under strong pressure from the different Bar Associations of the western region, the Government of Orissa wrote to the Registrar, Orissa High Court, for establishment of Circuit Court as soon as possible. The government stated that the demand was justified as the places in western region are distant from the principal seat of Orissa High Court situated in Cuttack in coastal Orissa. Further the demand was justified in accordance with the provisions of Article 39(A) of the Constitution of India and the recommendations of the Jaswant Singh Commission pertaining to setting up of Circuit Court or Benches at places other than the principal seat of a state High Court.[25] Also the backwardness of western region provides another suitable reason for the demand of Circuit Court. Nearly 50 per cent of the population of western Orissa belongs to Scheduled Castes and Tribes who cannot afford the cost of litigation at distant places due to economic backwardness. But all said and done the just demand of the people of western Orissa remains unfulfilled.

(iii) Sambalpuri Language and Culture

It may be recalled that the people of Sambalpur vehemently opposed the introduction of Hindi in Sambalpur area in the 1890s. They not only strongly favoured the restoration of Oriya but also wholeheartedly supported the inclusion of Sambalpur region with Orissa division of erstwhile Bengal Presidency. It was on the basis of Oriya language, the district of Sambalpur in 1936 and the rest of the Sambalpur area in 1948 were made a part of Orissa state. But as mentioned in Chapter Six, the form of Oriya spoken in Sambalpur area bears a distinct regional identity of its own. It not only differs from coastal Oriya but also provide a sense of unity among its speakers. Besides, it serves as the link language for a number of tribal languages such as Kissan, Kui, Mundari, Kharia, Oraon etc. prevalent in Sambalpur region. As this form of Oriya is spoken in the Sambalpur belt (i.e. western Orissa), it is popularly called Sambalpuri speech of Oriya language or the Sambalpuri-Oriya dialect. But the general feeling in Sambalpur area is that the Government of Orissa has done nothing or very little to protect, preserve and promote the Sambalpuri speech.

It is being alleged that, both at the official and elite level Sambalpuri speech has been undermined even though the people of western region use it as their mother tongue. Under the pre-eminent and predominant position of standard Oriya, the Sambalpuri speech by and large remains as a spoken dialect and till recently no serious written work appeared in this speech. The Sambalpuri people attribute this failure to the lack of official patronage and inattention. For instance, in the Census reports Sambalpuri is recorded as Oriya and not as a separate mother tongue. The Census enumerates Oriya as the principal language of Orissa. The people alleged that while languages with less than 100 speakers and having no script are listed in the Indian Census, the Sambalpuri speech is not even listed as a mother tongue, let alone as a distinct language.

Besides, Sambalpuri is spoken in an area which remained under feudal rule for centuries. The rulers for their vested interests patronised Oriya language and not Sambalpuri though the latter was spoken as a mother-tongue. The British also patronised the dominant Oriya language on account of administrative convenience and political expediency. The lack of official support and legitimisation thus led to the marginalisation of Sambalpuri speech. Not only that, the Sambalpuri culture comprising folksongs, folk music, folk dance, etc. face the fear of extinction due to the favourable treatment shown towards the dominant Oriya language and culture. To recall the evocative phrase of Oommen, this marginalisation of language and culture can be termed as 'culturocide'.[26]

In order to preserve and promote Sambalpuri language and culture serious attempts were made by a few leading activists and some socio-cultural organisations. For instance, in the 1970s and 1980s associations like 'Orissa Sanskrutika Samaj', 'Sambalpuri Lekhak Sangh', 'Koshali Bhasa Sahitya Parishad' and 'Sambalpuri Bhasa Suraksha Committee' were deliberately formed to protect and promote Sambalpuri speech. Similarly, cultural organisations like 'Koshal Sahitya Samaj' and the 'Paschim Orissa Sanskrutika Parishad' were formed to work for the improvement of Sambalpuri dance and music. These organisations mainly conducted seminars, conferences and symposia for creating cultural consciousness among the western people.[27]

In the 1970s, the Oriya department of Sambalpur University started a very ambitious project to highlight the language and folk-cultural tradition of western region through various publications. An Oriya monthly magazine called 'Saptarshi' was published under the aegis of Sambalpur University for the above purpose. Attempts were also made to publish newspapers, journals, periodicals, books and dictionary in Sambalpuri language. Some scholars have also made conscious efforts to develop the grammar, phonetics and forms of speeches in Sambalpuri so as to give it the status of a distinct language.[28] Some writers like Manglu Charan Biswal, Rahas Bihari Mishra, Murari Prasad Mishra, Radhesyam Padhee wrote Sambalpuri songs and plays for All India Radio and Television Centre. Leading literary figures like S.N. Bohidar and P.D. Joshi motivated the people through their examples to write in indigenous language. Short stories, plays, songs and novels were published in significant numbers. Local Oriya newspapers such as 'Agnisikha', 'Koshala' and 'Hirakhand' carried weekend columns in Sambalpuri literature. The 'Sambalpuri Lekhak Sangh' brought out a compilation of Sambalpuri poems glorifying Sambalpuri history, culture and festivals like 'Dalkhai', 'Puspuni' and 'Nuakhai'.[29] Sambalpuri plays like 'Gauntia Babu', 'Bhuka', etc. gained tremendous recognition and popularity. All these literary drive gave the needed thrust to arouse the cultural consciousness among the people of western Orissa.

The new cultural policy of the government for the preservation of folk culture has also helped the Sambalpuri culture of western Orissa. But a closer look reveals that the state government has done very little to develop the language and culture of western Orissa. The three Academies, viz, Orissa Lalit Kala Academy, Orissa Sahitya Academy and Orissa Sangeet Natak Academy were established primarily to promote cultural tradition, dance, drama, music, language and literature of Orissa state. The Orissa Sangeet Natak Academy took up various developmental schemes for the improvement of folk dances and music. For example, the Chhau Dance Training Centre played a crucial role in promoting the 'chhau' folk dance. Similarly, the Utkal Sangeet Mahavidyalaya and the Odissi Research Centre were established at Cuttack and Bhubaneswar respectively for codification, documentation and dissemination of various Odissi dance forms. The 'Konark dance festival' was also launched to popularise Odissi dance. But no such significant steps were taken to patronise and propagate the regional culture of Sambalpur. Excluding the 'Sambalpur Kala Parishad' and 'Sambalpur Kala Kendra', the numerous other cultural associations of western region seldom receive any cultural grant for promotion of local and regional culture. Under strong regional pressure the government has decided in 1989-90 to open district cultural centres in each district headquarters to provide incentives to cultural activities.[30] But by and large it was alleged that under pressure from mainstream culture the government pays scant attention to the promotion of Sambalpuri language and culture. It is also alleged that Gangadhar Meher, the famous Oriya poet from Sambalpur is not given due recognition compared to the litterateurs from coastal Orissa.[31] Discrimination is also noticed against Sambalpuri writers. Only two persons from western Orissa have received the Orissa Sahitya Academy award so far. The Orissa Sahitya Academy in 1987 awarded Prayag Dutta Joshi for his contribution to Sambalpuri language and literature. Under its aegis, the Sambalpuri Dictionary compiled by P.K. Tripathy and the study report 'Paschim Odissara Kathita Bhasa' by Gopabandu Rath were published in 1987.[32]

In the field of electronic media also the people of western region feel neglected. Demands for programme production centres at AIR and TV stations at Sambalpur have been made from time to time. As the production centre is located in Cuttack, even the programmes produced for Sambalpur region basically benefit the coastal people. The Radio and TV artists from Sambalpur area feel that their art forms have been neglected in comparison to that of coastal Orissa. The demands for news bulletin in Sambalpuri speech, adequate regional cultural programmes on Sambalpuri songs, dance and music were constantly made. Besides, demand was also made to translate many national TV and AIR programmes into Sambalpuri language.

In sum, the culture movement in western Orissa can be termed as an autonomist and not a separatist one. The movement basically aimed at the following things:

(a) recognition of the distinct status of Sambalpuri language; (b) government aid and patronage to development of indigenous Sambalpuri literature; (c) promotion and spread of Sambalpuri cultural tradition, art forms, dance, drama and music; (d) more TV and radio programme in Sambalpuri language; (e) non-interference of outsiders in Sambalpuri language and culture.

(iv) Demand for Development Council

In the meantime, the demand for a Development Council for the western region gathered momentum. The demand was seen as a part of the larger scheme of the autonomist perspective for the western region. The advocates of the Council maintained that the elected representatives of western Orissa have been denied proportionate representation in the successive ministries of Orissa. This has resulted in their exclusion from the decision-making process at the apex political level. Further, the economic and political domination of the culturally and educationally advanced coastal people frustrated the developmental aspirations of the western people. Hence the objective of the council is to secure regional autonomy within the constitutional framework for the economic, political, social and cultural development of the western region.

As regards Regional Developmental Council, Ashok Panda, senior Advocate in Supreme Court suggested that efforts should be made to create development council under the Constitution in terms of Article 371 with necessary modifications to ensure democratic and autonomous functioning. He maintained that Article 371 of the Constitution provides for special provisions for combating regional imbalances in the State of Maharashtra, Gujarat and Andhra Pradesh. Under Article 371(2), the Governor of these states is empowered to establish separate development boards for Vidarbha and Marathawada in Maharashtra; Saurashtra and Kutch in Gujarat with the provision that a report on the working of each of these Boards be placed before the State Legislative Assembly.[33]

In the case of Andhra Pradesh, Article 371-D (1) specifies provisions for giving special consideration to local residents of the different parts of the state in the matter of public employment and education. It is argued that the provisions under Article 371 are relevant to Orissa as widespread regional imbalance exists between the coastal and western Orissa districts. Also development in the traditional sense has not benefited the people of western region.[34]

Another group of autonomists led by Binod K. Pati harped more on the autonomous character of the regional council.[35] The demand for autonomous council according to this section aims at decentralisation of political, administrative, legislative and financial powers and ensuring regional financial autonomy and decision-making authority. The establishment of such a council would reasonably fulfill the need of the people of western region within the framework of Orissa state. The regional council would give power to the people and bring the western districts on an equal footing with the coastal districts. However, the Government led by Biju Patnaik set up the Gadhei Committee to examine the demand for regional council. The committee in its report in 1995 rejected the establishment of such a council.[36]

The draft constitution of the proposed council, however, provides that it shall have directly elected members for a period of five years and the nominated members should not exceed 5 per cent of the total strength of the council. Election to the regional council can be conducted along with the State Assembly. The Western Orissa Autonomous Development Council will have as its members all MLAs and MPs and all Chairmen of the Zilla Parishads of the western region. It will have a 15-member executive committee with Chairman and Vice-Chairman elected from amongst the members. The Chairman of the council shall have the status of a Cabinet Minister,[37] and its headquarters shall be located at Bolangir.

The council shall come into existence by an Act of Orissa Legislative Assembly and it shall be competent to frame rules and by-laws for its smooth and effective functioning. As regards finance, it is maintained that 80 per cent of the income derived from western region under non-plan head shall be spent by the council. For this purpose separate allocation should be made in the state budget. So far as the plan expenditure is concerned the council shall have the power to supervise the implementation of all central and state-sponsored schemes and projects. It shall also have the power to sponsor new development projects to be executed with the assistance of central and state governments.[38]

Further, the council shall have controlling power over the officials posted in western region and the Chairman shall have the powers to make entries in the character rolls of these officials. All class III and IV employees shall be recruited by the council from among the local inhabitants. The Executive Committee shall have the right to nominate an eminent person of western region to the State Public Service Commission, all Selection Boards and Selection Committees for the appointment to various important bodies and departments.[39] For proper administrative decentralisation a separate secretariat with recruits from the local region should be established. The Secretariat should be vested with powers of appointment, posting, transfer, etc. Some leading persons also demanded for a separate Planning Board with separate plan allocation in the union budget.[40]

On the whole the autonomists claim that the Regional Council would empower the people to have a say in matters concerning their own affairs, participate in the process of development and progress and have a share in economic prosperity. They rejected the demand for separate state, but emphasised that distinct regional identity of western Orissa be well recognised by the state leadership as well as by the mainstream coastal people. Finally, the Western Orissa Development Council was established in Bolangir in 1998. The establishment of this regional council satisfied the aspirations of certain sections of people in western Orissa.

2. The Separatist Trend: Movement for Separate State

In the late 1980s and early 1990s the regional movement in western Orissa took a significant turn as the demands for a separate Koshal state comprising the five districts of western Orissa were vigorously made by some separatist groups. The demand for a separate state for western Orissa was made on earlier occasions also. For example, during the anti-Hirakud dam agitation in 1948 some leaders of Sambalpur manifestly advocated for constituting Sambalpur and its adjoining areas into a separate state. The echoes for a separate state were also heard during the 1970s. Some Swatantra Party leaders demanded to constitute the coastal districts into a Union Territory and the rest of Orissa into a separate province.[41] Even some Swatantra MLAs from western Orissa made a strong plea for bifurcation of the state into Utkal and Koshal provinces.[42] They favoured a separate state for western Orissa on geographical, historical and socio-cultural grounds. The continuous neglect of western Orissa and the domination of coastal belt under successive governments were attributed as the main reasons for the separate state demand.[43]

However, the tone and the tenor of these earlier demands differ from the demand made in the recent times. The earlier demands for separate state were based on regional identity and material deprivation. But the recent demand is based on cultural deprivation and is rooted in the concept of 'Koshali nationalism'. In other words, the new demand is based on the assertion of separate identity in terms of Koshali identity and not just another regional Oriya identity. It aims at constitution of a separate Koshal state based on Koshali language and culture.

(i) Assertion of Koshali Identity

The assertion of Koshali identity dates back to the times of anti-merger struggle. The notion of Koshali identity, which paved the way for Koshali separatism, was first mooted by R.N. Singh Deo, the ruler of ex-state of Patna. The anti-merger group led by R.N. Singh Deo clamoured for a separate state for the Oriya-speaking princely states of the highland region in which Koshal tract comprising the district of Sambalpur and the ex-states of Patna, Kalahandi, Bamra, Sonepur, Rairakhol, Gangpur and Bonai formed the core area.

As noted earlier, western Orissa was formerly known as Koshal or Hirakhand kingdom in ancient and medieval times. The British broke this Koshal confederacy in 1818 when Marathas ceded the western part of Orissa to the British. Subsequently, Sambalpur was annexed by British under the 'doctrine of lapse'. Along with the Koshal states Sambalpur district was transferred to the Orissa division of Bengal Presidency in 1905. In 1946 R.N. Singh Deo with some other chiefs spearheaded the Eastern States Union movement with a view to reviving Koshal unity within the framework of Eastern States Union.

A closer examination reveals that the concept of Koshali separatism which Singh Deo engineered was based on distinct regional identity involving a segment of Oriya population in the ex-states of Sambalpur area. It was not based on a separate linguistic identity. According to this argument the notion of 'Koshali' identity emanated from the natural regional divisions of Oriya homeland into coastal plains and western highlands corresponding to the erstwhile kingdoms of Utkal-Kalinga and Koshal respectively. These two compact Oriya blocks differ historically, geographically and culturally. In addition, the Oriyas of the western part speak a tongue called Sambalpuri which can be distinguished from the speech of coastal Oriyas.[44] To put differently, Singh Deo's concept of 'Koshali separatism' was based on the regional differences which originated due to the divergence in political history, geographical distinctiveness and cultural differences between two Oriya blocks. Hence he favoured the idea of formation of two states, viz., Eastern States Union and the Orissa Province. In his scheme the Koshal states formed the nucleus of Eastern States Union.[45] Even the 'Koshal' or 'Mahakoshal' movements launched during the anti-Hirakud and the anti-merger agitations were grounded in the concept of Koshali separatism defined in terms of regional identity. The protagonists of these movements maintained that two Oriya-speaking provinces based on specific regional affiliation be created.

Thus it is clear that the notion of Koshali separatism at this stage was based primarily on regional plarticularism and not on any separate linguistic identity different from mainstream Oriya identity. Singh Deo's concept of Koshali identity was certainly based on geographical compactness, distinct historical experience and separate cultural practices under the broad rubric of one Oriya linguistic identity.

(ii) From Regionalism to Nationalism: The Movement for Koshal State

As mentioned earlier, the recent demand for separate Koshal state is based on Koshali identity which is conceived of as different from the Oriya nation/nationality. In this sense the Koshali identity is anchored on a separate cultural-linguistic identity and not distinct regional identity. The leading role in articulating this notion of separate Koshali nationality has been played by P.R. Dubey and his Koshal party. P.R. Dubey, a Supreme Court advocate and son of ex-Minister Bodhram Dubey, championed the 'two nationalities theory' which insists that the people of western Orissa (i.e. the 'Sambalpurias') and the people of coastal Orissa (i.e. the 'Katakias') belong to two different nationalities based on the objective conditions of common history, shared culture, common language and well-defined territory. The former belongs to the Koshali nationality and the latter to the Utkal-Kalinga nationality. Viewed from this perspective, the existence of a separate Koshali nationality logically implies the right to self-determination in cultural and political terms within the framework of the Indian Union. In other words, the Koshali separatism in nationality terms desired to have a well-demarcated provincial state of its own.

The protagonists of the separate Koshali nationality maintained that the regional imbalance, which has been accentuated under successive state governments, caused serious damage to the aspiration of the western Orissa people. It jeopardises their economic, political, social and educational developments. The apathetic political leadership and the attitudinal cleavages have further widened the gap between western and coastal Orissa. As a result, various separatist organisations like the 'Koshal Sangram Parishad', 'Koshal Sammilani', 'Koshal Liberation Front', and 'Western Orissa Liberation Front' have come up in support of the demand for separate Koshal state.

To realise the goal of separate Koshal state, the 'Koshal Sangram Parishad' under the leadership of P.R. Dubey and Rajiblochan Hota convened a meeting at Sambalpur on 10 November 1990 and a resolution supporting the demand for separate Koshal state comprising the five districts of western Orissa was passed in the meeting. The map of the proposed Koshal state (see Map No.2) was also adopted[46] and it was decided to send a delegation to Delhi to submit a proposal representing the case for Koshal state. Former MLA Rajiblochan Hota and leading advocates like Gorakhnath Sahu and Sanad Bihari Mohapatra

Map No. 2

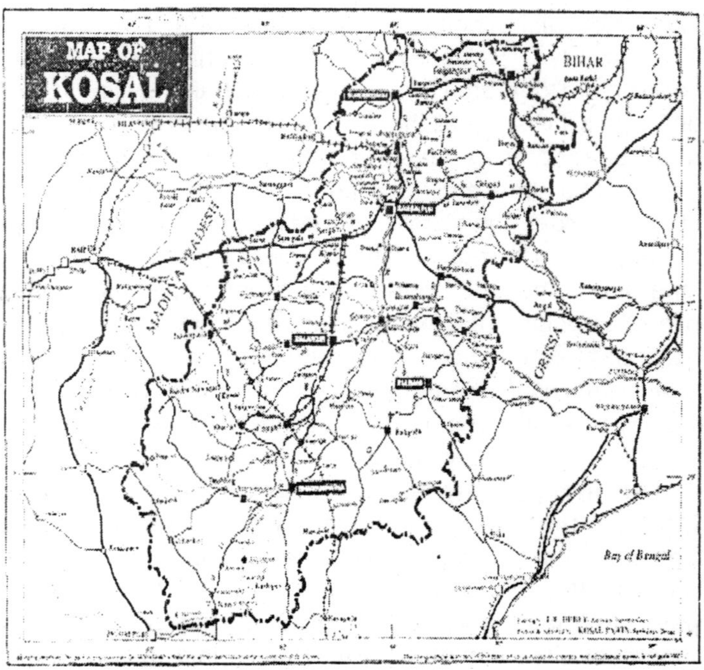

proposed to set up working committees at the panchayat level for creating awareness for the movement. Slogans like 'we want Koshal Pradesh', 'Koshali is our language' and 'Nuakhai is our festival' were popularised to arouse nationalist feelings among the members of Koshal Sangram Parishad. It was also resolved to urge all the MLAs and MPs of the areas of the proposed Koshal state to participate in the movement.[47]

To strengthen the case for separate state a regional political party called the 'Koshal Party' was launched on 24 October 1991 under the leadership of P.R. Dubey. The party was launched keeping the following objectives in mind: (a) to organise and bring together the people of Koshal region for their social, political, economic and cultural development within the framework of Indian Constitution; (b) to preserve, promote and protect Koshali (Sambalpuri) language, culture, music, art and literature; (c) to ensure equal educational and employment opportunities to the people of Koshal and to (d) conserve the natural resources of the Koshal region.[48]

In the meantime, another organisation called the Koshal Liberation Front (KLF) issued a pamphlet entitled, 'Fight for Separate State: The Only Alternative'. The Front observed that the Koshal region has been made a colony of coastal Orissa as the leaders from three dominant districts of coastal Orissa rule the entire Orissa and expropriate the wealth of western Orissa for the development of coastal Orissa. It castigated the government's decision to shift the proposed Aluminum Factory from Lanjigarh of Kalahandi district to a place in coastal area. It also condemned the forceful amalgamation of Koshal country with the province of Orissa.[49]

The front further alleged that the Koshali people (i.e. the people of western Orissa) have been treated as second-rate citizens in Orissa. The Koshali self-prestige and consciousness, on the one hand, and the continuous socio-economic exploitation, political discrimination and suppression of culture and language, on the other, have led the people of western Orissa to demand a separate Koshal state.[50]

Finally, the separate Koshal state movement was formally launched on 4 November 1991 under the aegis of the Koshal

Sangram Parishad and the Koshal Party. The leader of the movement, P.R. Dubey undertaken a 'Koshal Jana Jagaran Yatra' (People's Awareness Campaign) in an open jeep to explain the aims and objectives of the movement. The yatra covered the whole of western Orissa and lasted from 12 Febuary 1992 to 16 February 1992.[51] To create mass awareness and support for the movement the Koshal Sangram Parishad and the Koshal Party circulated the maps of the proposed state. Several pamphlets and leaflets focusing the attention on the plight of the Koshal people were also issued.

On 29 March 1992, the 'Koshal Sammilani' was convened by the Koshal Sangram Parishad and the Koshal Party at the Goyal Bhawan of Bolangir and a few resolutions supporting the formation of separate Koshal state were passed. The 'Koshal Sammilani' was organised on the lines of the Utkal Union Conference which was formed in 1903 to spearhead the Oriya nationalist movement. The 'Koshal Sammilani' was seen as a national conference by the Koshali activists to spread the ideals of 'Koshali nationalism'. The activists observed that in the state of Orissa the western (Koshal) region is exploited socio-economically and culturally. Further, after 1985 the political and administrative powers have been controlled by a group of corrupt politicians from coastal districts. It is also contended that the revenues obtained from Koshal region have been spent on the development of coastal districts.[52] Even it is alleged that the funds from Centre and development grants for STs and SCs of Koshal area have been spent for the development of coastal region.[53] Hence, the separatists argue that Koshal cannot flourish unless and until it is separated from Orissa. In other words, separation from Orissa is seen as the only alternative by the Koshali nationalists.

The second 'Koshal Sammilani' was held on 4 April 1993 at Nari Seva Sadan in Sambalpur. In this conference a resolution on separate state was unanimously passed. The resolution states that the Koshali people views with great concern the continuous neglect and exploitation of Koshal region ever since its merger with Orissa province. It also depricated the merger of Koshal region which was done in violation of the broad principle enunciated by

Indian National Congress in 1920 for constituting administrative units on linguistic basis.[54]

In this 'Sammilani', the idea of separation on the basis of Koshali nationalism was put forwarded in more explicit and concrete terms. The convention observes that historically and geographically Koshal region did not form a part of Utkal-Kalinga or Odra countries prior to the British rule.[55] The 'Sammilani' further noted that in post-merger Orissa, the leaders of the advanced coastal region have completely dominated the political and administrative machinery of the state by virtue of their numerical superiority in the legislative assembly and secretariat. The ministers and legislators of western region are marginalised at the decision-making level and this has resulted in exploitation of western Orissa by coastal region. As the western region has least control over the administration the budgetary allocation of the state and the distribution of central grants and assistance are strongly biased in favour of the coastal region.[56] The 'Sammilani' asserts that the Koshali people of western Orissa constitute a distinct nationality with distinct historical, linguistic and cultural identity of their own. Therefore, it resolves that a new state named Koshal be carved out on distinct linguistic-cultural basis within the constitutional framework of India in order to protect and promote the political, economic and cultural well-being of the Koshali people.

To substantiate its claim for separate state the 'Koshal Sammilani' emphasised on three sets of symbols which provide the objective basis for the notion of separate Koshali nationality. These symbols are: (a) historical glories, (b) linguistic unity and (c) cultural tradition.

(a) Historical glories

The glories of the ancient and medieval kingdoms of Koshal and Hirakhand, the historical legacy of Chauhan dynasty, the temples at the bank of Mahanadi river in Sonepur, the ruins of the temples around Patnagarh have provided the leaders of Koshal movement a vast pool of historical symbols to draw upon to feed the modern sense of Koshali identity and nationalism. The reference to Sambalpur kingdom as 'Sambalka' by Greek Geographer Ptolemy established the great antiquity of Sambalpur.[57]

History also shows that the Somavanshis who formed the first regional kingdom in western Orissa in 7th-8th centuries had their supremacy over the coastal part. The Somavamshis shifted their capital from Suvarnapur (modern Sonepur) in western Orissa to Jajatinagar in coastal Orissa and with that western Orissa was reduced to a peripheral area.[58]

Under the Chauhans, western Orissa reached the height of its glory. The illustrious Chauhan ruler Ramai Deo founded the powerful Patna state in 1325. Patna emerged as the nerve-centre of the 18 tributary states of Koshal confederacy which fell to the British in 1821.[59] The great literary works like 'Koshalanand Kavya' written by Gangadhar Mishra, the court poet of Sambalpur and 'Jayachandrika' written by Prahlad Dube depict the heroic glories of the Chauhans who ruled over Koshal for 453 years.[60] The sovereignty of Chauhan rule was acknowledged even by the rulers of Kalinga and Utkal.

Apart from this, the valour and courage shown by Surendra Sai, the heir apparent to the Sambalpur throne, during the Sepoy Mutiny in 1857 provided another basis for historical nostalgia for the present generation of western Orissa. Surendra Sai drove away the British forces from Sambalpur and waged guerrilla warfare to check British advance for a considerable time. He continued to fight against the British up to 1864.[61] Surendra Sai's historical fight against the British troops served as legends for the common people. It rejuvenates their historical roots.

The separatists claim that the average people in western Orissa now consciously identify themselves with ancient and medieval Koshal kingdom. They now consider themselves as people belonging to the 'Koshal Desh' which has a long recorded historical tradition of its own. This historical linkage with Koshal kingdom provided the requisite symbols, legends and myths which are carefully used in the construction of Koshali nationalism.

(b) Linguistic unity

Language plays an important role in the formation of regional national identity in India. The activists of Koshal movement therefore made serious efforts to define the identity of western

Orissa people in terms of separate language. They denounced Oriya identity and consciously attempted to re-cast their identity in 'Koshali' language. The name 'Koshali' has been preferred to 'Sambalpuri' for the purpose of creating distinction and differentiation from the Oriyas. The separatists argue that the nomenclature 'Sambalpuri' bears a regional identity[62] and blurs the distinction; whereas the name 'Koshali' evokes a national identity and provides a bond of unity among its speakers and draws a line of separation from the Oriyas.

To the separatist perception, Orissa is a bilingual state in terms of major link languages – Koshali is the link language of western region and Oriya is the link language of coastal Orissa. Apart from this some major tribal languages are also spoken in the Koshali area. But the leading Oriya litterateurs held that Koshali (Sambalpuri) is not an independent language but a dialect of Oriya. Conversely, some distinguished linguists of western Orissa like Prayagdutta Joshi and S.N. Bohidar claim that 'Koshali' is a self-sufficient complete language with an independent grammatical structure and alphabet.[63] It also possesses an autonomous structure and indigenous literature even though it does not have its own script.

Joshi convincingly argues that all eastern languages including 'Koshali' have originated from 'Ardha Magadhi' or 'Eastern Magadhi'. Koshali is a sister language of Awadhi, Bagheli and Chattisgarhi and belongs to the eastern group of languages of the Indo-Aryan family. The grammatical, morphological, syntactic and phonological features of Koshali language are identical with Hindi rather than with Bengali group.[64] Interestingly, Joshi claims that Oriya is a descendant of Koshali and Magadhi languages. He observes that both Oriya and Koshali originated from Sanskrit via 'Ardha Magadhi' and 'Koshali Bibhasa' (see Figure VII.1).[65]

During the rule of the later Chauhans the Koshali language was identified as Sambalpuri due to the political supremacy of Sambalpur in the erstwhile Koshal confederation. Some scholars have also established the distinct status of Koshali on the basis of comparative study of Koshali and other languages like Chattisgarhi, Bhatri, Kissan and Lariya.[66]

Figure VII.1: Linguistic Origin of Koshali and Oriya

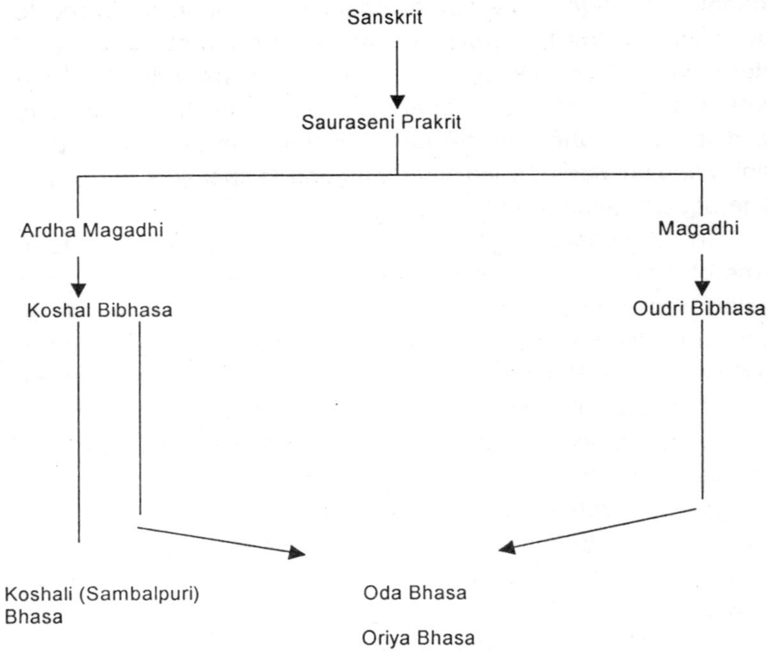

As Koshali language uses Oriya script, it is denied a distinct status by many people. But the fact of the matter is that script is not always considered as a necessary condition in defining a speech as a distinct language, though script plays an important role in distinguishing one language from another. The linguistic situation of India also reveals that many languages may share one common script and one language can be written in several scripts. For example, Hindi, Marathi, Sindhi, Gujarati share the common Devnagari script. Similarly, Bengali script is adopted by Assamese and Manipuri. Punjabi can be written in both Gurumukhi and Devnagari; Santhali uses both Bengali and Roman script in addition to its own script. K.S. Singh in his study of tribal languages observed that these languages mostly adopt the script of the dominant language in the state of their domicile.[67]

The protagonists of Koshali language maintain that Koshali can be written in either Oriya or Devnagari script. They also remark that historical evidences suggest that Oriya script was used in Utkal, Kalinga and Koshal regions.[68] In the quest for separate identity even some local writers have popularised the use of Devnagari script for Koshali language.[69] Some separatists, however, feel that since Koshali/Sambalpuri uses Oriya script, the average Oriya speakers treat it as a dialect of Oriya. In order to differentiate Koshali from Oriya, therefore, serious attempts were made in the second 'Koshal Sammilani' to evolve a separate script for Koshali language. One workshop for this purpose was arranged by the Koshal party.

The consciousness about Koshali language, quest for a separate script and development of indigenous literature should be seen as attempts by Koshali nationalists to reconstruct western Oriya identity in separate linguistic terms. The Koshali nationalists alleged that the dominance of Oriya language through official efforts reduced the Koshali language to the status of a dialect of Oriya. The hegemony of Oriya language and culture and the deliberate official and intellectual effort to suppress Koshali language posed serious threats to the existence of independent Koshali language. They further maintained that the Koshali speech community was brought into the Oriya fold due to the politics of language. After their integration the cultural identity of the Koshalis are deliberately defined in terms of mainstream Oriya language and culture. This not only led to undermining the utility of Koshali language but also poses a threat to its gradual extinction.[70]

Two leading literary organisations, viz, the 'Koshal Bhasa Sahitya Parishad' of Khariar and the 'Sambalpuri Lekhak Sangh' of Sambalpur took significant steps for the preservation and promotion of Koshali language. Under the aegis of these organisations, publication of periodicals, newspapers and journals are undertaken with an agenda to differentiate Koshali identity. Newspapers like 'Hakua', 'Sat Kahle Chhati Phate' and periodicals like 'Koshal Bharati' published from Sambalpur, Bolangir and Khariar respectively played vital roles in popularising Koshali language.[71]

For the recognition of Koshali as one of the official language in Orissa, the Koshal Party submitted a memorandum to the President of India. The memorandum stated that Article 347 of the Constitution empowers the President of India to direct a state of the Indian Union to accord official recognition to a language which is spoken by a substantial population of that state. The Constitution of India also provides for the preservation of the language of minority groups.[72]

Thus by claiming a separate status for the Koshali language the leaders of Koshal movement tried to provide an objective cultural basis to their demand for a separate Koshal state.

(c) Cultural tradition

The advocates of Koshali nationalism use some selective cultural symbols to root Koshali nationality in a distinct cultural mould. As noted earlier, the culture of western Orissa has grown out of the synthesis of Aryan and tribal elements which in turn has endowed the region with some cultural specificities and peculiarities.

Symbols like 'Sakti' worship (i.e. worship of mother goddess) and observance of festivals like 'Nuakhai', 'Puspuni' and 'Dalkhai', which reflected tribe and non-tribe integration, have been used to distinguish Koshali culture from the Oriya mainstream culture. 'Sakti' worship is seen as a dominant aspect of Koshali cultural identity. Goddess 'Samaleswari' is worshipped as a national deity and temples of 'Samaleswari' are found in all important places of western Orissa. Just as Oriya nationalism is identified with 'Jagannath Cult', so also Koshali nationalism is seen as identified with 'Sakti cult', i.e., Samaleswari worship.

To forge symbolic unity along cultural lines the 'Western Orissa Sanskrutika Parishad' made considerable efforts to celebrate 'Nuakhai', the most popular festival of western Orissa, on one single day. Earlier, each district of western Orissa observed 'Nuakhai' on different days. Hence, the common 'Nuakhai' festival celebration is seen as a symbolic tool for generating a sense of 'we feeling' and recasting Koshali identity.[73] Offering of 'Nuakhai' Bhet (gift) also promotes collective consciousness among the people. The 'Koshal Sammilani' in its first session even urged the state government to declare 'Nuakhai' as a public holiday all over the state.

Similarly, 'Puspuni' and 'Dalkhai' provide symbolic cultural values to define Koshali identity in separatist terms. Apart from this the rich cultural heritage of folksongs, music, dance, rituals, customs, ornaments, etc., provide some broad cultural symbols for construction of the cultural basis of Koshali nationalism.

To sum up, the activists of Koshal movement by using selective historical, linguistic and cultural symbols attempted to define Koshali separatism in nationalistic terms. They justified their separate state demand in terms of distinct Koshal history, territory, common culture and common Koshali language.

In support of their demand the members of second 'Koshal Sammilani' also submitted a memorandum to the President of India.[74] The memorandum reiterates the formation of Koshal state on the basis of Koshali nationality. It states that the Indian Constitution empowers the Parliament to create new state under Article 3 after seeking the views of the concerned state legislature(s). The Indian Parliament has exercised this power on many occasions in the past while forming states like Andhra Pradesh, Kerala, Maharashtra Gujarat, Punjab, Haryana, etc. Most of these states were created on the basis of linguistic unity. Hence, the protagonists urged the President to create a Koshali-speaking state to satisfy the political, cultural, economic and social aspirations of the people of western Orissa.[75]

The memorandum further notes that after the formation of greater Orissa in1948, the 'Mughalbandi' culture of coastal Orissa is glorified and imposed on the people of Koshal. The political identity of entire Orissa is also equated with the political identity of the mainstream nationality group, i.e. the Oriyas. No proportionate floor-time in the Orissa Legislative Assembly is allotted to the legislators of Koshal region to present their problems. A perusal of the proceedings of the Assembly conclusively proves that the debates are mostly monopolised by the representatives of coastal region.[76] Further, the state level leadership of all national parties is monopolised by the leaders of coastal Orissa. The memorandum also highlighted that the Koshali people have no share in the state administration in proportion to the area, population and resources of the region.[77] The Koshalis have almost no representation in the ranks of Secretaries, Additional Secretaries and Joint Secretaries in Orissa government. At the district level most of the crucial and key civil posts are manned by officers of the dominant nationality group.[78]

Hence, the 'Koshal Sammilani', on behalf of the oppressed Koshali people, requested the President of India to take suitable steps to carve out a new Koshal state. The 'Sammilani' observed that the creation of a Development Board or an Autonomous Regional Council under Article 371 will not bring any permanent solution to the problem. Therefore, the solution lies in granting full-fledged statehood to Koshal, according to them.[79] It further states that the liberation struggle of the Koshali people is not a mere struggle against under-development or regional imbalance. It is a struggle for preservation of Koshali nationality, culture and language; it is a struggie for self-survival through self-rule.[80]

In the meantime, the agitation for the regional development council picked up momentum. The autonomist denounced any attempt to divide or reorganise Orissa. They raised the slogan, 'we do not want Uttaranchal, Bananchal or Chhatisgarh, but we want regional council for better development.' At this juncture another separatist organisation called the 'Koshal Bhumi Mukti Sangathan' strongly supported the separate Koshal state demand. It rejected outright the autonomous council demand as in its opinion such a council will not solve the long standing problems of western Orissa. Its members wholeheartedly supported the division of Orissa along linguistic lines.[81]

In an interview to the editor of an Oriya weekly, Sibasankar Bagh, the President of 'Koshal Bhumi Mukti Sangathan' categorically stated that separate state will be the answer to the all-round development of western region.[82] According to him, the only alternative to get rid of the cumulative exploitation is separate Koshal state. In March 1998, a delegation led by S.S. Bagh and Kishalay Nanda visited Delhi and a memorandum demanding separate state was submitted to the Prime Minister.[83]

On 1 April 1998, the separatist boycotted Orissa day celebration. Thereafter, in a meeting arranged at Sambalpur the leaders of 'Koshal Bhumi Mukti Sangathan', 'Vir Surendra Sai

Manch' and Koshal Party unanimously rejected the idea of development council. Later a procession attended by P.R. Dubey, S.S. Bagh, Balgopal Mishra, Subash Chandra Nayak was taken out from Samaleswari temple to the district collector office and the agitators submitted a memorandum to the Prime Minister through the district collector.[84] Not only that, a militant organisation called the Western Orissa Liberation Front (WOLF) was formed under the 'Koshal Bhumi Mukti Sangathan' to spread awareness among the people at the grass root level. Massive efforts were made by WOLF to circulate leaflets to mobilise support for a separate state.[85]

The Koshal movement was intensified due to some other issues as well. Some of the decisions undertaken by the Biju Patnaik government in 1990-93 were viewed seriously by the Koshal activists. For example, the state government closed down the special Yojana cell for Kalahandi. Further, the government decided not to set up TV studio at Sambalpur and withdrew the facilities to make programmes. Security circle of Hirakud Dam was shifted from Sambalpur to Bhubaneswar. Also, funds released for flood victims in Orissa during 1980-85 were diverted for beautifying roads of Cuttack and Bhubaneswar; for constructing a ring road at Cuttack and an elephant sanctuary at Chandaka.

The coastal leaders wish away the demand for separate state as a non-issue raised by some disgruntled politicians to score political mileage. Some also remark that it is the handiwork of some people who do not have political or social base in western Orissa.

To conclude, it may be said that though the Koshal movement is still in low-key and confined to a few urban elites, yet the bogey of Koshali separatism in nationalist terms may seriously jeopardise the political unity and territorial integrity of Orissa state. Further, the rise of Koshali nationalism resulted in the existence of two parallel regional nationalisms in the state of Orissa. That is, Koshali nationalism now runs parallel to the mainstream Oriya nationalism. Earlier, Oriya identity united the people of western Orissa with the rest of Orissa, but now some of them are searching for a new identity under the banner of Koshali nationality. The Koshali separatists contend that the dominant coastal Oriya group made a conscious attempt to marginalise and destroy Sambalpuri-Koshali identity with a view to build an overarching Oriya identity coinciding with the political identity of Orissa. To safeguard their Koshali identity therefore these separatists in western Orissa raised the banner of separate Koshali nationalism.

It follows that within the provincial framework of Orissa Koshali nationalism is growing along side the mainstream Oriya nationalism. Mainstream Oriya nationalism is broadly identified with Oriya linguistic-cultural identity and with the state of Orissa. However, the Koshal separatists identify Oriya nationalism with the people and region of coastal Orissa. In their perception, since nationalism is inextricably linked with home territory, culture and language, Oriya nationalism is associated with coastal Orissa and Koshali nationalism is identified with western Orissa (i.e. Koshal). They further contend that Oriya nationalism is defined in terms of the identity of the people of the coastal districts of Balasore, Cuttack and Puri (i.e., the heartland of 'Utkal-Kalinga desh') and that this identity is being imposed on the Koshali people. It is also alleged that, the coastal people, who champion the cause of Oriya nationalism, insist that the Koshali identity should be sacrificed for the larger cause of Oriya nationalism, as the existence of a separate Koshali identity will pose a serious threat to Oriya nationalism

The Koshali nationalists further maintain that the political merger of Koshal with Orissa does not necessarily mean its cultural eclipse. Culturally and linguistically the Koshalis are different people and hence their identity should not be merged into Oriya identity. The dominant coastal people, however, stress that since Oriya nationalism is coextensive with Orissa province, the collective nationalist identity of the minority, i.e., Koshali-Sambalpuri people, is undesirable and unwarranted. Their political merger with Orissa in1948 automatically meant their cultural and linguistic merger and hence question of separate Koshali nationality simply does not hold good.

But sections of the Koshali-Sambalpuri people still assert their Koshali identity and they strongly emphasise upon separate Koshali nationalism and separate Koshal state. As a result, two language-based regional cultural nationalisms— Oriya and Koshali— are seen in the state of Orissa. While Oriya nationalism is broadly associated with the formation of Orissa state and maintenance of Oriya identity in general; Koshali nationalism is mainly linked with the movement for separate Koshal state for the protection of a distinct Koshali identity within Indian Union.

Notes and References

1. See, *The Samaj* (Oriya Daily), 30 September 1973. It may be recalled that clause (2) was inserted to Article 371 of Constitution of India for removing regional disparities in the states of Andhra Pradesh, Maharashtra and Gujarat.
2. See, Sumit Ghosh, "Regional Demands in Orissa", *Hindustan Standard*, 5 October 1973, The Western Orissa People's Front mainly raised the issue of "mulki rule" and "sons of the soil" preferences for the people of western Orissa.
3. *Ibid.*
4. *The Samaj* (Oriya daily), 2 October 1973. The Sambalpur Bar Association in a meeting in September 1973 adopted a resolution seeking preference for students of Sambalpur University for admission in medical and technical colleges located in the region.
5. *Koshala* (Oriya weekly), 21 September 1973.
6. *Amrit Bazar Patrika*, 11 November 1973; *The Prajatantra* (Oriya daily), 10 November 1973. The allegations were made against the coastal districts in general and the Cuttack districts in particular. The Front acused the state leadership of regional bias which endangered the unity and integrity of the state.
7. See the Leaflet issued by the *Western Orissa United Youths Front*, 26 March 1973.
8. See, M.B. Bohidar, *Our Sorrow is Our Plight*, Sambalpur, 1973.
9. See the *Bargarh Conference Proceedings*, 17 July 1978, pp.2-4.
10. See, the *Revenue Department Notification*, Cuttack, 22 February 1954. It states that for the establishment of steel plant and allied and ancillary factories at Rourkela, an area measuring 78 sq. miles covering 92 villages was acquired. See also the *Orissa Extraordinary Gazette Notification*, 22 February 1954.
11. *Memorandum of Rourkela Displaced Persons Welfare Committee* to the President of India, 3 February 1959.
12. Leaflet circulated by Rourkela Displaced Persons Committee, Jhirpani, Rourkela, 25 June 1992.
13. See the representation of Nagra Mukti Sangathan to Orissa Chief Minister dated 25 May 1982.

14. *Memorandum*, submitted by Adivasi and Harijan Youth Welfare Association of Rourkela to Chief Minister Orissa dated 21 September 1992.
15. *Memorandum* of Hirakhand Nagarik Parishad, Sambalpur, submitted to Governor of Orissa dated Sambalpur the 7th January 1992.
16. *Joint Memorandum*, submitted to Information and Broadcasting Minister by "Paschim Orissa Yuba Ekta Parishad", "Paschim Orissa Krushak Sangathan" and "Sambalpur Artist Forum", 7 April 1990.
17. See, *Orissa Police Records*, DIB No.5374, dated 4 September 1991, Sambalpur Headquarters.
18. *Orissa Police Records*, 7 September 1991.
19. See *Letter of Orissa High Court*, No.4994 dated 20 November 1959 to Government of Orissa.
20. See the Letter of Registrar, Orissa High Court, dated 5 November 1979, No.86661, XXX-7 to the Secretary to Government of Orissa, Home Department, Bhubaneswar.
21. The Bolangir Bar Association did not join the campaign launched by Sambalpur Bar Association because the latter wanted to have the circuit sitting of the High Court at Sambalpur. See for details, the Annexures of the *Memorandum of the Action Committee*, Sambalpur Bar Association to the Prime Minister of India dated 18 December 1991.
22. Letter of Biju Patnaik, leader of opposition, OLA, No.459 dated 15 March 1989 to President, Sambalpur Bar Association.
23. *Chief Minister's Letter No.7309*, dated 22 December 1990 to the Honourable Chief Justice of Orissa High Court.
24. *Representation* of the MLAs from western Orissa to the Orissa Chief Minister dated 23 March 1990.
25. See the Letter of the Secretary to Government of Orissa, Home Deptt., Bhubaneswar to the Registrar, Orissa High Court, Cuttack No.802-89, dated 11 December 1990.
26. T.K. Oommen, "Insiders and Outsiders in India: Primordial Collectivism and Cultural Pluralism in Nation-Building", *International Sociology*, Vol.1(1), 1986, p.67.
27. See the Leaflet of Western Orissa Sanskrutika Parishad, 27 August 1982.

28. Scholars like S.N. Bohidar, Prayagdutta Joshi, Manglu Charan Biswal, P.K. Padhee, N.P. Guru and others wrote prolificly on the distinct status of Sambalpuri language. See for details, S.N. Bohidar, "Sambalpuri Bhasare Dwanda Samasa" (Oriya), *Saptarshi*, Vol.1(2), 1972, pp.19-20; P.D. Joshi, "Koshal Anchalra Lok Bhasa" (Oriya), *Saptarshi*, Vol.10(6), pp.15-19; M.C. Biswal, "Sambalpuri Upa Bhasa" (Oriya), *Saptarshi*, Vol.8(3), 1974, pp.70-73; M.K. Churia, "Paschimaanchaliya Upabhasare Bibhakti Pratyayara Rupatatwa" (Oriya), *Saptarshi*, Vol.13(10), 1984, pp.26-33; P.K. Padhee, "Sambalpuri Bhasara Ketoti Baishistya" (Oriya), *Saptarshi*, Vol.11(5), 1982, pp.12-16.
29. On literature development, see B.S. Pradhan, *Purnakalia Lok*, Tarun Sahitya Sansad, Sambalpur, 1980; Lala Raghunandan Saideo, *Purnahuti*, Oriya Sanskrutika Samaj, Sambalpur, 1981.
30. *Annual Plan Report, 1989-90*, Government of Orissa, Planning and Coordination Department, Bhubaneswar.
31. See P.K. Das, "Upabhasa Adhyayana Kshetrare Paschimanchalia Odiya Upabhasa" (Oriya), *Saptarshi*, Vol.11(5), 1982, pp.5-11.
32. See Gopabandhu Rath, *Paschim Odissara Kathita Bhasa* (Oriya), Orissa Sahtiya Academy, Bhubaneswar, 1988.
33. See the letter of Ashok Panda, Advocate, Supreme Court to Prof. Rajni Kothari, Member, Planning Commission, New Delhi, 4 April 1990.
34. *Ibid.*
35. Binod Kumar Pati, *Autonomous Development Council for Western Orissa*, Pamphlet, Sambalpur, N.D.
36. *Ibid.*
37. See the *Draft Constitution of the Western Orissa Autonomous Development Council*, prepared by Prafulla Kumar Pati, dated Sambalpur the 3rd April 1995.
38. *Ibid.*
39. *Ibid.*
40. *Ibid.*
41. *The Samaj* (Oriya daily), 14 October 1972.
42. *Kosala* (Oriya weekly), 11 October 1972 and 21 October 1972.
43. See, Muralidhar Panda, *Orissa Mantrimandal 'O' Purbatana Garjat* (Oriya), Bolangir, 1972; also see his booklet, *Abahelitara Pantha*

Ka'an? (Oriya), Patnagarh, 1977. Complaining against the parochial attitude of the state leadership, Panda in this booklet advocated for bifurcation of the state into two Oriya-speaking states on the basis of regional affiliation. It further stated that linguistic unity and uniformity should not be the only principle in carving out states in India. States can be created on the basis of regional identity and for the development of a backward region. This is because unequal treatment is always disadvantageous to the weaker side.

44. See Koshali, *Whither Koshal*?, Bolangir, 1946, pp.24-26.
45. See the pamphlet, *Formation of Hirakhand or Koshal Province*, Bolangir, 1933, pp.11-13; Also see the pamphlet, Koshal Sangh, *Koshal Tract*, Bolangir, 1946. It was pleaded at that time that if all areas with the same language should be brought under one administration, then all Hindi-speaking regions in India should be joined together to form one provincial unit.
46. The Map of the proposed Koshal state was prepared by Koshal activists at the Paikmal meeting on 30 October 1990. The proposed state covers an area of 73,480 sq. km. and includes the five western Orissa districts of Bolangir, Kalahandi, Phulbani, Sambalpur and Sundargarh and the Athamallik subdivision of Dhenkanal district and Phuljhar and Bindra-Nawagarh of Madhya Pradesh (now in Chhatisgarh).
47. See the *Rudra Aawhaan* (Oriya weekly), Bolangir, 19 November 1990.
48. Interview with P.R. Dubey, the President of Koshal Party.
49. See the pamphlet, *Why Separate Koshal State*?, issued by Koshal Liberation Front dated 15 January 1991.
50. Leaflet, *Swatantra Koshal Pradesh Kahinki*? (Oriya), Koshal Liberation Front, dated 1 November 1991.
51. Interview with P.R. Dubey, President, the Koshal Party.
52. See the *Resolutions of First Koshal Sammilani*, dated 29 March 1992.
53. *Ibid*.
54. See the *Resolutions of Second Koshal Sammilani*, dated 4 April 1993. It may be noted here that from 1 April 1993 the number of districts in Orissa rose from 13 to 27 and subsequently to 30.

Consequently, the number of western Orissa districts gone up from 5 to 11 and that of the coastal districts from 4 to 11. As a matter of fact, these new districts formed the subdivisions in the former undivided districts. In some cases new districts are carved out by joining two or more subdivisions, and in some cases bigger subdivisions are organised into new districts. Following the reorganisation of districts, the Koshal Sammelani included the western districts of Sundargarh, Sambalpur, Bargarh, Jharsuguda, Deogarh, Bolangir, Suvarnapur, Kalahandi, Nuwapara, Boudh and Khandhmals in their proposed Koshal state.

55. *Ibid.*
56. *Ibid.*
57. See N. Senapati and B. Mohanty, *Orissa District Gazetteers, Sambalpur*, Cuttack, 1971, p.53.
58. See Herman Kulke, "Early State Formation and Royal Legitimisation in late Ancient Orissa", in M.N. Das (ed.), *Sidelights on History and Culture of Orissa*, Cuttack, 1977, p.258.
59. On Ramai Deo see L.E.B. Cobden-Ramsay, *Bengal District Gazetteers, Feudatory States of Orissa, 'Patna State'*, Calcutta, 1910, pp.281-303.
60. See J.K. Sahu, "Historical Value of Jayachandrika", *Orissa Historical Research Journal*, Vol.XV, Nos.3&4, p.38.
61. S.P. Das, *Sambalpur Itihas* (Oriya), Sambalpur, 1962; J.P. Singh Deo, "Veer Surendra Sai Was Direct Descendant of Manik Rai", *Souvenir Oriya Sankrutika Samaj*, Sambalpur, 1984, pp.10-15.
62. As far as distinct linguistic identity is concerned there exists intra-regional differences in western Orissa. The people of Sambalpur district favour the name 'Sambalpuri'; whereas the people of Bolangir and Kalahandi districts prefer the 'Koshali' nomenclature.
63. See P.D. Joshi, "Koshali Bhasa (Oriya)", *Saptarshi*, Vol.II(1), 1982, pp.19-21; "Swatantra Koshali Bhasa", *Saptarshi*, Vol.12(11), 1983, pp.1-6; "Swatantra Koshali Bhasa (Oriya)", *Saptarshi*, Vol.13(9), 1984, pp.1-10; and S.N. Bohidar, "Sambalpuri Bhasare Dwanda Samasa", *Saptarshi*, Vol.1(2), 1972, pp.19-23.
64. P.D. Joshi, *op. cit.*
65. See P.D. Joshi, "Hai Koshali Bhasa (Koshali)", *Koshal Bharti*, Vol.1(1), 1987, pp.1-10.

66. See L.P. Nayak, "Sambalpuri 'O' Chattisgarhi Bhasayi Sankramita Kshetrara Boli Manankara Tulanatmaka Rupatatwika Adhyayana" (Oriya), *Saptarshi*, Vol.14(2), 1985, pp.22-28.
67. K.S. Singh, "Tribal Identity Movements based on Script and Language", *Man in India*, Vol.62(3), 1982, pp.234-45.
68. P.D. Joshi, "Koshali Lipi Samasya Bichar" (Koshali), *Hame Koshali Hamar Bhasa Koshali* (ed.), N. Panigrahi, Sambalpur, 1992, pp.30-33.
69. L.P. Nayak, "Koshali Bhasa Aur Sanskriti: Aaj Ke Paripreksshi Mein" (Devnagari), *Koshal Bharati*, Khariar, 1987, pp.29-32. It may be noted that alphabets are specific to a particular language but script can be used by many languages.
70. See the Memorandum submitted to the President of India by Koshal Party for the recognition of Koshali language as an official language in Orissa, published in N. Panigrahi (ed.), *Hame Koshali, Hamar Bhasa Koshali* (Koshali), Sambalpur, 1992, pp.44-49.
71. See Koshal Bharti, *op. cit.*; *Sambalpuri Kabita Sankalana*,Sambalpuri Lekhak Sangha, Sambalpur, 1986.
72. See Memorandum submitted to President published in *Koshal Bharti, op. cit.*
73. "Simmering Discontent in West Orissa", *The Statesman*, 11 August 1991.
74. See, *The Memorandum* submitted to the President of India by Koshal Sammelani for the formation of Koshal State, Sambalpur, 1993.
75. *Ibid.*
76. *Ibid.*
77. *Ibid.*
78. *Ibid.*
79. *Ibid.*
80. *Ibid.*
81. See the Leaflet issued by "Koshal Bhumi Mukti Sangathan", Daldalipada, Kshetrajpur, Sambalpur, N.D. Also its leaflet "Pruthak Koshal Rajya Dabi", Sambalpur, dated 8 May 1998.
82. See Interview of Sibasankar Bagh in *Madhujyoti* (Oriya weekly) No.12, Wednesday, 10 December 1997.
83. Koshal Bhumi Mukti Sangathan leaflet, *op. cit.*

84. *Ibid.*
85. See *Ganabarta* (Oriya weekly), 28 February 1989; *Sunday*, 23-29 September 1990; *Bolangir Katha* (Oriya weekly), 12 December 1990.

8

Conclusion

In the preceding pages the phenomena of nationalism and regionalism have been analysed in the empirical situation of Orissa within the multicultural context of India. In the course of the analysis attention has been mainly focused on the following important questions. In which sense of the term the Oriyas constitute a nation and the movement launched by them to preserve their identity qualifies for the label of nationalism given the fact that these notions in India are exclusively identified with Indian state and Indian identity? Another pertinent question relates to the conditions under which nationalism and regionalism, as sentiment or as movement, emerges and thrives in a multicultural state or a part thereof. The differing levels of competing identities situated in a multicultural set-up such as India are also highlighted in the course of the study.

To understand the content and goal of Oriya nationalism and to underscore the critical variables of regionalism in Orissa the study begins with a conceptual clarification on such key terms as nation, nationalism and regionalism. It has been noticed that scholars confuse nationalism with regionalism and more often than not dub the former as regional movement in multicultural and/or multi-national contexts. To allay such confusion, it has been made amply clear in this study that nationalism results from a sense of cultural deprivation, real or perceived, leading to 'culturocide' in nationality terms. Assertion of cultural identity thrives on the concept of homeland, distinct language and shared history which may lead to a political motivation for self-rule in either independent or autonomous sense. That is, nationalism as a political movement may not always be sovereign-state-seeking in character.

On the other hand, regionalism emanates from a sense of relative material deprivation accruing from socio-economic disparities and political inequality. Regional identity is invariably anchored to a geographical area and it engulfs a people who may belong to a section/portion of the same nation/nationality or a group having minor regional, cultural and dialectal differences. A national identity is invoked in the case of a national movement; while a regional movement stresses upon a regional identity.

The basic argument made in this study is that nation and state need not and should not be viewed as coterminous terms. A state by definition and implication is a sovereign body; whereas sovereignty is not an essential attribute of nation. State and nation can be combined in a variety of ways. The experience of many non-European countries substantiates this point beyond doubt.

By and large, in most parts of Europe nations emerged as culture-congruent sovereign states. But, in several non-European countries, particularly the countries of Asia, Africa and Latin America, nation acquired a sovereign-political connotation at the macro-political level and a primordial-cultural form at the regional-cultural level. Unlike Europe, many distinct territorially rooted cultural communities in Asia, Africa and Latin America did not tend to acquire their own states but preferred to retain their distinct cultural identities inside a sovereign federal state. Even in Europe, in the case of the U.K., distinct nationalities like the Scots and the Welsh prefer to be a part of the common British state.

Hence, going by the experience of several multicultural and multi-national countries of the world, it is suggested that nation can be conceptualised either in political terms using a set of political variables such as sovereignty, common citizenship and common legal-administrative system, or in cultural terms using a set of socio-cultural criteria such as cultural homogeneity, shared history and a distinct language, territory being common to both. Needless to say, the former represents the sovereign macro-political unit, and the latter represents the multiple nationalities contained in the macro unit. In other words, the macro unit is viewed as nation in political terms and the regional-cultural units are viewed as nations in cultural terms.

It is further suggested that a nation is essentially a territorially rooted cultural community which tends to have a politically self-ruling unit. As a matter of fact, the potentiality for political self-rule is significant in the understanding of nation, but political self-rule can be realised either in independent or autonomous terms. Hence, the sovereignty criterion should not be used as an essential condition in the understanding of nation. A nation can exist without being endowed with sovereign statehood and this variety of nations is widely referred to as cultural nations or nations without states. It is in this latter sense that the Oriya people constitute a nation vis-a-vis the broader Indian nation.

Given this double connotation of nation, in many multicultural and/or multi-national countries nationalism is also understood in a dual manner. Consequently, two broad varieties of nationalism are found in these countries: (a) nationalism seeking sovereign states; and (b) nationalism seeking provincial states. Analytically, the former may be referred to as political nationalism and the latter as regional cultural nationalism. The former resulted from a unified political articulation and is interwoven with sovereignty, the most important pre-requisite of the political content of nation. The latter emerged from the cultural view of nation and it basically aimed at protection of cultural distinctiveness within the provisions of self-determination in either independent or autonomous terms. In most of the instances these cultural nationalisms pursued the goal of self-determination in provincial terms within a common sovereign state. These two varieties of nationalism were found in several multicultural and/or multi-national countries in colonial times and they continue to exist in such countries even in the postcolonial and contemporary times.

In such a scenario, it is quite unlikely that an overarching 'terminal' loyalty to the common state is going to emerge in several ex-colonial multicultural and/or multi-national countries. What is emerging, on the contrary, is a set of multiple cultural nations/ nationalities coexisting under a common state or civil-political identity thereby allowing two levels of loyalties, a dual notion of identity, a dual conception of nationality and finally double interpretation of nationalism. This shows that from its birth in Western Europe to the time it flourished in several ex-colonial multicultural or multi-national countries, nationalism underwent a metamorphic transformation and assumed different connotation at different contexts in a single multicultural country.

It follows, then, that nationalism in multicultural and/or multi-national countries cannot be singularly equated with one form of loyalty to the sovereign nation-state. Further, because of the different connotation and contextualisation of nationalism, the sole interpretation of nationalism as a sovereign-state-seeking political movement (as in the case of most parts of Europe) does not hold good in the case of multicultural and/or multi-national countries of Asia, Africa and Latin America. Besides being a political movement for sovereignty, nationalism in such countries is also seen as a movement for retention of cultural identity within a denoted cultural 'homeland'.

It is made clear in this study that the concept of nation – political or cultural – is central to nationalism. As an ideology, or as a movement, all nationalisms underline the principle of co-terminality between culture and polity. In our opinion, this co-terminality between cultural and political unit (i.e. governance unit) can be attained in independent or in autonomous terms. In other words, nationalism may be directed at achieving a culture-congruent sovereign state or culture-congruent a provincial state within a larger sovereign state. Our basic contention is that while political nationalism invariably aims at sovereign state, the goal of regional cultural nationalism may vary from levels of autonomy to provincial self-rule to complete independence. Both 'sovereign-state seeking' and 'provincial-state seeking' nationalisms are found in concrete empirical situations in different parts of the world.

In India, regional cultural nationalism assumes the form of irredentist, autonomist, separatist and secessionist movements. The irredentist type aims at unification of vivisected territories of a cultural nation under a provincial roof. The autonomist and separatist types also desire to protect cultural-linguistic identity in a provincial boundary. But the secessionist type strives to seek a sovereign state of its own and in that case it turns into political nationalism.

The emergence of Oriya national movement under British colonialism is a telling example of regional cultural nationalism in colonial India. It has been noted in chapter four that nationalism in British Orissa emerged to protect and preserve Oriya cultural-linguistic identity within the parameters of a provincial boundary in multicultural India. There is no denying that, the Oriya people at the macro level embraced the common anti-colonial nationalist struggle for India's independence. But at the same time they indulged in nationalist mobilisation to safeguard their distinct cultural identity vis-à-vis other cultural communities in India. Under the British colonial rule, the Oriyas were doubly deprived as their territory was apportioned between different administrative units. On the one hand, they faced cultural deprivation in nationality terms as outsiders, especially the Bengalis, posed considerable threats to their linguistic identity. On the other, they faced material deprivation as the outsiders mostly occupied the jobs in their land under colonial administration.

In princely Orissa, however, there was no apparent external threat to Oriya language and culture. Nationalism here resulted from an extreme material deprivation because of massive socio-economic exploitation unleashed by the native feudal rulers. Nonetheless, there was an anticipated danger of losing Oriya identity had these Oriya territories been integrated to any non-Oriya speaking provincial unit, e.g. the Eastern States Union. Importantly, on both occasions, i.e., formation of Orissa province in 1936 and integration of princely states with Orissa province in 1948-49, the common Oriya language had united all sections of Oriyas for a united Orissa province.

The Oriya experience shows that the major hypotheses proposed in the study have been proved correct. For example, the existence of several cultural nations such as Oriyas, Bengalis, Telugus and Tamils under Bengal and Madras Presidencies in British times resulted in nationalistic mobilisation by the deprived Oriyas. The Oriya national movement led to a quest for united

Orissa as the Oriyas, who are distinct both by objective and subjective criteria, faced threat to their language and culture from the dominant Bengali nationality. The projection of Bengali language and culture as superior and the denial of distinct identity to Oriya language and culture created disaffection among the Oriyas.

But the Oriya national movement was not the only example of regional cultural nationalism in India. Several such examples are available in colonial as well as independent India. The first spark of cultural nationalism in India came in the wake of Bengal partition in 1905. This was followed by the rise of national consciousness among the Oriyas, the Telugus, the Sindhis, the Kannadigas, etc. The reunion of Bengal in 1911 and the formation Orissa and Sind provinces in 1936 marked the beginning of regional cultural nationalism seeking provincial states in India.

After independence, India faced the greatest task of maintaining her territorial unity and integrity by accommodating the numerous diverse cultural nationalities thriving within her soil. The political map of independent India retained several multi-lingual provinces such as Bombay, Madras, Punjab, Assam and a few larger princely states such as Hyderabad, Mysore, Patiala and East Punjab States Union (PEPSU), etc. This apart, some portions of different nationalities were retained in different administrative units. It is well known that the British through different constitutional reforms had provided the basic framework of India as union of autonomous provinces. The government of independent India adopted the same political framework and hence the regional cultural nationalisms seeking separate provinces gathered momentum in the post independent period. The Indian political leadership mainly accommodated people's demand for separate provinces within the framework of the Indian Constitution. The political environment in India had changed after independence. The establishment of a federal democratic polity, introduction of electoral politics and the emphasis on self-governance contributed to a great extent to the strengthening of regional cultural nationalism in different parts of India. The Constitution of India in fact acknowledged and established cultural pluralism and hence cultural nationalism by enlisting originally fourteen major Indian languages in the Eighth Schedule under Article 344(i) and 351. Subsequently, the number rose to twenty-two as Sindhi (in 1967), Konkani, Nepali and Manipuri (in 1992), Maithili, Santhali, Dogri and Bodo (in 2003) were added to the Schedule. In the changed political atmosphere, people having distinct linguistic-cultural identity increasingly became desirous of distinct status in terms of having a separate province and inclusion of their languages in the Eighth Schedule. The rationale behind these demands is maintenance of cultural distinctiveness within the provision of self-rule inside the Indian Union.

The rise of Telugu nationalism calling for a separate Telugu province was the first notable case of regional cultural nationalism in independent India. Despite being the largest linguistic community in the erstwhile composite Madras Presidency, the Telugus felt deprived vis-à-vis the dominant Tamils ever since the colonial days. In the case of Telugus there was no serious threat to language and culture as such, but they were dominated socio-economically and politically by the Tamils. The Telugu nationalism bears some similarities with Oriya nationalism. In both the cases, a portion of the homeland of the concerned nationality, i.e. Telangana in the case of the Telugu nationality and western Orissa in the case of the Oriya nationality remained under the control of the former princely areas. As a result, in both the cases, nationalist mobilisation spread to those erstwhile princely areas so as to include them under the separate provinces for Oriya and Telugu people, respectively. The Telugu cultural nationalism finally led to the establishment of the Andhra province in 1953.

After the formation of Andhra province, regional nationalist aspirations sprang up in several parts of India. The situation went to such unprecedented heights that the Indian central leadership had finally accepted linguistic-cultural homogeneity as the chief basis of provincial reorganisation. The first significant step to realise this end was taken when the States Reorganisation Commission (SRC) was set up in 1953. The SRC followed four broad principles in the matter of provincial reorganisation: (a) preservation and strengthening of the unity and integrity of India; (b) linguistic and cultural homogeneity; (c) financial, economic and administrative viability; and (d) successful working of the national plan. The SRC recommended the formation of sixteen states and three union territories. But the States Reorganisation Act of 1956 created fourteen states and six union territories in the Indian Union.

The provincial reorganisation of 1956 in India was widely known as 'linguistic reorganisation'. However, on a closer look one finds that the provincial reorganisation in 1956 created some linguistic provinces such as Kerala, Karnataka and Tamil Nadu, while some other provinces like Orissa, Bengal, Bihar and Uttar Pradesh preceded the reorganisation. The major Hindi-speaking provinces of Bihar, Madhya Pradesh, Uttar Pradesh and Rajasthan were formed following historical and geopolitical reasons. The 1956 reorganisation was also carried out on the basis of some constitutionally rcognised scheduled Indian languages. The numerous non-scheduled languages were left out of the scheme of reorganisation at that time. It may be noted that the1991 Census of India reported 1,576 languages and mother tongues which were further grouped into 114 languages following appropriate linguistic methods. Of these, twenty-two languages are recorded in the Indian Constitution as scheduled languages and rest ninety-two remained as non-scheduled languages. Of course, this is not to say, that as many provinces should be formed for as many languages spoken in India. Nevertheless, the people with a distinct language, sizeable numerical strength and a specific cultural homeland would stand a better chance for having a separate province of their own. Further going by the linguistic principle the regions with distinct languages such Maithili, Bhojpuri, Awadhi, Bundelkhandi, Santhali, Coorgi Dogri, etc., should have been constituted into separate provinces. Again, some scheduled languages are identified with two or more provinces, whereas some languages like Maithili, Santhali, Bodo and Dogri, although spoken in distinct regions, are not identified with specific provinces of their own. Besides, the identification of a scheduled language with a particular province in India has reduced many languages as minority languages or dialects. Several tribal languages are also left out of the scope of the Constitution even though they are spoken by quite a large number of people.

Thus, the scheme of reorganisation adopted in 1956 only benefited the mainstream nationalities; the smaller and peripheral nationalities largely remained outside the purview of the reoganisation.

At the time of 1956 reoganisation, Bombay and Punjab were kept as bilingual provinces and Assam was retained as multi-lingual province notwithstanding people's demand to divide them into separate provinces. In the case of bilingual Bombay province the two principal linguistic communities, namely, the Marathis and the Gujaratis, were pitted against each other. The Samyukta Maharashtra Movement, which symbolised Marathi national consciousness against the cumulative domination of the Gujaratis, rejected the idea of bilingual Bombay and fought tooth and knell for the formation of a separate Marathi-speaking province. Finally, the bilingual province of Bombay was divided in 1960 to form the new provinces of Maharashtra and Gujarat on linguistic basis to satisfy the Marathi and the Gujarati nationalist aspirations. The 1956 reorganisation and later the formation of Maharashtra and Gujarat in 1960 have legitimised language as an important ingredient of regional cultural nationalism and hence basis for formation of province in the Indian polity. But in course of time, due to tremendous popular pressure the Indian government has accepted some other ingredients of cultural nationalism such as religion (in somewhat covert manner), tribe and region as bases of provincial reoganisation in India.

It is popularly known that free India has adopted secularism as the basic foundation of her liberal-democratic polity and society. Keeping the secular policy in view, the Indian political leadership disapproves formation of separate provinces based exclusively on regional religious nationalist aspiration. Yet, instances of cultural nationalism using religious identities and the Indian leadership acceding, somewhat tacitly, to the demands of separate province formation on the basis of linguistic-cum-religious identity or tribal-cum-religious identity are significantly found in India. For example, the Sikh-Punjabi nationalism led to the formation of the province of Punjab in 1966; and the nationalistic mobilisation by the Christian tribes of Naga, Garo, Khasi, Jaintia and Mizo led to the formation of the provinces of Nagaland, Meghalaya and Mizoram in 1963,1972 and 1987, respectively.

After the partition of India, the Sikh-Punjabis, who mainly concentrated in the north-west part of the erstwhile Indian Punjab province, carefully used selective religious symbols such as *'kesh'* (unshorn hair), *'kachha'* (underwear), *'Kangi'* (comb), *'Kara'* (iron bangle) and *'Kripan'* (sword) to differentiate themselves from the Punjabi-Hindus and define their national identity in religious terms. Finally, after a prolonged movement, the Sikh-Punjabis were able to get a separate Punjab province for them. But in granting the formation of the Punjab province and later the provinces of Nagaland, Meghalaya and Mizoram, the Indian leadership acknowledged religious basis of regional cultural nationalism to some extent. Further, recently the proposal for the trifurcation of the state of Jammu & Kashmir is raised by several people. As per this proposal, the state should be reorganised into the provinces of Jammu, Kashmir and Ladakh. If this reoganisation is carried out, the proposed provinces will definitely have specific religious identities apart form the linguistic and tribal identities of the people. Incidentally, the religion-based cultural nationalism in India invariably develops secessionist goal. For example, the supporters of the Khalistan nationalism never accepted the Punjab province, they strongly press for the sovereign Sikh state. The Nagas also continuously demand for the formation of sovereign Naga state.

The nationalistic mobilisations by several communities in Northeast India are some of the other after leading examples of regional cultural nationalism in India. Among the Assamese people in Northeast India cultural nationalism emerged in the context of the imminent danger to Assamiya national identity posed by the Bengali migrants in the initial period and the foreigners and the illegal infiltrators later. Assamese national consciousness did not emerge to achieve a separate province for Assamese people; it was rather directed at safeguarding Assamese nationality from the onslaught of Bengali expansionism and the regular incursions by the illegal foreign infiltrators. The Assamese faced stiff resistance from the Bengalis, especially in the Barak valley, when Assamese language was declared as the official language of the state in 1960 and as the medium of instruction in 1972. Like the Oriyas, the Assamese too faced both cultural and material deprivation because of Bengali domination.

However, in the 1980s, the Assamese nationalism turned more economic in orientation and centered more on the issue of nativism, that is, local reaction against the economic exploitation of Assam by the outsiders and illegal foreign infiltrators. In the 1980s, two regional organisations, the All Assam Students Union (AASU) and the All Assam Gana Sangram Parishad (AAGSP), launched the most powerful Assamese nationalist movement against the foreigners and illegal migrants. The agitators demanded for the detection and immediate deportation of the illegal foreign migrants from Assam as they were causing socio-economic imbalance and affecting regional electoral politics of the state. After a widespread violent agitation for a pretty long time, the Assam accord was finally signed between ASSU and the Government of India in 1985. The accord prescribed for the detection and deportation of the illegal infiltrators. Following the accord AAGSP entered into the state politics under its new name Asom Gana Parishad (AGP) and the AGP continued to be a powerful political force in Assam ever since. Subsequently, secessionist ideology has crept into Assamese nationalism. The secessionist plank was mainly projected by a militant organisation, the United Liberation Front of Asom (ULFA). In sharp contrast to the autonomist nationalism of ASSU-AGP, the ULFA pursues clearly secessionist nationalism and presses for the constitution of a sovereign state of Assam.

Articulation of nationalism among several tribes is also available in various parts of India. Tribal nationalism mainly emerges in India on the basis of common tribal identity, common culture and common territorial bonds. Several tribes in India have also been able to define their nationality in terms of their distinct language as well as tribal identity. Tribal nationalism mostly emerged in India to protect the tribal communities from the cumulative domination of the non-tribal and other distinct tribal people. In Northeast India, for example, nationalism among some tribal communities rose in protest against the introduction of the Assam State Language Bill of 1960, which declared Assamese as the official language of the erstwhile multi-lingual state of Assam. Fearing Assamese cultural domination, the Khasi, Garo and Jaintia tribes of the erstwhile hill districts of Assam constituted the All Party Hill Leaders' Conference and demanded for the formation of a separate province for them inside the Indian Union. Responding to the hill people's agitation in erstwhile Assam, the Government of India decided to go for a major territorial reorganisation of Northeast India. The Northeastern Reorganisation Act was passed in 1971 and a new province of Meghalaya comprising the Khasi-Jaintia and the Garo Hills districts of Assam was created; the same year Manipur and Tripura were elevated to full-fledged provincial status and Mizoram and Arunachal Pradesh (formerly NEFA) were made into union territories.

Similarly, the rise of Mizo nationalism led to the formation of the Mizoram province. Initially, Mizo nationalism, under the stewardship of the insurgent outfit Mizo National Front (MNF), harped vociferously on the idea of a sovereign Mizo state, but with passage of time its trajectory changed and it accepted self-determination in provincial statehood terms within India. The province of Mizoram was created following the Rajiv-Laldenga accord in 1986. With the formation of Mizoram province in Northeast India, the MNF rebels gave up arms and joined the state electoral politics. Henceforth, MNF as a regional political party identifies itself with Mizo nationalist sentiment and works for the development of the Mizo tribe.

The Naga tribes, however, have not been able to accept so far the Indian political identity and the Indian nation-state. The radical elements of Naga nationalism always persisted with the idea of secessionism and formation of an independent Naga state. In the case of the diverse Naga tribes, nationalism is articulated on the basis of a common Naga tribal identity, a traditional Naga 'homeland', shared historical experience and a spoken lingua-franca called Nagamese. The leadership of Naga tribes from the beginning rejected the provisions of the Sixth Schedule of the Indian Constitution and overtly mobilised for creation of sovereign Naga state soon after the independence of India. Under the aegis of the Naga National Council (NNC) and the leadership of Angami Naga leader A. Zapu Phizo an armed rebellion for Naga independence was launched in 1949. At the time of the 1956 states reorganisation, the Naga territories were not touched. As a result, the Naga armed rebellion intensified further.

To accommodate Naga nationalist aspiration, finally the Indian government constituted the province of Nagaland in 1963. Nagaland became the first tribal province in independent India, but the radical Nagas rejected the idea of self-determination for the Naga tribes in provincial terms. Subsequently, the National Socialist Council of Nagaland (NSCN) was formed in 1980 to continue the armed struggle for Naga independence. Later, the NSCN was split into two factions: the NSCN-IM, led by Th. Muivah and Isak Swe, and the NSCN-K, led by S. S. Khaplang. Both the factions of NSCN insist on the sovereignty issue of the Nagas and the NSCN-IM deliberately uses the word 'Nagalim' to cover the entire Naga inhabited areas in India and Myanmar. But the Indian government categorically rejects the sovereignty issue and is ready to solve the problem of Naga nationality within the territorial boundary and the constitutional framework of India. The Naga nationalism combines the traits of both secessionist and irredentist nationalism. Its secessionist ideology insists on secession of Naga territories from India and its irredentist goal highlights the unification of all the Naga inhabited areas in India and Myanmar under the sovereign state of Nagalim.

Some other tribes in the Northeast such as the Bodos, the Karbis, the Kukis, the Rabhas, the Reangs, the Hmars, etc., and the numerically dominant Bengali people of the Cachar region of Assam also persist with their separatist cultural nationalism and the quest for 'homeland'. For example, since 1986, the Bodos, a Tibeto-Burman tribal group living in the north-west parts of Assam, clamoured for a separate province of Bodoland to save the Bodo language and culture from the domination of the majority Assamese nationality and the outsiders living in the Bodo areas. The creation of Bodo Autonomous Council (BAC) in 1993 and later the establishment of the contiguous unit of the Bodoland Territorial Council (BTC) in 2005 were steps taken to safeguard the regional interests of the Bodo nationality to some extent. But a militant section of the Bodos disapproves the formation of BTC; this section clearly advocates for the constitution of a sovereign Bodoland state.

Like the Bodos, the Garo (A'chik) tribes in Meghalaya and the Reang tribe in Mizoram are also engaged in nationalist mobilisations for the preservation of their respective tribal-national identity. The Reang nationalism strongly presses for the recognition of the Reang (Bru) cultural-national identity and calls for protection of the Hindu Reangs from the oppression of the Christian Mizo tribes. The Reang (Bru) nationalism has been demanding an autonomous district council for the Reang tribe within the province of Mizoram. In Meghalaya, the A'chik Matgrik Liberation Army (AMLA) and the A'chik National Volunteer Council (ANVC) spearhead the Garo (A'chik) nationalist movement to separate the Garo hills districts from Meghalaya and establish an independent Garoland (A'chikland) state covering the Garo tribe inhabited areas in India and Bangladesh. Subsequently, the ANVC changed the stand of Garo (A'chik) nationalism and demanded for the constitution of a Garo (A'chik) homeland comprising the present Garo hills districts of Meghalaya and the adjoining Garo inhabited areas in some parts of the border districts in Assam. Similarly, the Hynniewtrep National Liberation Council (HNLC) representing the Khasi tribe in Meghalaya wishes to free the Khasi (Hynniewtrep) nation from India and establish a 'Bri Hynniewtrep', i.e., a sovereign Khasi state comprising the Khasi inhabited areas in Meghalaya and the adjoining areas.

In Manipur, secessionist nationalism has been pursued by various sections of the people since India's independence. The province of Manipur in Northeast India represents ethnically and culturally one of the most heterogeneous places in India. Its territory is mainly divided into the Meitei (Manipuri) dominated Imphal valley and the Naga and Kuki tribes dominated hill areas. Manipur remained a principality in colonial times and it became a union territory in 1956. Following the large-scale territorial reorganisation in Northeast India in 1972, it became a full-fledged province in the Indian Union. Some sections of the people in Manipur, however, resented the accession of Manipur with India. Besides, there exists in Manipur continuous ethnic clashes between the dominant Meitei community, who constitute little more than 50 per cent of the total population, and the Naga and Kuki tribes, who form nearly 40 percent of the population. All these factors motivated several insurgent organisations representing the interests of the principal Meitei community in Manipur to indulge in secessionist nationalism calling for the separation of Manipur from India and establishment of the sovereign Manipur (Kangleipak) state. One such leading insurgent organisation in Manipur, the United National Liberation Front (UNLF), even demands a plebiscite under United Nations supervision on the issue of Manipur's sovereignty. On the other hand, the Naga tribes are fighting for inclusion of the Naga inhabited areas of Manipur in the proposed 'Greater Nagaland' demand made recently by the NSCN-IM Naga leaders. The Kuki militant tribals also press for the establishment of sovereign Kuki nation-state comprising parts of Manipur and Mizoram. Apart from these nationalist movements, the United People's Democratic Solidarity (UPDS), which consists of two secessionist outfits: the Karbi National Volunteers (KNV) and the Karbi People's Front (KPF), seeks the secession of the Karbi nation located in the Karbi-Anglong and North Cachar Hills districts of Assam.

The above appraisal of regional nationalist movements shows that both varieties of nationalism: nationalism seeking independent state and nationalism seeking provincial state are seen in Northeast India. In other words, both autonomist and secessionist nationalisms are found in Northeast India. But as a matter fact, most of the cultural nationality groups in Northeast India are developing the desire for political independence from the Indian Union. This may be due to the fact that Northeast India is strategically located and connected to international boundary on three sides.

In the case of the Uttaranchal region of former province of Uttar Pradesh, nationalist aspiration for internal self-determination in provincial terms was articulated by the people on the basis of regional identity, ethnic differences, cultural distinctiveness and historical experiences. Similarly, in the Jharkhand region of the erstwhile Bihar province and in the Chhattisgarh region of former province of Madhya Pradesh, cultural nationalism seeking provincial statehood developed on the basis of common territorial identity, regional economic backwardness, tribal identity and cultural differences and different historical background than the rest of the people.

In western part of India, the tiny province of Goa came into being in 1985 due to the rise of Konkani cultural nationalism spearheaded by the Maharashtrawadi Gomantak Party. The Gorkha National Liberation Front (GNLF) launched popular movements since the 1980s to attain a provincial statehood for the distinct Gorkha-Nepali nationality living in the Darjeeling district and its adjoining areas in the state of West Bengal. To accommodate the Gorkhali-Nepali regional nationalist aspiration, the Indian government created the Gorkhaland Autonomous Hill Council, but the GNLF nationalist leaders are not satisfied with this limited version of the internal self-determination.

Further, the recent demand raised by the supporters of Koshali nationalism for a separate Koshal province in western Orissa brings into limelight another variety of cultural nationalism in India. This variety of cultural nationalism establishes the fact that even in a linguistically homogeneous province like Orissa, nationalism may crystallise from conflict over developmental disparities between regions. The people of the relatively deprived region in this case try to reconstruct their identity in more objective cultural-linguistic terms and not in regional backwardness terms. Once this development takes place, the regional consciousness for developmental gains turns into a regional cultural nationalism calling for protection of the newly constructed nationality.

As far as regionalism in India is concerned, the crux of the problem lies in regional imbalance. But unfortunately, going by the popularly accepted political understanding of nationalism, several cultural nationalisms seeking provincial statehood to protect distinct regional-national identity within the framework of the Indian Union are often viewed as regionalism. But it is profoundly argued in this study that regionalism, as a sentiment or as a movement, largely originates from a feeling of material deprivation resulting from wide-range socio-economic disparities and political disadvantages. Further, regionalism or sub-regionalism differs from regional cultural nationalism in that the former primarily seeks to obtain balanced regional development and equal share in political power and administration; the latter basically seeks protection of distinct regional nationality in autonomous terms. The possibility of a regional movement demanding separate provincial statehood cannot however be ruled out. As already mentioned, recently a few provinces in India were formed primarily on the basis of regional factors.

Most of the states in India show wide socio-economic disparities because of historical, geographic, economic, political and administrative reasons. Historically, India inherited uneven levels of development from colonial administration. India emerged as a single political unit only under the British colonial rule. But for politico-administrative reasons, the British divided India into 'British India' and 'Indian India'; the former was ruled by them directly and the latter was controlled by the Indian princes under British paramount power. The package of modernisation programmes launched by the British brought rapid socio-economic development in the territories under their direct rule. Conversely, under feudal rule the territories in the 'Indian India' lagged far behind in developmental matters. After independence of India, although a good deal of investment through planned development programme was made, 'Indian India' could not keep pace with the already developed 'British India' and hence the regional imbalance perpetuated.

The natural tendency of capitalism to produce uneven development widened the regional gaps further. In addition, the already developed areas produced political elites who not only influenced development decision-making considerably but also remained favourably biased towards their own regions. Hence, in most regional movements the popular cry centers on the demand to have an autonomous decision-making body for developmental purposes in the deprived regions. In other words, deprived and disadvantaged people of several backward regions increasingly support political and administrative decentralisations for removal of regional imbalance in several parts of India.

People of a geographically distinct and socio-culturally different region are likely to develop deep regional discontent if they face socio-economic disadvantage and political discrimination. It is noted in chapter six that barring a few pockets in one or two districts, the remaining areas of western Orissa lag far behind the coastal region in the fields of education, irrigation, agricultural development, road density and urbanisation. In spite of planned development, the historical differences in development between coastal and western regions of Orissa persist more or less.

In the political sphere the people of western Orissa remain as underdogs ever since the British times. The British influence made the coastal Orissa people politically more conscious and advance. Obviously therefore after independence the coastal people controlled the political machinery in the Orissa province. This has resulted in political polarisation along regional lines. Moreover, the participation of the people of western Orissa in government and decision-making is far from satisfactory. Thus, the sense of relative backwardness in socio-economic and political sphere provided the requisite bases for the growth of regionalism in Orissa.

As noted earlier, a regional movement may demand a separate provincial state, but such a demand is necessarily based on regional identity and articulation of relative regional backwardness and not on distinct regional cultural-national identity. In some instances of regionalism in India, however, elements of regional culture and speech are used as reinforcement variables to arouse popular sentiment. A regional movement may also be projected as a cultural national movement. In such a situation the people of the less developed region reconstruct their identity by redefining their cultural-linguistic boundary in clear separatist terms. This is exactly what happenes in western Orissa when a group of separatists recently began to transform the regional articulation against regional imbalance into a cultural-nationalistic mobilisation for a separate Indian province under the banner of 'Koshali nationalism'. It may be recalled that in chapter two we have noted that a national movement may grow from a pre-existing cultural identity or it may be launched for search of such an identity. The emergence of 'Koshali nationalism' in western Orissa falls in the latter category. Here the separatist groups bring cultural deprivation in nationality terms to the forefront. They argue that the material deprivation of the western region continues because of the lack of separate cultural-national identity of the western Orissa people.

Here, the shift in emphasis on identity seems to have been made precisely for two reasons: (a) the socio-economic advantages involved in defining collective identity in cultural-national terms; and (b) distinct language and cultural homogeneity are considered as chief bases of formation of provinces in India.

Like the western Orissa case, instances of prolonged regional movements are also found in other parts of India. For example, the Telangana agitation in north-western Andhra Pradesh broke out on the issue of regional discrimination and backwardness. Like Orissa, the issue here is the domination of Telangana region by the developed coastal Andhra region. Formerly, Telangana belonged to the old Hyderabad state and during the periods of states reorganisation in India in 1956 it was made a part of Andhra Pradesh following the 'Gentlemen's Agreement' which upheld the 'Mulki rule' safeguards in the matters of education, employment and property rights. The agitation flared up following the non-implementation of the 'Mulki rule' safeguards.

In many respects the Telangana movement bears resemblance with regionalism in western Orissa. First, in both instances material deprivation accruing from regional imbalance is attributed as the main cause of the movement. Second, in both cases the backward regions formerly belonged to princely areas and the developed regions experienced the influence of British colonial rule. Naturally, therefore, the pace of development between the two regions differed in both the provinces. Third, the difference in political history of the two regions in both the cases created attitudinal sub-cultures and stereotypes among the respective peoples. Finally, regional differences in day-to-day speech, customs and cultural practices are invoked in both the instances. However, the Telangana regional agitation differs from western Orissa movement in one important respect. That is, in Telangana region backwardness is cited as the chief basis of the demand for separate Telangana province. Whereas, in the case of western Orissa two distinctly separate trends in regional articulation are noticeable: (a) the demand for regional autonomous council for development and (b) the efforts to transform the regional movement to a separatist cultural-nationalistic mobilisation.

Another regional movement which shares some commonalities with that of western Orissa is the Vidarbha movement in Maharashra. The Vidarbha region in the province of Maharashtra as compared to western Maharashtra region is backward socio-economically and politically. Prevalence of low-level of industrial development, poor irrigation and communication facilities ever since colonial times created discontent among the people in the Vidarbha region. The States Reorganisation Commission in its report to the central government in 1955 recommended for the creation of Vidarbha province comprising the Marathi-speaking Nagpur and Berar districts. Despite that, Vidarbha region was made a part of the bilingual Bombay province at the time of states reorganisation in 1956 and then it was merged with the province of Maharashtra formed in 1960. The activists of the separate Vidarbha movement maintain that, despite common linguistic identity with rest of Maharashtra the people of Vidarbha constitute a separate entity based on historical, geographic and economic grounds. The case of Vidarbha again shows that even in a linguistically homogeneous province like that of Maharashtra regional separatism among the people of a deprived region can grow to the extent of demanding separate province on the basis of their regional backwardness. Like Vidarbha, the demands for separate provinces of Vindhyachal and Bundelkhand are also based on the factor of regional backwardness.

It may be noted here that the creation of the provinces of Uttaranchal, Chhatisgrarh and Jharkhand recently in 2000 has established the factor of regional identity and economic backwardness as yet another basis of provincial reorganisation in India in addition to the previously accepted bases of language, tribe and to some extent religion. The states reorganisation in 1956 created fourteen states (provinces) and six union territories in the Indian Union. But by 2000 the number of provinces in India went up to twenty-eight, and demands for the formation of more provinces are constantly made. Thus in India, between 1956 and 2000, i.e., in a span of forty-four years, as many as fourteen new provinces have been formed, in addition to the already existing seven union territories. Looking at the contemporary mobilisations for separate province demands, based on either the factor of distinct cultural nationality or the factor of regional identity and backwardness, it seems the redrawing of the provincial map of India is not complete so far.

It follows that regional cultural nationalism seeking provincial statehood in India is an empirical reality and it cannot be simply wished away at the altar of the larger all-India political nationalism. Even after the formation of so many provinces based on language, tribe and region, still provinces in India retain distinct cultural minorities who demand separate provinces. This apart, demands for separate provinces are also continuously made on the basis of backwardness or specificity of a region.

Most of these separate province demands, based on either distinct regional nationality or backwardness and/or specificity of a region, continue to exist in India precisely because of the (a) disjuncture between provincial governance unit (or in some cases local administrative unit) and the regional cultural-nationality, (b) the desire to become a recognisable collectivity, (c) regional socio-economic and political backwardness, and above all (d) the practical socio-economic benefits involved in maintaining distinct identity and autonomy.

On the basis of our analysis of nationalism and regionalism in Orissa the following broad conclusions can be made:

(i) The territorial dismemberment of Orissa in colonial times led to domination of Oriyas by cultural outsiders which in turn posed external threat to Oriya cultural-linguistic identity.

(ii) Cultural nationalism seeking provincial autonomy crystallised in colonial times in both parts of Oriya homeland—British Orissa and Princely Orissa—to protect distinct Oriya cultural-national identity vis-à-vis other Indian cultural nationalities.

(iii) Regional discontent in contemporary times emerged in the province of Orissa due to relatively low level of development in western Orissa.

(iv) The growth of regional political parties, the struggle for power and political polarisation along regional lines and the disadvantageous position of the people of western Orissa in government and decision-making accentuated regional discontent further.

(v) The regional tension in contemporary Orissa has produced two attitudinal sub-cultures such as 'Sambalpuri' and 'Kataki'. The former is identified with the coastal region and the latter is associated with the western region of Orissa.

(vi) Regional mobilisation in western Orissa reveals two broad trends: 'autonomist' and 'separatist'. The former focuses on development council for western Orissa, while the latter demands formation of separate Koshal province comprising western Orissa districts.

(vii) Protection of material interests of the people of western Orissa was the main issue of regionalism in Orissa in its initial stage; whereas in recent times the emphasis of regionalism has been shifted to assertion of separate Koshali nationality.

(viii) Rise of regional consciousness seems to have eroded common linguistic identity in Orissa. The demand for Koshal province testifies this.

On the whole, it may be said that in colonial times if the threats to Oriya nationality came from external sources, especially from the Bengalis, in contemporary times the threats largely come from within, i.e., from the growing discontent among the western Oriyas. Initially the internal threat was seen in terms of regional tension over developmental gains and distribution of political power. But now the internal threat is perceived in terms of a parallel identity as a group of separatists began to circulate the idea of 'Koshali nationalism' and demand a separate Koshal province on that basis. This latter development seems to be more dangerous from the point of view of Orissa as it not only poses a threat to Oriya identity but also seeks the division of the province along notions of separate nationalities.

Our analysis suggests that both integrative and alienative processes are at work in present-day Orissa. The mainstream coastal group sees integration in terms of a monolithic Oriya identity and well-integrated Oriya state. The alienated group in western Orissa on the other hand started thinking in terms of their own integrative process by raising a counter regional cultural nationalism. All these developments give rise to the notions of double identity and bipolarised loyalty and in turn pose serious threats and challenges to Oriya identity and unity and integrity of Orissa province in the Indian Union. It may be realised that an authentic Oriya nationality and an integrated Orissa state cannot be sustained by perpetuating the dominance of the mainstream coastal group and depriving the legitimate shares of the peripheral group. After all, the whole of Orissa, and for that matter, the concept of Oriya identity and homeland cannot be identified with a particular section of Oriyas only.

Finally, our study highlights some broad conceptual-theoretical issues which contain some far-reaching sociological implications. For example, it shows that in multicultural states/ countries such as India three levels of identity operate. First, at the macro-national level an overarching civil-political identity operates. This civil-political identity binds the people as common citizens of a multicultural state/country. Second, at the meso/ middle-level (i.e. at the provincial level) a cultural-national identity operates. This identity focuses on loyalty of a distinct cultural community to its culture, homeland and language. this identity often expresses the desire for provincial self-rule. Third, at the micro-level, a regional identity operates. This identity focuses on local-regional interests and it emphasises equality and elimination of regional disparity.

As far as collective mobilisations for recognition of cultural-national identity in provincial space, or, movements for elimination of regional disparity in India are concerned, five possibilities can be visualised. One, there may be real cultural distinctiveness and the community in question faces actual threats to its cultural identity. In such a situation the community will indulge in nationalistic mobilisation to protect its separate cultural boundary. Two, there may be no cultural distinctiveness but the community in question feels dominated and discriminated. Such a situation will lead to a regional mobilisation against domination and inattention. Three, there may be negligible cultural differences and the concerned people face material deprivation. The people in this case will invoke their regional identity and call for balanced regional development. Four, there may be common cultural-linguistic identity but the people in question possess distinct historical background. Given the divergence in history, regional imbalance in this case will lead to a regional mobilisation by the less developed region. Finally, there may be regional socio-cultural differences and the community in question faces both material and cultural deprivation. This situation will give rise to nationalistic mobilisation as the affected community may indulge in search for a new distinct cultural nationality.

As a matter of fact, all forms of nationalism and regionalism in a multicultural county like India are seen in the context of equality and identity. There is no denying that modernisation, with its twin forces of industrialisation and urbanisation, considerably affected the traditional ascriptive values and institutions in India, but the increasing doses of modernisation could not dismantle primordial-cultural ties. In fact, under the influence of the forces of modernisation, the primordial-cultural identities are getting strengthened day by day. In some cases in India equality is demanded on the basis of an already existing distinct identity; and in some cases a distinct identity is constructed for equality. In yet other instances, a broader collective identity is accepted, but the dominated group demands equality on the basis of a regional identity. For example, the autonomists in western Orissa accept the broader Oriya identity and show allegiance to Orissa state, but they demand equitable share in material resources and balanced development. The separatists, however, disown Oriya identity and demand for complete separation from Orissa. The separatists in western Orissa are claiming for equality on the basis of a newly constructed regional-national identity.

In the end, it may be suggested that both nationalism and regionalism result from a sense of relative deprivation which in turn originates from domination, discrimination, disadvantage and disaffection. In the case of regional nationalism in a multicultural country/polity, cultural deprivation resulting from differences in nationality acts as the crucial variable; whereas in the case of regionalism in a multicultural country/polity, material deprivation in socio-economic and political terms acts as the crucial variable. In the former, material deprivation may be used as a reinforcement variable; in the latter, cultural deprivation may act as reinforcement variable. However, depending upon the context and nature of the movement in a multicultural country/state the nature of variable may change.

Bibliography

Anderson, B.	1991	*Imagined Communities: Reflections on the Origin and Spread of Nationalism (rev. ed.),* London: Verso
Amin, Samir	1978	*The Arab Nation*, London: Zed Press.
Armstrong, John	1982	*Nations Before Nationalism*, Chapel Hill.
Acharya, P.	1953	"The Antiquity of the Words 'Odissa' and 'Oriya'," *Orissa Historical Research Journal*, Vol. 2, No.364, pp.56-58.
Acharya, P.	1969	*Studies in Orissa History, Archaeology and Archives*, Cuttack: Vidyapuri.
Aitchinson, C.U.	1909	*A Collection of Treaties, Engagements and Sanads Relating to India and Neighbouring Countries*, Vol.I, Calcutta.
Alam, J.	1964	"Class, Political and National Dimensions of the State" in A. Majeed (ed.), *Regionalism and*

		Developmental Tensions in India, New Delhi: Cosmo pp.37-51.
Azam, Kauser J.	1981	*Political Aspects of National Integration*, Meerut: Minakshi.
Beams, John	1872	*A Comparative Grammar of the Modern Aryan Languages*, London.
Buckland, C.F.	1902	*Bengal under the Lieutenant Governor*, Vol.1, Calcutta.
Breuilly, J.	1985	*Nationalism and the State*, Chicago: University of Chicago Press.
Blaunt, James A.	1987	*The National Question*, London: Zed Books.
Banaji, Jairus	1974	"Nationalism and Socialism", *Economic and Political Weekly*, 7 September, 1538-39.
Banerjee, Kishalay	1984	*Regional Political Parties in India*, New Delhi: B.R. Publishing.
Birch, A. H.	1989	*Nationalism and National Integration*, London: Unwin Hyman.
Baboo, B.G.	1979	"Geography of Sakti Cult in the Sambalpur District of Orissa", *Folklore*, Vol.20(9), pp.191-200.
Biswal, M.C.	1974	"Sambalpuri Upa Bhasa" (Oriya), *Saptarshi*, Vol.8(3), pp.70-73.
Bohidar, S.N.	1972	"Sambalpuri Bhasare Dwanda Samasa

		(Oriya)", *Saptarshi*, Vol.1(2), pp.19-20.
Banerjee, R.D.	1930	*History of Orissa*, Vol.II, Calcutta.
Barnett, Ross M.	1976	*The Politics of Cultural Nationalism in South India*, New Jersey: Princeton University Press.
Baskin, D.	1970	"American Pluralism: Theory, Practice and Ideology", *Journal of Politics*, pp.71-95.
Bhardwaj, Krishna	1982	"Regional Differentiation in India: A Note", *Economic and Political Weekly*, Annual No.1, Vol.17, pp.605-14.
Brubaker, Roger	1996	*Nationalism Reframed: Nationhood and the National Question in the New Europe*, Cambridge: Cambridge University Press.
Bailey, F.G.	1963	*Politics and Social Change: Orissa in 1959*, Bombay: Oxford.
Bailey, F.G.	1959	"The Oriya Movement", *Economic Weekly*, 26 September, pp.1331-33.
Bailey, F.G.	1959	"Orissa Politics: Congress Loses Majority", *Economic Weekly*, 29 August, pp.1204-5.
Bailey, F.G.	1959	"Orissa Politics: The Ganatantra Parishad",

		Economic Weekly, 24 October, pp.1469-71.
Bailey, F.G.	1963	"Parliamentary Government in Orissa – 1947-56", *Journal of Commonwealth Political Studies*, Vol.1(1), pp.112-123.
Bailey, F.G.	1959	"Orissa Politics: The Feudatory States", *Economic Weekly*, 19 September, pp.1298-1301.
Beiner, Ronald (ed)	1999	*Theorising Nationalism,* Albany: State University of New York Press.
Billig, Michael	1995	*Banal Nationalism,* London: Sage Publications.
Brass, Paul	1974	*Language, Religion and Politics in North India*, New Delhi: Vikash.
Brass, Paul	1966	*Factional Politics in an Indian State: The Congress in Uttar Pradesh*, Bombay: Oxford University Press.
Brass, Paul	1991	*Ethnicity and Nationalism: Theory and Comparison*, New Delhi: Sage.
Chatterjee, S.K.	1947	"The Language and the People of Orissa", *Indian Historical Quarterly*, Vol.XXIII.
Chakravarti, M.M.	1898	"The Language and Literature of Orissa", *Journal of Asiatic Society*

		of Bengal, Vol.XXVI, Part I, pp.339-45.
Chakravarti, Tapas	1984	"Social Content of Oriya Literature of the late 19th Century" in B.S. Das (ed.), *Life and Culture in Orissa*, Calcutta: Minerva.
Chatterjee, Partha	1975	"Bengal: Rise and Growth of a Nationality", *Social Scientist*, Vol.37, August.
Coleman, J.	1958	*Nigeria: A Background to Nationalism*, Berkeley: University of California Press.
Conner, Walker	1978	"A Nation is a Nation, is a State, is an Ethnic group, is a...", *Ethnic and Racial Studies*, 1 October, pp.381-82.
Conner, Walker	1972	"Nation-Building or Nation-Destroying", *World Politics*, pp.319-55.
Churia, M.K.	1984	"Paschimanchaliya Upabhasasre Bibhakti Pratyayare Rupatatwa" (Oriya), *Saptarshi*, Vol:13(10), pp.26-33.
Cobden, Ramsay L.E.B.	1910	*Bengal District Gazetteers, Feudatory States of Orissa*, Calcutta.
Cohn, B.S.	1967	"Regions Subjective and Objective: Their Relation to the Study of Modern Indian History and Society" in R.I. Crain (ed.), *Regions and Regionalism in South Asian Studies: An*

Exploratory Study, Duke University, pp.104-36.

Chatterjee, A.K. 1976 "Sociological Context of Regionalism in India – A Conceptual Framework" in Satish Chandra et. al. (eds.), *Regionalism and National Integration*, Jaipur: Alekh Pub.

Clark, Audrey N. 1990 *Penguin Dictionary of Geography*, London: Penguin Books.

Das, S.P. 1969 *Sambalpur Itihas* (Oriya), Sambalpur: Vishwabharti.

Deutsch, K. 1953 *Nationalism and Social Communication*, Cambridge: Cambridge University Press.

Davis, H.B. 1978 *Towards a Marxist Theory of Nationalism*, New York.

Dash, S.C. 1965 "Government and Politics in Orissa", *Indian Journal of Political Science*, Vol.26, pp.83-100.

Das, M.N. 1952 *Utkal Gaurav Madhusudan* (Oriya), Utkal University.

Das, M.N. (ed.) 1977 *Sidelights on History and Culture of Orissa*, Cuttack: Vidyapuri.

De, S.C. 1952 "Cowry Currency in Orissa", *Orissa Historical Research Journal*, Vol.1, No.2, pp.10-21.

De. S.C. (ed.) 1964 *Diary of Political Events in Orissa, 1936-47*, Cuttack.

Das, P.K.	1982	"Upabhasa Adhyayana Kshetrare Paschimanchalia Odiya Upabhasa" (Oriya), *Saptarshi*, Vol.11(5), pp.5-11.
Deo, P.K.	1961	*My Humble Contributions, Ganatantra Parishad, 1956-61*, Bhawanipatna.
Despande, Madhav N.	1983	"Nation and Region: A Socio-linguistic Perspective on Maharashtra" in Milton Israel (ed.), *National Unity: The South Asian Experience*, New Delhi: Promilla.
Desai, A.R.	1966	*Social Background of Indian Nationalism*, Bombay: Popular Prakashan.
Edmonds, C.J.	1962	"Kurdish Nationalism", *Journal of Contemporary History*, Vol.6, pp.87-107.
Ejai, Mostafa and Enole, Cynthia	1969	"Nation States and State Nations", *International Studies Quarterly*, 13 June, pp.141-42.
Emerson, Rupert	1960	*From Empire to Nation*, Boston.
Erdman, H.L.	1967	*The Swatantra Party and Indian Conservatism*, London: Cambridge.
Forrester, Duncan B.	1970	"Sub-Regionalism in India: The Case of Telengana", *Pacific Affairs*, Vol.XI, No.1, pp.5-17.

Finer, S.E. 1975 *Comparative Government*, Middlesex:Penguin Books.

Gellner, Ernest 1983 *Nation and Nationalism*, Oxford: Basil Blackwell.

Geertz, Clifford 1971 "The Integrative Revolution: Primordial Sentiments and Civil Politics" in Clifford Geertz (ed.), *Old Societies and New States*, New Delhi: Amerind.

Ghosh, Sumit 1973 "Regional Demands in Orissa", *Hindustan Standard*, 5 October.

Guha, A. 1983 "Little Nationalism Turned Chauvinist: Assam's Anti-Foreigner Upsurge (1970-80)", *Economic and Political Weekly*, Vol.15, Special No.1701-9.

Ghosh, A. and Sengupta N. 1982 "The Nationality Question in India" in N. Sengupta et. al. (eds.), *Fourth World Dynamics: Jharkhand*, Delhi: Authors Guild.

Grierson, G.A. 1922 *Linguistic Survey of India*, Vol.I, Calcutta.

Govt. of India 1955 *Report of the States Reorganisation Commission*, New Delhi.

Govt. of India 1971 *Census of India*, (Orissa Series-16), New Delhi.

Govt. of India 1981 *Census of India*, (Orissa Series-16), New Delhi.

Govt. of India 1991 *Census of India*, (Orissa Series-19), New Delhi.

Govt. of India	2001	*Census of India,* (Orissa Series-22), New Delhi.
Govt. of India	1932	*Report of the Orissa Boundary Committee*, Vol.I, Delhi.
Govt. of Orissa	1981	*Statistical Abstract of Orissa*, Bhubaneswar.
Govt. of Orissa	1991	*Statistical Abstract of Orissa*, Bhubaneswar.
Govt. of Orissa	2005	*Statistical Abstract of Orissa,* Bhubaneswar.
Govt. of Orissa	1967	*Who's Who of Freedom Workers in Orissa*, Cuttack.
Govt. of Orissa	1954	*Orissa Extraordinary Gazette Notification*, 22nd February.
Govt. of Orissa	1991	*Assembly-wise and District-wise Party Position in Orissa Assembly*, Bhubaneswar: Secretariat of Orissa Legislative Assembly.
Govt. of Orissa	1972	*Report of the Sarjoo Prasad Enquiry Commission*, Home Department.
Hayes, C.J.	1948	*The Historical Evolution of Modern Nationalism*, New York: Macmillan.
Hechter, M.	1975	*Internal Colonialism*, London: Oxford University Press.
Hechter, M.	2000	*Containing Nationalism,* New York: Oxford University Press.
Harrison, Selig S.	1968	*India: The Most Dangerous Decades*, Princeton, New Jersey

Habib, Irfan	1975	"Emergence of Nationalities", *Social Scientist*, August.
Hroch, Miroslav	1996	"From National Movement to the Fully-formed Nation: The Nation-building Process in Europe", in Balakrishnan, Gopal, (ed), *Mapping The Nation*, New York: Verso, pp. 78-97.
Irslchik, E.F.	1969	*Politics and Social Conflict in South India*, Bombay: Oxford.
Jena, B.B.	1966	"Feudal Grip", *Seminar*, November, pp.26-33.
Jena, B.B.	1968	"General Elections in Orissa" in S.P. Verma and Iqbal Narain (eds.), *Fourth General Election in India*, New Delhi: Orient, pp.349-61.
Joshi, P.D.	1981	"Khadial Anchalara Lok Bhasa" (Oriya), *Saptarshi*, Vol.10(6), pp.15-19.
Joshi, P.D.	1987	"Hai Koshali Bhasa" (Koshali), *Koshal Bharti*, Vol.1(1), pp.1-10.
Joshi, P.D.	1982	"Koshali Bhasa" (Oriya), *Saptarshi*, Vol.11(1), pp.19-21.
Joshi, P.D.	1983	"Swatantra Koshali Bhasa" (Oriya), *Saptarshi*, Vol.12(11), pp.1-6.
Joshi, P.D.	1984	"Swatantra Koshali Bhasa" (Oriya), *Saptarshi*, Vol.13(9), pp.1-10.

Joshi, P.D.	1992	"Koshali Lipi Samasya Bichar" (Koshali) in N. Panigrahi (ed.), *Hame Koshali, Hamar Bhasa Koshali*, Sambalpur.
Kedourie, Elie	1960	*Nationalism*, London.
Kohn, Hans	1961	*The Idea of Nationalism*, New York.
Kohn, Hans	1962	*The Age of Nationalism*, New York.
Koshali Sangh	1946	*Whither Koshal?* Bolangir.
Koshal Sangh	1946	*Koshal Tract*, Bolangir.
Koshal Sammilani	1993	*Memorandum Submitted to the President of India for formation of Koshal State*, Sambalpur.
Kulke, H.	1977	"Early State Formation and Royal Legitimisation in late Ancient Orissa" in M.N. Das (ed.), *Sidelights on History and Culture of Orissa*, Cuttack :Vidyapuri.
Karve, I.	1953	*Kinship Organisation in India*, Poona.
Karna, M.N.	2000	"Language, Region and National Identity" in S.L. Sharma and T.K. Oommen (eds.), *Nation and National Identity in South Asia*, New Delhi: Orient Longman, pp.75-96.
Lambert, Richard D.	1967	"Methods of Determining Regions with Special Reference to India" in R.I. Craine (ed.), *Regions and Regionalism in South*

		Asian Studies: An Exploratory study, Duke University, pp.271-83.
Lele, J.	1986	"Regional Disparities and National Identity in Maharashtra", *Journal of Social and Economic Studies*, Vol.3, No.2, pp.175-89.
Meher, R.K.	1999	*Development Disparities in A Backward Region*, New Delhi: APH Publishing Corporation.
Mittal, A.C.	1962	*An Early History of Orissa*, Banaras.
Mohanty M and L.N. Mishra	1968	"Orissa: Politics of Political Stagnation" in Iqbal Narain (ed.), *State Politics in India*, Meerut: Meenakshi, pp.240-61.
Mishra, P.K.	1983	*Orissa (1900-1936): A Study in Political Development*, Calcutta: Punthi Pustak
Mohanty, Nibedita	1984	*Oriya Nationalism: A Quest for United Orissa*, New Delhi: Manohar.
Mishra, R.N.	1984	*Regionalism and State Politics in India*, New Delhi: Ashish Publishing.
Mill, J.S.	1958	*Considerations on Representative Government* (1861), New York.
Mishra, A.K.	1979	"Madhusudan and the Growth of Economic Nationalism in Orissa",

		Orissa Historical Congress Proceedings, Bhubaneswar, pp.90-95.
Mohapatra, Baikoli	1976	*Odiya Andolanara Itihas* (Oriya), Cuttack.
Mohapatra, J.N.	1941	*Orissa in 1936-37 to 1938-39*, Cuttack.
Mohapatra, M.	1952	"General Economic Condition of Orissa: 1803-1818", *Orissa Historical Research Journal*, Vol.1, No.2, pp.171-75.
Maddox, S.L.	1901	*Final Report on the Survey and Settlement of the Province of Orissa, 1890-1900*, Calcutta.
Mitra, N.N. (ed.)	1929	*Indian Quarterly Register*, Vol.II, Calcutta.
Mishra, M.K.	1989	*Folksongs of Kalahandi*, Bhubaneswar: Mayur Publications.
Mazumdar, B.C.	1925	*Orissa in the Making*, Calcutta.
Minohan, J.	1996	*Nations Without States: A Historical Dictionary of Contemporary National Movements*, Westport: Greenwood Press.
Mudalkar, A. and R. Vora	1984	"Regionalism in Mahatrashtra" in A. Majeed (ed.), *Regionalism and Developmental Tensions in India*, New Delhi: Cosmo, pp.90-112.
Mukherji, Partha N.	1999	"Nation-State Reformulated: Interrogating Received

		Wisdom", *Man and Development*, December, 51-68.
Mukherjee, P.	1959	"Employment of the People of Orissa in the 19th Century", *Orissa Historical Research Journal*, Vo..3, pp.110-17.
Mukherjee, P.	1964	*History of Orissa in the 19th Century*, Cuttack.
Mukherjee, P.	1981	*The History of the Gajapati Kings of Orissa*, Cuttack: Kitab Mahal.
Mahtab, H.K.	1957	*History of Freedom Movement in Orissa*, Vol.1, Bhubaneswar.
Mahtab, H.K.	1959	*History of Orissa: Part-I*, Cuttack.
Mahtab, H.K.	1959	*History of Orissa: Part-II*, Cuttack.
Mahtab, H.K.	1972	*Sadhanara Pathe* (Oriya), Cuttack.
Mahtab, H.K.	1972	*Beginning of the End*, Cuttack.
Menon, V.P.	1968	*Transfer of Power in India*, Delhi: Orient Longman
Menon, V.P.	1961	*The Story of the Integration of the Indian States*, New Delhi: Orient Longman
Nairn, Tom	1977	*The Break-up of Britain: Crisis and Neo-Nationalism*, London: New Left Books.
Nanda, Sukadev	1979	*Coalitional Politics in Orissa*, New Delhi: Sterling.

Nanda, Subrat K. 1986 "Punjab: The Case of a Fractured Nationality", *Mainstream*, 1986, pp.22-25.

Nanda, Subrat K. 2005 "Cultural Identity and Nationalism in Multi-national context: The Indian Experience" *The NEHU Journal*, Vol. III, No.1, Jan., pp. 67-88.

Nanda, Subrat K. 2006 "Cultural Nationalism in a Multi-national Context: The Case of India" *Sociological Bulletin*, Vol.55, No. 1 Jan-Apr, pp. 24-44.

Nayak, L.P. 1985 "Sambalpuri 'O' Chattisgarhi Bhasayi Sankramita Kshetrara Boli Manankara Tulanatmak Rupatatwika Adhyayan" (Oriya), *Saptarshi*, Vol.14(2), pp.22-28.

Narain, Iqbal 1984 "Regionalism: A Conceptual Analysis in the Indian Context" in A. Majeed (ed.), *Regionalism and Developmental Tensions in India*, New Delhi: Cosmo, pp.20-32.

Narain, Iqbal (ed.) 1967 *State Politics in India*, Meerut: Minakshi.

Narain, Iqbal 1978 "Cultural Pluralism and National Integration in India" in K.R. Bombwall

		(ed.), *National Power and State Autonomy*, Meerut: Minakshi, pp.186-98.
Namboodripad, E.M.S.	1975	"Class Character of the Nationalist Movement", *Social Scientist*, August
Nag, Sajal	1999	*Nationalism, Separatism and Secessionism*, Jaipur: Rawat.
O'Malley, L.S.S.	1921	*Bengal District Gazetteers, Puri*, Calcutta.
Oommen, T.K.	1989	"Political Alienation and the Internal Threats to the Indian Nation State: Towards a Non-Alarmist Perspective", *The Indian Journal of Social Science*, Vol.2, No.2.
Oommen, T.K.	1988	"Nation, State and Ethnicity: Towards a Conceptual Clarification and an Empirical Explication", *Social Action*, Vol.38, pp.333-43.
Oommen, T.K.	1997	*Citizenship and National Identity: From Colonialism to Globalism*, New Delhi: Sage.
Oommen, T.K.	1994	"State, Nation and Ethnie" The Processual Linkages", *in P. Ratchiffe (ed.), Race, Ethnicity and Nation*, London: University College London Press, pp. 26-46.

Oommen, T.K. 2000 "Conceptualising Nation and Nationality in South Asia" in S.L. Sharma and T.K. Oommen (eds.), *Nation and National Identity in South Asia*, New Delhi: Orient Longman.

Oommen, T.K. 1997 *Citizenship, Nationality and Ethnicity: Reconciling Competing Identities*, Cambridge: Polity Press.

Oommen, T.K. 1986 "Insiders and Outsiders: Primordial Collectivism and Cultural Pluralism in Nation-building", *International Sociology*, Vol.1(1), pp.53-74.

Oommen, T.K. 1990(a) *State and Society in India: Studies in Nation-building*, New Delhi: Sage.

Oommen, T.K. 1990(b) *Protest and Change: Studies in Social Movements*, New Delhi: Sage.

Parekh, Bhikhu 2000 *Rethinking Multiculturalism: Cultural Diversity and Political Theory,* New York: Palgrave.

Patra, K.M. 1970 "Growth of Social Consciousness in Orissa in 19th Century", *Proceedings of the Indian Historical Records Commission*, Vol.II, pp.148-61.

Patra, K.M. 1979 *Orissa State Legislature and Freedom Struggle: 1912-1947*, New Delhi: ICHR.

Patra, K.M. 1971 *Orissa Under the East India Company*, New Delhi: Munshiram Manoharlal.

Peggs, James 1859 *History of the Baptist Mission*, Cuttack.

Patra, S.C. 1978 *The Formation of Orissa Province*, Calcutta: Punthi Pustak.

Patnaik, P. 1968 *Odiya Sahitya* (Oriya), Cuttack.

Peterson, William 1975 "On the Sub-nations of Western Europe" in Nathan Glazer and D.P. Moyinihan (eds.), *Ethnicity: Theory and Experience*, Cambridge: Harvard University Press.

Pye, L.W. 1968 *Politics, Personality and Nation Building*, Princeton: Princeton University Press.

Pati, Binod K. n.d. *Autonomous Development Council for Western Orissa* (Pamphlet), Sambalpur.

Pati, Prafulla K. 1995 *Draft Constitution of the Western Orissa Autonomous Development Council*, Sambalpur.

Panigrahi, N. (ed.) 1992 *Hame Koshali, Hamar Bhasa Koshali* (Koshali), Sambalpur.

Patnaik, Dhirendranath	1982	*Festivals of Orissa*, Bhubaneswar: Orissa Sahitya Academy.
Patel, B.	1987	"Bhasa" Sambalpuri 'O' Kissan" (Oriya), *Saptarshi*, Vol.14(2), pp.1-5.
Panda, Muralidhar	1977	*Abahelitara Pantha Ka'an?* (Oriya), Patnagarh.
Panda, Muralidhar	1972	*Orissa Mantrimandal 'O' Purbatana Garhjat* (Oriya), Bolangir.
Pradhan, P.M.	1972	"Freedom Struggle in the ex-States of Orissa", *Orissa Review*, Vol.XXIIX, No.1, Bhubaneswar.
Pradhan, Sadasib	1986	*Agrarian and Political Movements: States of Orissa (1931-1949)*, Delhi: Inter-India.
Pati, Satyabhama	1987	*Democratic Movements in India*, Delhi: B.R. Publishing.
Patnaik, Lalmohan	1941	*Resurrected Orissa*, Cuttack.
Patnaik, S.N.	1972	*Odissare Swadhinata Andolan* (Oriya), Cuttack.
Padhee, P.K.	1985	"Sambalpuri 'O' Bhatri" (Oriya), *Saptarshi*, Vol.14(4), pp.9-22.
Padhee, P.K.	1982	"Sambalpuri Bhasare Ketoti Baishistya" (Oriya), *Saptarshi*, Vol.11(5), pp.12-16.
Pathy, Jagannath	2000	"Tribe, Region and Nation in the Context of the

		Indian State" in S.L. Sharma and T.K. Oommen (eds.), *Nation and National Identity in South Asia*, New Delhi: Orient Longman, pp.97-111.
Phadnis, Urmilla	1989	*Ethnicity and Nation-building in South Asia*, New Delhi: Sage.
Padhi, A.P. (ed.)	1985	*State Politics in India: A Case Study of Orissa*, New Delhi: B.R. Publishing.
Rath, R.N.	1964	*Late Utkalmani Gopabandhu Das*, Cuttack.
Rath, R.N.	1964	*The Story of Freedom Movements in Orissa States*, Cuttack.
Roy, B.C.	1960	*Orissa under the Marathas*, Allahabad.
Roy, B.C.	1960	*Foundations of British Orissa*, Cuttack.
Ray, Amal	1974	"Sub-regional Politics and Elections in Orissa", *Indian Journal of Political Science*, October-December, pp.340-51.
Ray, Amal	1971	"Coalitional Politics in Orissa: Decision-making and Change", *Economic and Political Weekly*, 9 January, pp.904-11.
Rath, Gopabandhu	1988	*Paschim Odissara Kathita Bhasa* (Oriya), Bhubaneswar: Orissa Sahitya Academy.

Rao, K.V.N.	1973	*Emergence of Andhra Pradesh*, Bombay: Popular Prakashan.
Rao, K.V.	1965	"Politics in Orissa: Social Ecology and Constitutional Compulsions", *Indian Journal of Political Science*, Vol.26, pp.101-11.
Rao, K.V.	1968	"The Pattern of Orissa Politics" in Iqbal Narain (ed.), *State Politics in India*, Meerut: Minakshi, pp.209-16.
Rama Reddy, G. and Sharma, B.A.V.	1979	*Regionalism in India: A Study of Telengana*, New Delhi: Concept.
Renan Ernest	1996	"What is a Nation?" in Eley Geoff and Suny, Ronald Grigor, (ed), *Becoming National: A Reader,* New York: Oxford University Press, pp41-55.
Snyder, L.L.	1982	*Global Mini-Nationalism: Autonomy or Independence*, Westport: Greenwood Press.
Snyder, L.L.	1954	*The Meaning of Nationalism*, New Brunswick.
Sahu, N.K.	1964	*History of Orissa*, Vol.1, Cuttack.
Sahu, N.K.	1977	*Odiya Jatira Itihas* (Oriya), Bhubaneswar: Orissa State Bureau of Textbook

		Preparation and Production.
Samantray, N.	1964	*Odiya Sahityara Itihas* (Oriya), Cuttack.
Sterling, A.	1846	*An Account:Geographical, Statistical and Historical of Orissa Proper or Cuttack*, London.
Sitaramaya, Pattabhi B.	1946	*The History of the Indian National Congress, 1885-1935*, Bombay.
Shills, Edward	1957	"Primordial, Sacred and Civil Ties", *British Journal of Sociology*, Vol.3, pp.130-45.
Stalin, J.	1955	"Marxism and National Question", *Collected Works*, Vol.3, Moscow, pp.300-84.
Shafer, Boyd C.	1955	*Nationalism : Myth and Reality*, New York.
Seton-Watson, H.	1977	*Nations and States*, London: Methuen.
Satyamurthy, T.V.S.	1983	*Nationalism in Contemporary World*, London: Frances Pinks.
Samal, J.K.	1988	*Princely States of Orissa*, Allahabad.
Senapati, N. and B. Mohanty	1968	*Gazetteers of Orissa, Bolangir*, Cuttack.
Senapati, N. and B. Mohanty	1971	*Orissa District Gazetteers, Sambalpur*, Cuttack.
Supakar, S.	1956	*Sambalpur Budi Anchalara Lokankara Durdasha* (Pamphlet), Cuttack.

Supakar, S.	1988	*Itihasra Parihas* (Oriya), Sambalpur.
Sambalpur Lekhak Sangh	1986	*Sambalpuri Kabita Sankalana* (Sambalpuri), Sambalpur.
Singh Deo, J.P.	1984	"Veer Surendra Sai was direct Descendant of Manik Rai", *Souvenir Oriya Sanskrutika* Samaj, Sambalpur. pp.10-15.
Singh, K.S.	1982	"Tribal Identity Movements Based on Script and Language", *Man in India*, Vol.62(3), pp.234-45.
Smith, A.D.	1972	"Ethnocentrism, Nationalism and Social Change", *International Journal of Comparative Sociology*, Vol.13.
Smith, A.D.	1983	*Theories of Nationalism*, London.
Smith, A.D.	1981	*The Ethnic Revival*, Cambridge: Cambridge University Press.
Smith, A.D.	1986	*The Ethnic Origins of Nations*, London: Oxford University Press.
Smith, A.D.	1973	"Nationalism" in *Current Sociology*, Vol.XXI, No.3, pp.5-185.
Smith, A. D.	1994	"Gastronomy or Geology? The Role of Nationalism in the Reconstructions of Nations", *Nations and Nationalism*, Vol. 1, No. 1, pp 3-23.

Smith, A.D.	1998	*Nationalism and Modernism: A Critical Survey of Recent Theories of Nations and Nationalism*, London: Routledge.
Schwartzberg, J.	1967	"Prolegomena to the Study of South Asian Regions and Regionalism" in R.I. Crain (ed.), *Regions and Regionalism in South Asian Studies: An Exploratory Study*, Duke University, pp.86-101.
Schwartzberg, J.	1968	"The Geography of Caste in North Indian Plain" in B.S. Cohn et. al. (eds.), *Structure and Change in Indian Society*, Chicago, pp.103-25.
Smiley, D.	1980	*Canada in Question: Federalism in the Eighties*, Toronto.
Spate. O.H.K.	1954	*India and Pakistan*, London.
Toynbee, G.	1928	*A Sketch of the History of Orissa, 1803-1828*, Calcutta.
Two Bachelors of Arts	1919	*The Oriya Movement*, Aska.
Tilly, C. (ed.)	1980	*The Formation of National States in Western Europe*, Santa Barbara.
Talcher Prajamandal Committee	1950	*History of Talcher Prajamandal*, Cuttack.

Worsely, Peter	1974	*The Three Worlds: Culture and World Development*, Chicago.
Wolf, Ken	1976	"Hans Kohn's Liberal Nationalism: The Historian as a Prophet", *Journal of the History of Ideas*, Vol.37, pp.651-72.
Weber, Max	1947	*From Max Weber: Essays in Sociology*, London: Routledge and Kegan Paul.
Warner, Lee W.	1894	*The Protected Princes of India*, London.
Weiner, Myron	1963	*Politics of Scarcity: Public Pressure and Political Response in India*, Bombay: Oxford
Weiner, Myron (ed.)	1968	*State Politics in India*, Princeton: Princeton University Press.

Reports, Proceedings and Memorandums

1. *Report of the Royal Institute of International Affairs on Nationalism*, London, 1939.
2. *Report of Orissa States Enquiry Committee*, Cuttack, 1939.
3. *Journal of Asiatic Society of Bengal Proceedings*, Vol.XXIX, 1870.
4. *Report of the Indian Statutory Commission*, Vol.IV, 1930.
5. *Report on the Constitutional Reforms*, Calcutta, 1928.
6. *Proceedings of the Legislative Council, Bihar and Orissa*, Vol.1, 1927.
7. *Indian Annual Register*, Vol.I, 1939.
8. *General Review of the Administration of the Feudatory States of Orissa, 1931-32*.
9. *Memorandum submitted to the President of India by Koshal Party for the recognition of Koshali Language as an Official language in Orissa*, Sambalpur, 1992.

Index